The Saints,
Humanly Speaking

To Marc,
Have faith everyday!.
Believe, Trust, Inspire.
From your priestess
Alison

The Saints, Humanly Speaking

THE PERSONAL LETTERS OF

St. Teresa of Avila
St. Thomas More
St. Ignatius Loyola
St. Thérèse of Lisieux
St. Francis de Sales
and many more

Selected and Arranged by
FELICITAS CORRIGAN, O.S.B.

CHARIS

SERVANT PUBLICATIONS
ANN ARBOR, MICHIGAN

© 2000 by The Trustees of Stanbrook Abbey
All rights reserved.

Charis Books is an imprint of Servant Publications especially designed to serve
Roman Catholics.

Servant Publications
P.O. Box 8617
Ann Arbor, MI 48107

Cover design: Alan Furst Design

00 01 02   03 10 9 8 7 6 5 4 3 2 1

Printed in the United States of America
ISBN 1-56955-205-3

Library of Congress Cataloging-in-Publication Data

Letters from the saints
The saints, humanly speaking : the personal letters of St. Teresa of Avila, St.
Thomas More, St. Ignatius Loyola, St. Thérèse of Lisieux, St. Francis de Sales,
and many more / selected and arranged by Felicitas Corrigan.
      p. cm.
Originally published: Letters from the saints. New York : Hawthorn Books,
1964.
Includes bibliographical references.
ISBN 1-56955-205-3 (alk. paper)
1. Christian saints—Correspondence.   I. Corrigan, Felicitas.
BX4655.2 .L45 2000
282'.092'2—dc21
[B]   99-086136

Contents

3. The Christian in the Church

4. The Christian in Life

5. The Christian in Death

Acknowledgments

The compiler desires to express her thanks to the Right Reverend Father Abbot of Mount St. Bernard Abbey, Leicester, and to Reverend Père André Louf, O.C.S.O., of the Abbaye Ste. Marie-du-Mont, Godewaersvelde, France, for their kind permission to include Letter 82; to the Very Reverend Father Provincial, S.D.B., for permission to translate Letter 38; to the Very Reverend Father Provincial of the Society of Jesus, British Province, for the use of Letters 2, 67 and 91; to the English Provincial of the Sisters of Charity of St. Vincent de Paul for Letter 8; to the Mother Superior of the Missionary Sisters of the Sacred Heart, Honor Oak, for letters 7 and 12. She also thanks Burns & Oates for permission to publish Letters 13, 14, 31, 36, 43, 52, 54, 56, 60, 64, 65, 72, 77, 81, 85, 88, 89, 91, 92, 104, 108, 112 and 113.

The compiler and publisher have made every effort to secure permission from copyright holders to letters that appear in this collection. If any copyright holder notifies the publisher of a failure to obtain permission for any letter, we will gladly correct the oversight.

Introduction

Experience goes to show that letters will always find a reading public. Why? Is it because they are the literature of the common man? Under the compulsion of deep or strong feeling, we have all at some time found an outlet for self-expression in a letter: it may have been evoked by love, the death of a friend, some spiritual aspiration, or simply by a chord of music or a sunset-touch; but whatever the cause, words have come unbidden because our hearts are full and we can't help it. Even those who shirk letter-writing will at least agree that receiving letters is one of the never-failing joys of life. How often do we sit in silence and examine the script—it may have something about it familiar and dear, puzzling or pleasurable—and then with quickened heartbeat we draw out the letter and slowly savor it word by word. All of a sudden the whole room becomes transfigured with warmth and light, the personality of the writer is present to us in a moment of unique encounter, we know and are known.

If that be true of the letters of our humdrum selves, how much truer of those of the famous. Yet possibly to some ears the sound of letters from saints strikes a discordant note, as if the saints were far removed from the concrete and tarmac fly-overs and runways of this clamorous modern world. But if we have tended to make the saints pure abstractions, embodiments of ethical perfection purged of all human ties and lovable weaknesses, the best way to shatter the illusion is precisely by reading their letters. "I am a piece of twisted wire," St. Aloysius explained, "and I have entered religion to get twisted straight." To his daughter Meg, Thomas More made this admission: "My nature struggles so mightily against suffering that a fillip on the nose almost makes me to quake." Placid Riccardi considered it a bad joke if people spoke as if they venerated him, and would promptly produce a bad photograph of his very plain face to turn the praise to ridicule. Inwardly and outwardly, the saints are very like any other Christian.

. Some of them reveal their human qualities at first sight, they walk straight into the room and fill it with genial warmth and love; others are more reserved and call for study. It often helps to know a little of their background. St. John of the Cross, seemingly so remote in his frightening austerity, stood a good deal of teasing from his exuberant partner St. Teresa, who nicknamed him her little Seneca. Even smaller than St. John of the Cross was the stern St. Alphonsus Liguori, for when he graduated in Civil and Canon Law at the precocious age of sixteen, he was so tiny that he upset the equilibrium of the grave judges assembled by suddenly disappearing through his robes; he played the harpsichord beautifully, was fond of painting and sword-play, and if he sounds rigid and unbending, it is well to remember that no one showed greater tenderness to poor sinners, or more truly verified in his own experience the program he once mapped out for a nun: "Contradiction, sickness, scruples, spiritual aridity, and all the inner and outward torments are the chisel with which God carves his statues for paradise."

•Letters which compress within a few lines sorrows, doubts, disillusionment, hopes, and fears all so amazingly like our own, bring human beings to life before our very eyes, making them more vividly present than the crowd which jostles our elbows every day. The saints were very busy people and they dashed off their letters in a hurry like most of us. "You must not give yourself the trouble of rereading the letters you write me," Teresa of Avila tells her brother Lorenzo. "I never reread mine. If a word here or there should have a letter missing, just put it in, and I will do the same for you, for your meaning is quite clear.° This down-to-earth quality, this simplicity and directness, this complete absence of humbug is characteristic of all the saints. There are no platitudes, no talking for talking's sake, no long faces; on the contrary, even the most serious expositions are often salted with delicious humor. Who but a Frenchman could have allayed the scruples of a high-born lady of the Court as to powdering her hair, with such deadly wit accompanied by such a disarming smile as St. Francis de Sales when he asked: "After all, don't pheasants, those pretty creatures, give their feathers a good dust bath to stop their breeding lice?" We are tempted to think of the saints as being always and perhaps boringly edifying. Are they? Read St. Jerome's letter to his aunt Castorina, and you will understand why a pope once halted before his picture in the Vatican gallery, wagged a reproving finger at the naked form depicted striking his breast with a stone, and remarked: "Aha! You do well to beat your breast with that stone, for without it the Church would never have canonized you!" Jerome's letter to his aunt raises a nice problem (Letter 48). Who preserved the letter? One imagines a rather acid spinster perusing her nephew's ultimatum with eyebrows upraised and thin lips pursed, and then casting it into the flames with an indignant exclamation of, "The impertinent young scamp!" Hardly could she foresee that in the centuries to come many a hooded scribe seated in the carrel of his monastic cloister would chafe his frozen fingers, sharpen his quill, and laboriously transcribe Epistola XIII "Ad Castorinam Materteram" among the Opera Omnia of the Father of our Vulgate translation of the Bible, Eusebius Hieronymus Sophronius. Does the letter contain a moral, by any chance, for those aunts tempted to look down their noses at the angry young men who happen to be their sisters' sons?

The group of English Jesuit martyrs of the sixteenth century exercises a peculiar attraction. High spirited, of deep feeling and burning zeal, of keen cultured intellect and sensitive human frailty, recoiling from suffering yet going forward with youthful eagerness to meet it, they seem to have been turned out one and all from some celestial Officer's Training Corps. St. Ignatius Loyola, their military commander, possibly founded it to train none but heroic graduates for their earthly apostolate. Among them Robert Southwell, only thirty-three at the time of his death, stands out as a gentle, lovable combination in the sixteenth century of Gerard Manley Hopkins and G.K. Chesterton. His paradoxes, like G.K.C.'s, may fascinate some and repel others, but few will deny the splendor of his prose. This is the English of Shakespeare, the tongue of the persecuted Catholics who set sail for America, the land of freedom beyond the seas. By much study, Southwell has obviously made himself proficient in the elegant euphemisms fashionable at the court of Elizabeth I, determined that his contemporaries should listen to his voice; we can but admire the fire and energy with which he forges his skillful, harmonious language in order to fight with the weapons of his time.

Many of the contributors to this book fall naturally into friendly companies bound by race, similar aims and religious ideals, and it is intriguing to trace their action one upon another. Such, for example, were the English martyrs, the Jesuit martyrs of North America, and the missioners in China and Vietnam drawn from the French Lazarists and the Missions Etrangères of Paris. Here it is only possible to select one group in order to show this soft intercourse from soul to soul.

St. Robert Bellarmine, professed under St. Francis Borgia, friend of St. Charles Borromeo, confessor of St. Aloysius Gonzaga, first met St. Francis de Sales when the latter was summoned to Rome in 1600 to face a barrage of abstruse theological questions propounded by the reigning pope, Clement VIII, assisted by the three cardinals, Baronius, Bellarmine and Frederick Borromeo. St. Francis acquitted himself with such modesty and ability that he was promptly confirmed in his appointment as coadjutor to the Bishop of Geneva, and at once returned to France. Four years later he met the Baroness de Chantal, and in 1610, with her cooperation, he founded the Order of Visitandine nuns. "In Madame de Chantal," he declared, "I have found the perfect woman whom Solomon sought in Jerusalem and found not." His desire had been to provide a new kind of religious life for women who should be free from enclosure and the usual obligations of the Divine Office, and at liberty to leave their convents to look after the sick and poor.

When St. Jane Frances de Chantal went to set up her first convent in Paris, Francis entrusted her spiritual guidance to a priest fourteen years his junior, named Vincent de Paul. In July 1616, St. Francis wrote from Annecy to Robert Bellarmine at Rome to consult him about the advisability of providing his nuns with a Rule, and of introducing solemn vows and enclosure as the only means of giving them full canonical status. With the practical wisdom born of long association with Roman ways, St. Robert gave him the excellent advice, which went unheeded, to let well enough alone and keep the nuns in simple vows as they were. Perhaps because he was thinking more about the nuns than about the poor, Francis de Sales found himself finally forced to do what he never intended, namely, to found one more religious Order for nuns who should be strictly enclosed.

Meanwhile his friend Vincent de Paul, busily at work in Paris, stood appalled at the misery and poverty all round him. To provide a remedy and organized help, he enlisted the aid of a widow of high social standing, Louise de Marillac, who was to prove herself his courageous and self-effacing partner. Together they assembled and trained a band of helpers to go into the hospitals and streets, nurse the dying, feed the poor, house the orphans and outcasts. "Your convent," St. Vincent told them, "will be the house of the sick; your cell, a hired room; your chapel, the parish church; your cloister, the city streets or hospital wards; your enclosure, obedience; your grating, the fear of God; your veil, holy modesty." Thus it came about that under Francis's very nose, as it were, Vincent de Paul and Louise de Marillac—perhaps because they were thinking more about the poor than about the nuns—carried his plans into effect, and did it all so quietly that they themselves did not know that they had launched a mighty enterprise of Christian charity which would win the admiration of people of the most divergent views the whole world over.

These saints all happen to be contemporaries, but as we read a collection of letters such as this, we make a discovery which opens up new horizons in the Communion of Saints and involves ourselves in a strange and intimate way. It is that the members of Christ's family recognize and call to one another across all boundaries of space and time; whether they belong to the second century or the nineteenth matters little, for being united by the same love and bound by the same loyalties, they speak the same language. The saints are not mere memories, over and done with; they are gloriously alive and present. Thus the voice of the gay little Frenchman put to death but yesterday in Vietnam becomes one with that of John the Evangelist's disciple in the Roman Coliseum. To St. Ignatius of Antioch's cry:

"I am God's wheat, to be ground by the teeth of wild beasts that I may be found pure bread!" Théophane Vénard answers in echo: "The grain of wheat must be ground, the bunch of grapes trodden in the wine press. May I become pure bread and wine fit to serve the Master."

Clearly Ignatius was filling Théophane's mind as he sat in his cage at Tonkin and spoke of himself to his sister as standing in the arena already intoning the hymn of triumph as if assured of victory (Letter 110). And little though he could foresee it, Théophane Vénard in his turn was to send a phrase ringing over the world in our own day. Raised to the priesthood on June 5, 1852, at the early age of twenty-two, he was sent almost immediately to Tonkin. There he spent years of heroic labor under overwhelming difficulties (Letter 16), until he was betrayed and captured on November 30, 1860. Chained by neck and ankles in his cage of bamboo he daily expected execution, but was kept in cruel suspense until the morning of the feast of Our Lady's Purification, February 2, 1861. When he saw the convoy of elephants and soldiers drawn up to escort him to his death, he rose and dressed in wedding garments of white cotton beneath a long robe of black silk, and in a sweet strong voice sang Latin hymns and psalms as the procession forced its way through the enormous crowds gathered to watch the spectacle. With a covetous eye on the new clothing, the executioner, a horrible hunchback, asked what Théophane would give him to dispatch him quickly. "The longer it lasts, the better," came the mocking reply.

He was a prolific letter-writer, and during the long days and nights he spent in captivity he managed to procure the necessary writing materials to send firsthand and first-rate accounts of the life within and around him to his relatives and friends at home. Less than a fortnight before his death he wrote to reassure his aged father: "We are all flowers planted on this earth which God collects in his own time, some earlier, some later. The crimson rose is one thing, the virginal lily another, the humble violet another." A young countrywoman of his would soon enough catch the sound of his voice, applaud it to the very echo, and—since there is no law of copyright among the saints—would make Théophane Vénard's little flower her self-chosen if somewhat embarrassing title.

For before the century was out, as a Carmelite nun lay dying of tuberculosis in her monastery at Lisieux, she repeatedly kissed the photograph of Théophane Vénard, which was one of her greatest treasures, and spoke to those around of his coming very soon to take her to heaven. During her twenty-four years, she had lived a sheltered and unknown life, yet had been filled with seemingly wild aspirations: "I want to be a warrior, a priest, a doctor of the Church, a martyr. I want to go to the ends of the earth to preach your name, to plant your glorious Cross on pagan shores." And now she was bidding life farewell, having accomplished none of these heroic tasks. By way of leave-taking, she copied out for her sisters, passages from Saint Théophane's last letters to his family. "He is a *little* saint," she explained to them. "His life contains nothing out of the ordinary. He loved Our Lady and he loved his family as well. So do I. I simply cannot understand those saints who didn't. As a farewell keepsake for you, I have copied some passages from his last letters to his relatives; they are my very thoughts. My soul is like his soul."

When St. Thérèse spoke of her desire for martyrdom, she was thinking in terms of the pagan lands of the Far East. Yet the opening section of this book entitled "The Christian in the World" is concerned almost exclusively with the surrender, not only of goods, but of very life itself for God's sake. For the gospel leaves us in no doubt that the Christian position everywhere is one of opposition to the world; the Christian is a citizen of the country which is above, and at any time he may be called upon to give that supreme witness to Christ which is known as "martyrdom." If any have been tempted to label the early centuries of the Christian era "the Church of the martyrs," and to think of the martyrs themselves as men of a different stamp, of a different age, bred in a different atmosphere, warriors stronger and greater than ourselves, our own eyes, if we use them aright, must necessarily disabuse us; we have witnessed in our times a martyrdom more terrible by far than that of bodily torture, and it has come to our very doors. Although one look into our own souls is enough to convince us that we are not built on the heroic scale, that we are miserable things with nothing magnificent about us, yet God in His inscrutable designs may already have marked some of us for sacrifice. He makes the choice and He gives the strength to fulfill, as He gave it to Philip Howard, an unfaithful husband (Letter 105), to Philip's litigious grandson William (Letter 106), and to many a sinner beside. The martyr is a triumph of divine grace, the perfect Christian, so he stands at the head of this book as a challenge and a model to any person who, in obedience to faith, would freely surrender his own life in exchange for the fullness of life in Christ.

For the rest, the book may be left to speak for itself, but there would seem to be one serious omission—it contains no letter which deals satisfactorily with human love. Obviously love occupies a central position in human life and human sanctity, for marriage is a Christian state of life, and in it and by it most Christians attain to eternal glory; it is not as if there were one Christian life for priests and religious and another for people in the world, since there is but one holiness to which all Christians are bound to tend by virtue of their baptism. St. Francis points out that within this framework of the Christian life common to all, whether in the cloister or the world, there are diverse conditions, vocations and duties; yet among his hundreds of letters, even he fails to treat of love and marriage convincingly. St. Thomas More, a twice-married man, would seem outwardly at least to let one down badly. He married Jane, eldest daughter of John Colt of Netherhall, Essex. However, his son-in-law William Roper informs us that More's mind most served him to the second daughter, for though he thought her the fairest and best favored, yet when he considered that it would be both great grief and some shame also to the eldest to see her younger sister preferred before her in marriage he, then, of a certain pity, framed his fancy toward her, and soon after married her. He loved her tenderly yet, when she died four years later leaving him with four children, he at once found them a mother in Alice Middleton, a sensible, kindly, unimaginative widow, seven years his senior, whose main fault seems to have been that common wifely failing, an inability to appreciate her husband's jokes. The whole story provokes reflection. Standards have shifted, and today concepts of love and marriage are dictated by the celebrities of TV and sport. There is a difference of emphasis between the two statements: "We are married because we love each other," and, "We love each other because we are married"; if St. Thomas More's life exemplifies the second, then his happy children and harmonious household are sufficient proof of the wisdom of his sacramental philosophy. Until better times befall, however, one must accept the already canonized maxims which occasionally remind one of the newly ordained curate whose sermon on marriage sent the old lady chuckling out of church with the comment: "I wish I knew as little about it as he does!"

In the main, the reader will not have to acclimatize himself to the contents of the letters; he will respond easily enough to their warmth and light. Whether it be Augustine or Jerome, Bernard or Anselm, Francis de Sales or John Bosco, the saints talk our own language, however various their intonations or different the timbre of their speech. There is perhaps one exception which may call for mental adjustment, the letter of St. Ammonas the Hermit (Letter 82). It might be possible to read it, to try to decipher and reconstruct it, without arriving at any real understanding. Contemporary interest in the Paschal mystery and the Christian initiation of baptism may well find in this unusual exposition of the contemplative ideal a mine of spiritual wisdom. Ammonas spent some time in the desert of Scete, living the life of a hermit before he joined St. Antony whose disciple and successor he became; he was probably Bishop of Oxyrhynchus, but the facts of his life have not been fully established. The first Egyptian monks lived almost exclusively in the atmosphere of the Bible from which they borrowed their formulas, but the doctrine they expressed was no theoretical abstraction. In this letter the saint starts from the concrete fact of his own experience. He is aware that he is a sinner; he has not brought to fruition the seed he received at baptism, or he may even have lost it completely through his own fault. He sees the seed as dynamic. It should develop according to the rhythm set forth in the gospel: it begins with the spirit of penance seen as the fulfillment of John the Baptist's preaching, and continues by the gift of the Holy Spirit to the crowning experience of the baptism of the Holy Ghost and of fire received by the Apostles on the day of Pentecost. The path leading to this final grace is depicted as a progressive realization of one's own state of sinfulness, hand in hand with intensive, ever-increasing petition to God to be healed and clothed once more in the heavenly garment of the Spirit of truth. This must be accompanied by unremitting effort to keep watch over one's thought-desires, in order to discern which of them come from God, from ourselves, or from the devil. The soul's interior struggle, the growing awareness of what Walter Hilton was later to call "the lump of sin," so purifies it, that with all its powers gathered into unity, it is enabled to turn its gaze Godward and await the divine response, namely, the final opening of the eyes of the heart and the contemplation of God in all purity. This Johannine teaching of the relationship between the gifts of the Holy Spirit received at baptism and the highest gifts of contemplation is of enduring relevance.

The selection of letters closes on the triumphant chord of resurrection, for however drab and mean and sorry the life of a Christian may appear in the eyes of the world, it will end in everlasting glory. Physical death consummates the sacramental death of baptism, and far from being the end of things, it is but the beginning; the believer's last breath destroys the flesh and inaugurates life, because it is breathed out in the death of Christ himself. "If we have died with him," St. Paul tells Timothy, "we shall also live with him." Thus, when we have passed through death's lowly gate, we may hope to join the procession that is ever making its way into the high Jerusalem, the everlasting city of heaven.

In conclusion, it should be observed that this book makes no claim to be a work of critical scholarship. Its aim is purely practical. The compiler has occasionally treated sources with considerable freedom, condensing or omitting passages which made the extract too long or robbed it of general application. The title of any book is a matter for serious consideration, and rarely does the final choice meet with unqualified approval. Strictly speaking, this book might have been called *Letters to the Saints,* for that man, whose words of burning exhortation and encouragement to Christians were written under the direct inspiration of the Holy Ghost, opens one of his letters thus: "Paul, an apostle of Jesus Christ by the will of God, to all the saints who are at Ephesus, the faithful in Christ Jesus: grace be to you and peace from God our Father and the Lord Jesus Christ." The faithful in Christ Jesus and the saints—in St. Paul's mind, the two are synonymous, whether they be in Ephesus, Corinth, London, New York, Paris, Tokyo, or Timbuktu. We, the faithful, are the saints. If you object: "Yes, but *saints,*" the answer is that all the men and women in this book are our brothers and sisters, one with us in the Communion of Saints, and because by our baptism we put on Christ Jesus, then potentially every one of us, like them, is a saint.

Felicitas Corrigan, O.S.B.
Feast of Our Lady of Consolation,
July 5, 1999

The Christian
in the World

1. Christianity a Rough Profession

ST. ROBERT SOUTHWELL
To his fellow-Catholics in prison, A.D. 1584

When we come to the service of Christ, we come to a rough profession, that is found to have a continual defiance and enmity with the pleasures, vanities, and praises of this world, and therefore we can look for nothing else at their hands who are friends to the same, but only trouble, hatred, and persecution. The friendship of this world is an enemy to God, and St. Paul himself said, that if he would have pleased men, he could not have been the servant of God. It is no disgrace to the sun to be hated by the birds of night, nor to the jewel to be trodden on by swine.

Wherefore whosoever hath entered a virtuous course, let him prepare his mind for all manner of temptation, for we know that the devil will never agree with those who in God's cause are his enemies, howsoever he fawned upon them while they were in his power. As long as the lion has the prey in his power, he can dally and play with it, but if he sees it offer to escape from him, he forthwith fixes his claws into it. The devil kisseth when he meaneth to kill; he giveth us a draught of poison in a golden cup, and in a sumptuous and stately ship wafteth his passengers upon the rock of eternal ruin. Oh, how much are worldlings deceived that rejoice in the time of weeping, and make their place of imprisonment a palace of pleasure; that consider the examples of the saints as follies, and their end as dishonorable; that think to go to heaven by the wide way that only leadeth to perdition!

The example of Christ and the title of Christian are motives sufficiently forcible to make us suffer adversity. The path to heaven is narrow, rough, and full of wearisome and trying ascents, nor can it be trodden without great toil; and therefore wrong is their way, gross their error, and assured their ruin, that after the testimony of so many thousands of saints, will not learn where to settle their footing. It were enough to have the example of Christ alone, "who," as St. Augustine saith, "crieth always unto us, Which way wilt thou go? I am the way. Whither wilt thou go? I am the truth. Where wilt thou stay? I am the life." And if this way lead us through austere and painful passages; if this truth teacheth humility; if this life be not achieved without a doleful and dying pilgrimage: *Woe be unto you that laugh, for you shall weep; and happy are they that mourn, for they shall be comforted.* For in truth, the contentments of this life are but real misery and feigned felicity; assured sorrow, and doubtful delights; rough storms and timorous rest; solace full of sadness, and hope full of hazard. They are like fair weather in winter, nothing durable; like a calm in the sea, always uncertain; like the steadiness of the moon that is ever changing.

Seeing therefore that all our troubles, penalties, restraints, and afflictions are but means to remind us of our state and the dangers of our profession, and but seeds of eternal glory, how much soever they may seem covered and corrupted here on earth, let us solace ourselves in hope of our joyful harvest. We are but pilgrims here; we have no place of abode, but seek a future place of rest. If the way had been filled with pleasures, with true delights, we should easily have been drawn aside in our journey towards heaven, attracted and withheld by the pleasant view and desire of these allurements. God hath therefore made our journey tedious, uncomfortable and distressing, that we may hasten to our repose, and swiftly run over the course of this life.

Christianity is a warfare, and Christians spiritual soldiers. In its beginning, our faith was planted in the poverty, infamy, persecution, and death of Christ; in its progress, it was watered by the blood of God's saints; and it cannot come to the full growth unless it be fostered with the showers of the martyrs' blood. Our flowers, that foreshew the happy calm of our felicity, grow out of thorns, and of briars must we reap our fruit. But if the stalk wound, the flowers heal; if the gathering be troublesome, the fruit is the more delightsome. We know that the flower of Jesse gave its most pleasant scent, and came to its full growth upon the cross; we know that the fruit of life was not gathered without thorns. We must now ascend to the mount of myrrh, which is in taste bitter, and to the hill of frankincense, which giveth no sweet savor but when it is by fire resolved. Now cometh the winnower with his fan to see who is blown away like light chaff, and who resisteth the blasts like massy wheat. That which lieth hid in the young blade of corn is displayed in the ripe ear; and that which is concealed in the flower is uttered in the fruit. The cunning of the pilot is not known till the tempest riseth; nor the courage of the captain till the war beginneth; nor the constancy of the Catholic till the persecutor rageth.

We must not suffer Christ's flock either to be scandalized by our example, or destitute of our necessary endeavors. Suppose a serious and earnest battle, whereupon the state of the common-weal depended, and where the king himself was in complete armor, ready in person to fight for his kingdom: should any of his nobles come into the field with a fan of feathers instead of a buckler, and a posy of flowers instead of a sword, and, in every respect, more like a carpet-knight than a man of arms, surely the king could not take it but in very evil part: even so will Christ, if in this spiritual war against his Church, for which he fought in person and received so many wounds, we should look more like worldly wantons than true soldiers, and not be as ready as our king and captain to venture our lives in the same contest. Now therefore is the time that it becometh us to show proof of ourselves. Now must it be known whether we be vessels of honor or reproach; whether we be signed with the seal of the lamb, or branded with the mark of the beast; whether we be of the wheat or of the tares; and, finally, whether we belong to the flock of Christ or to the herd of Belial.

2. Life, What Is It?

ST. PETER CANISIUS
To the Jesuits in Cologne, A.D. 1552

The several sorts of great misery incident to this life are before us. We have bitter experience of the difficulties of our generation and know the appalling changes of fortune to which practically everything is subjected, just as if the world was in its last delirium and about to collapse into nothingness. In this place we hear with what terrible cruelty the Turk rages against our next neighbors of Hungary, often butchering many thousands of Christians in the most brutal way. And is there to be any measure or end to the multitude of stormy mutinies that have now begun? We are borne down and disquieted from every side by a thousand treacheries and evil designs, and there is no place of rest and solid peace for us except in the wounds of our Crucified Lord. In them is our home of refreshment, our harbor, our sanctuary. Let the world indulge its madness. Let it wear itself out, for it cannot endure and passes like a shadow. It is growing old and, I think, is in its last decrepit stage. But we, buried deep in the wounds of Christ, why should we be dismayed?

3. Riding the Storm

ST. JOHN CHRYSOSTOM
June 404

To the most worthy deaconess, beloved of God, Olympias, John the Bishop sends greetings in the Lord.

Come now, I am going to ease the soreness of your despondency and scatter the thoughts which have given rise to this somber cloud. What bewilders your mind, why do you grieve and torment yourself? Because the storm that has rushed upon the Churches is fierce and threatening, because it has shrouded all in moonless darkness and is working up to a crisis, day after day bringing cruel shipwreck while the whole world is toppling over into ruin? I am aware of this too; there is no one to deny it. Whenever you hear that one of the Churches has been submerged, another tossed in dire distress, this one drowned by the angry flood, that mortally injured in some way, that a certain Church has received a wolf instead of a shepherd, a second a pirate instead of a helmsman, a third an executioner instead of a physician, be saddened by all means, for one ought not to endure such things without pain. But since grieve you must, at the same time set a limit to your sorrow. If you like, I will sketch the present position for you to depict the tragedy in even clearer lines.

We see the ocean upheaved from its very bed, we see the dead bodies of sailors floating on the surface, others overwhelmed by the waves, ships' decks split asunder, sails rent, masts broken in pieces, the oars slipped out of the hands of the rowers, the helmsmen sitting idle on the decks opposite their tillers, hands folded on knees. Before the hopelessness of the situation they can only groan aloud, utter piercing shrieks, wail, lament. No sky visible, no sea: everything lies in deep, obscure, and gloomy darkness; no man can descry his neighbor. The roaring waves swell and thunder, sea beasts rise on every side to threaten the voyagers. Why try to find words for what cannot be expressed? For whatever simile I choose for present-day evils, words elude and fail me altogether.

I am conscious of these disasters, yet for all that I do not relinquish a most firm hope. I keep my mind fixed on the Pilot of all things; He does not ride the storm by steersmanship, but by a mere nod He breaks the surging of the sea, and if not immediately, if not at once, that precisely is His way. He does not cut calamities short at the outset, but averts them only as they approach their climax when almost all have abandoned hope. Only then does He show forth wonders and miracles and display that power which is His alone, while He schools the sufferers in patience.

Do not lose heart then. There is only one thing to be feared, Olympias, only one trial, and that is sin. I have told you this over and over again. All the rest is beside the point, whether you talk of plots, feuds, betrayals, slanders, abuses, accusations, confiscation of property, exile, sharpened swords, open sea, or universal war. Whatever they may be, they are all fugitive and perishable. They touch the mortal body but wreak no harm on the watchful soul. Hence when blessed Paul wanted to stress the insignificance of earthly weal and woe, he summed it up in a single phrase: *The things that are seen are temporal* (2 Cor 4:18). Why then fear the things that are temporal which will roll on in an ever-flowing stream? Whether pleasant or painful, the present does not last for ever.

Do not be perturbed therefore by all that is going on. Give up crying for help to this person or that and chasing shadows—for such is all human endeavor. Rather should you incessantly invoke Jesus whom you adore, that He may but turn His face towards you. Then, in one decisive moment, all your trouble is ended.

4.The Acid Test

St. Philip Neri
To his spiritual son, Rome, November 6, 1556

Jesu Maria! I doubt whether I ought to address you as "Dearest," the term people usually employ at the beginning of a letter, seeing that because of the war you have the heart to keep away from us all—from father, friend, and brothers—with the idea of preserving your own skin safe and sound. Dutiful sons ordinarily help their father in his need with their possessions, their strength, their life. I shall say nothing of the man who, though ignorant of Christ, gave himself as hostage to redeem his father's dead body; nor shall I add many more besides. Their example would merely cover you with confusion, you who profess to be spiritual yet hang back irresolute because of what others may say, you who tremble for your own skin whereas you should have snatched at an opportunity like this to come and, if needs be, gain the crown of martyrdom.

It is obvious from all this that you have not as yet even made a beginning, for death scares only those who are still in a state of sin, not those who, like St. Paul, desire to die and be with Christ, or lament with Job that their days are prolonged, much as they long to depart. Indeed, were you a man such as I should wish to see you, the heaviest cross you could bear would be the powerlessness to die for Christ, as you possibly might if you came here. All men are anxious to stand on Mount Tabor and witness Christ's transfiguration, but few are willing to go up with Him to Jerusalem and accompany Him to Calvary. A true Christian is proved in the fire of tribulation. As to the consolations which filled you on your journey with Brother Alexis, you shed a few crocodile tears in the course of your reading, and thrilled with an emotion strange to you—well, there is nothing remarkable about that. Christ was merely enticing you with this sweet invitation to bear a little of His cross. As a rule, people who aim at a spiritual life begin with the sweet and afterwards pass on to the bitter. So now, away with all tepidity, off with that mask of yours, carry your cross, don't leave it to carry you. Moreover, practice discretion. Don't impose on others, and do your best to give rather than to receive, for a spiritual man has possessions simply in order to benefit his neighbor. If, as your letter tells me, you have been treated with so much kindness and courtesy, then learn from it to be gracious and humble in your own bearing; and if the friend whom you praise to the skies kept you nine days in Florence in return for the one you once spent on him in Prado, remember that you owe him eighty-one days' board at Prado by way of exchange.

But I must end my letter since I have a secretary who, I am sorry to say, is not up to much, and possesses just sufficient wit to ruin the pithiest proverbs of Solomon himself. And I shall end the more readily because I am in bed, ill and afflicted by God. Pray to Him for me, for I am sick in body, and in soul far removed from all I should like to be. Simon and Ludovico, who have written this letter for me, send you their best remembrances.

5. Soldier of the Cross

BLESSED ALEXANDER BRIANT
To the Superiors of the Society of Jesus, A.D. 1581

Pax Christi. Whenever I reflect, Reverend Fathers, how ardently and by what manifold means our good and great God seeks our salvation, desires our love, and the possession of our hearts, and yearns to reign within us, I am confounded with amazement that we wretched men, neither moved by His benefits nor allured by His rewards, nor even compelled by fear of His judgements, serve Him not with all our strength as living sacrifices and perfect holocausts. More than two years ago, I asked my then director whether, if I should return from foreign parts I might hope that the Fathers of the Society would admit me to holy obedience. And when he assured me that he had not the least doubt of it, my hope and courage increased, and for these two years during which I have lived in England, I have very frequently renewed my resolution. But now, since by the divine disposal I am deprived of my liberty and can no longer spend my labor usefully, the desire has revived and my soul is again inflamed by it, so that I may at length "vow a vow to the Lord my God." I made a vow indeed, that should it one day please God to deliver me from prison, I would within the space of a year resign myself entirely to the Fathers of the Society of Jesus, and would freely and with extreme joy, deliver up my whole will, unreservedly and for ever, to the service of God and their obedience. And this, I trust, will be accomplished by God, because the vow was made by me in time of meditation on heavenly things. For thus it happened.

The first day that I was tortured upon the rack, before I came to the torture-chamber, giving myself up to prayer, I was filled with a supernatural sweetness of spirit, and even while I was calling upon the Most Holy Name of Jesus and upon the Blessed Virgin Mary (for I was saying my Rosary) my mind was cheerfully disposed, well comforted, and readily inclined and prepared to suffer and endure those torments, even at the moment when I most certainly expected them. At length the resolution I have spoken of occurred to my mind, and I willingly renewed the vow with the same condition. It seemed to me that God was pleased instantly to approve this act.

Whether what I am relating be miraculous or no, God knoweth, but true it is, and thereof my conscience is a witness before God. And this I say that in the end of the torture, though my hands and feet were violently stretched and racked, and my adversaries fulfilled their wicked desire in practicing their cruel tyranny upon my body, yet, notwithstanding, I was without sense and feeling well nigh of all grief and pain; and not only so, but as it were comforted, eased, and refreshed of the grief of the past torture. I continued still with perfect and present senses, in quietness of heart and tranquillity of mind. In the meantime, as well as I could, I did muse and meditate upon the most bitter Passion of our Savior, and how full of innumerable pains it was. And whilst I was thus occupied, methought that my left hand was wounded in the palm, and that I felt the blood run out. But in very deed there was no such thing.

Now, therefore, that my petition may be made known to you, I address your paternities as though present; I humbly submit myself to you, earnestly begging that if it can be done, being absent, I may be able to be enrolled and received into your Society. I demand it with a suppliant mind and with my whole heart, that thus I may think humbly with the humble, resound the praises of God with the devout, may return continual thanks to Him for His benefits, and that I may also be the more assisted by suffrages to run with greater safety the course of the appointed combat. There is no cause for hesitation on account of my health, because I have now, by the goodness of God, nearly regained my former vigor and strength, and I continue to improve daily. As to the rest, commending myself to your prayers, I bid you farewell in the Lord, anxiously expecting what may be your decision regarding me. Farewell.

6. Jesuits in Disguise

ST. EDMUND CAMPION
To his Jesuit Superior, June 20, 1580

Father Robert, with Brother George his companion, had sailed from Calais after midnight on the day before I began writing this; the wind was very good, so we hope that he reached Dover some time yesterday morning. He was dressed up like a soldier—such a swaggerer, that a man needs must have very sharp eyes to catch a glimpse of any holiness and modesty shrouded beneath such a garb, such a look, such a strut. Yet our minds cannot but misgive us when we hear all men, I will not say whispering, but crying the news of our coming. It is a venture which only the wisdom of God can bring to good, and to His wisdom we lovingly resign ourselves. I will go over and take part in the fight though I die for it. It often happens that the first rank of a conquering army is knocked over. On the twentieth of June I mean to go to Calais: in the meantime I live in the College at St. Omer, where I am dressing up myself and my companion Ralph. You may imagine the expense, especially as none of our old things can be henceforth used. As we want to disguise our persons and to cheat the madness of this world, we are obliged to buy several little things which seem to us altogether absurd. Our journey, these clothes, and four horses which we must buy as soon as we reach England, may possibly square with our money; but only with the help of Providence which multiplied the loaves in the wilderness. This indeed is our least difficulty, so let us have done with it.

Today the wind is falling, so I will make haste to the sea. I have been thoroughly well treated in St. Omer College, and helped with all things needful. We purposely avoided Paris and Douai. I think we are safe, unless we are betrayed in these seaside places. I have stayed a day longer than I meant, and as I hear nothing good or bad of Father Robert, I persuade myself that he has got through safely. I pray God ever to protect your reverence, and your assistants, and the whole Society. Farewell.

7. As Others See Us

ST. FRANCES XAVIER CABRINI
To her nuns, Liverpool, November 8, 1898

This is the seventh time that I leave Europe to go to the Missions of America. Yielding to a secret inspiration of the soul, I visited this country, England, that was once the island of saints and lost its faith, alas, through the pride and passion of its king. Pray, dear daughters, pray much for the conversion of England. It breaks one's heart that this country is deprived of the true Faith. England has all the qualities that make it worthy to be a portion of Christ's fold. Her only fault is that of having but half the Faith, and no longer being joined to the Head which forms the perfect union of the Church with Christ.

I left Paris on October 27th for America via England for, although there was no time for me to work in England, I felt I wanted at least to visit this country where I longed so much to do some good. After breakfast I went out with my companion to see London. The first thing I wanted to do was to buy a trunk in place of the one I had left at Victoria Station. With this initial experience in shopping, we began to learn something about prices in London, which to us appeared fabulous. Leaving the Sisters' house to go to the center of the city where all the commerce is transacted, we entered a small station. Having taken our tickets, we stood with many others in what appeared to us a room, waiting to start. Suddenly we felt ourselves descending into the earth. Then there was a stop. People began to run as if they were running for their lives, and without saying a word. In London everybody seems to move about in silence. So we too followed and took our places in the train, and as quick as lightning we found ourselves in the center of the city, having gone all the way underground. Then we rose and came out into the daylight. When we asked people the way, they not only answered kindly, but even offered to carry our bag and umbrella. We asked one man the way, and after pointing in the right direction, he apologized at not being able to accompany us, saying he had urgent business on hand. We entered a shop about six times the size of Bocconi's in Milan to buy something we needed, and were treated with great kindness and courtesy. We were offered chairs and shown whatever might interest us. In other countries they speak of nobility and courtesy, in London they practice it. In one shop where we were unable to get a trunk, the manager made one of his clerks accompany us and gave him instructions to help us get what we wanted. I could cite similar examples by the hundred. This is how they treat Sisters in England, and God, who considers whatever is done to His servants as done to Himself, will bless this nation. On August 2nd, we left London to go to Manchester where some friends awaited us. At nine A.M. we were at Victoria, where we gave orders with regard to our luggage. The porters were going to weigh it to ascertain the cost of transport, when the clerk gave them orders to take it as it was to the train. "The Sisters," he said, "can go as they are"; and he gave me a ticket to reclaim the luggage at the end of the journey. I was astonished at the courtesy shown me, and interiorly implored blessings on this country of England which I should love to call if possible the "Land of Angels."

8. Bound for Warsaw

St. Louise de Marillac
To Sisters Margaret, Magdalen, and Frances,
Sisters of Charity, servants of the sick poor at Warsaw
August 19, 1655

Well, the moment appointed by divine Providence for our Sisters' departure is here at last. We watch them set forth with grief at the parting, but with joy in the certain knowledge that they are going to carry out God's will and unite their efforts to yours, that His sacred plans may be accomplished in the Kingdom of Poland. O my dear Sisters, those plans are of such great consequence! I beg God's goodness to manifest itself to you, for I feel confident that the revelation will give rise to deep humility and embarrassment at seeing yourselves selected for such a task, and will inspire you with the resolution never to fall short of your calling. And how must you—and I too—set about that? In this way: we must completely crush our evil passions and desires by mortifying our senses; our hearts also must be athirst if, by God's grace, they are to be filled with love. Then His goodness will be able to look with favor upon the sacrifice of self you offer up frequently to His divine Majesty, and upon the services you render to the poor.

Dear Sisters, you have always told me that you had but one heart in your three persons. In the name of the Blessed Trinity to whom you paid honor and owe honor, I beg you to open your ranks and admit our three Sisters to this union of heart so that the three last may be indistinguishable from the three first. I assure you they are carrying out the project in a frame of mind which aims solely at pleasing God; no one is out for herself, no one wants personal satisfaction, any more than you do. That doesn't mean to say that at times human nature won't provide occasions of struggle, even to the most perfect, but that, as you know, tests the loyalty of those who would belong entirely to God. Don't be taken by surprise then; however self may rebel, it is precisely then that our souls must rise to ever more generous heights in the practice of heroic virtue. We must straightway humble ourselves, calm our feelings, and give proof that we intend to be real Christians; thus we shall pay homage to Jesus Christ by exercising the virtues He has Himself set before us in His sacred humanity.

One thing seems to me necessary. Will you allow me to ask it of you, dearest Sisters? It is this: never speak Polish among your three selves without explaining what you say to the others, for in this way they will learn the language more quickly, and you will avoid the pitfalls which might cause trouble were you to act otherwise. You realize these Sisters' attitude towards God as they set out? They go to perform His holy will by serving the poor in a spirit of love. And their attitude towards you? They appreciate the choice God has seen fit to make of you to be the corner stones of this new foundation, they believe that you should be given all the credit for it, and that God's providence has sheltered you under His wings to guide you as you go without companionship and in blind trust, having no clear knowledge of the road. These considerations, however, cause them no jealousy whatever; on the contrary, the Sisters derive consolation from treading in your footsteps and look forward to finding you practicing the customs and duties that God requires both of you and of themselves. They hope moreover that you, dear Sister Margaret, will not refuse them a timely word of advice when they need it, any more than will the other Sisters, for they have no idea, you know, how the sick are nursed in that country.

I believe, dear Sisters, that I can never be sufficiently glad at the unity I foresee will bind you in word and deed, both at home (where it will show itself openly and edify all) and abroad. In other words, as regards your own six selves, no secrets whatever; as regards the world outside, everything kept secret that passes within the family circle of the six. Oh, if you do that, what great things lie in store!

I implore the goodness of our Lord to bestow on you the blessings necessary to the task He lays upon you, and am in His holy love, dearest Sisters, your humble and very affectionate servant,

Louise de Marillac

P.S. I assume that there is no need to ask you to pray God for the well-being of our revered Father, Monsieur Vincent.

9. A Call From Canada

St. John de Brébeuf
To the Jesuits in France, A.D. 1636

When you reach the Hurons, you will certainly find hearts full of charity; we shall welcome you with open arms as an angel of paradise, we have every intention of doing all we possibly can for you; but our position is such that we can do precious little. However careworn and weary you may be, we can offer you nothing but a poor mat, or at best a skin rug for bed; added to that, you will arrive at a time of year when fleas will keep you awake almost all night. And this petty martyrdom, to say nothing of mosquitoes, sandflies, and suchlike gentry, lasts usually not less than three or four months of the summer.

As for the winter, how do you imagine you will spend it? I am not exaggerating when I tell you that five to six months of winter are passed in almost continual discomforts—bitter cold, smoke, and vexation from the natives. We have a simple log cabin, but so well jointed that we have to send someone outside to see what the weather is like. The smoke is very often so thick, so stifling, and so persistent, that for five or six days at a time, unless you are completely hardened to such conditions, it is all you can do to decipher a line or two of your Breviary. And from morning until night, our hearth is almost always surrounded by natives, and of course, they seldom fail to appear at mealtimes. The food is not so bad. We are usually satisfied with a little corn, or a morsel of smoked fish, or some fruit. Strawberries, raspberries, and blackberries according to the season are to be found in almost incredible quantities. We gather plenty of grapes which are fairly good; the squashes last sometimes four or five months, and are so abundant that they are to be had for almost nothing.

So far we have looked only on the bright side. As we have

Christians in almost every village, we have to reckon on making the rounds at all seasons, and on staying in any place if necessity demands for two or three whole weeks, amid indescribable annoyances. Moreover our lives hang upon a single thread. Apart from the fact that your cabin is merely, so to speak, a thing of straw, and may be burned down at any moment, the ill-will of the natives is enough to keep us in a state of almost perpetual fear. A malcontent may set you on fire, or choose some lonely spot to split your skull open. And then you are held responsible for the barrenness or fruitfulness of the earth on pain of your life: you are the cause of droughts; if you cannot make rain, they go so far as threatening to do away with you. I leave you to imagine if we have any grounds for feeling secure.

There is no inducement whatever here to the practice of virtue. We live among tribes who have no idea of what you mean when you speak to them of God, and whose mouths are often filled with horrible blasphemies. You are occasionally forced to forgo offering the holy Sacrifice of the Mass; and when you are able to say it, a little corner of your cabin must serve you as chapel, although the smoke, snow, or rain will hinder you from adorning it even had you the means of doing so. I need not warn you that there is not much chance of privacy with the natives all round; they scarcely ever leave you, and hardly know what it is to speak in a low tone. One point I dare not discuss: the risk of disaster from falling into their impurity, if a man's heart is not sufficiently filled with God to be steadfast in resisting this poison.

"Well, and is that all?" someone will exclaim. "Do you think such arguments are likely to quench the fire that consumes me? All you have told me seems to me nothing in comparison with what I am ready to endure for God. If I knew a place under heaven where there was yet more to be suffered, I would go there." Ah, you to whom God has given this desire and this light, come, come, dear Brother. It is workmen like you we want out here. Have no fear of the difficulties. There will be none, since you look for comfort only in being crucified with the Son of God. You who have learned to commune with God and converse in heaven with saints and angels will find silence sweet. As for the diet, it might well be insipid did not the gall endured by our Lord render it more savory and delicious than the most appetizing food in the world. What joy to shoot these rapids and scale these rocks for one whose mind is on his loving Savior, tormented by cruel enemies, and mounting Calvary bowed beneath His Cross. The discomfort of a canoe is very easy to bear, to him who recalls our Lord crucified. What a consolation—for unless I use such terms I shall not satisfy you—to be perhaps abandoned on the journey by the natives, exhausted by illness, or dying from hunger in the woods, and to be able to say to God, "My God, since I have come to do Your holy will, here I am in this extremity." Then with your whole thought upon the God-Man who died upon the Cross, you will re-echo His cry to His Father, "My God, my God, why hast Thou forsaken me?"

I tell you that if Truth Himself had not declared that there is no greater love than to lay down one's life for one's friends, I should conceive it a thing equally noble to do what the Apostle tells the Corinthians: "I die daily, I affirm it, by the very pride that I take in you, brethren, in Christ Jesus our Lord." It would be equally noble, in other words, to drag out a life full of suffering, amid continual likelihood of a violent death, which those whom you have come to save will probably inflict on you. I sometimes recollect what St. Francis Xavier once wrote to Father Simon, and please God the same thing may one day be written even of ourselves, unworthy though we be. His words were: "The best of news comes from Molucca: John Beira and his companions are constantly in peril and in danger of death, and the result is great progress in the Christian religion."

10. Capture by the Mohawks

ST. ISAAC JOGUES
To his Jesuit Provincial, August 5, 1643

We set out from the Hurons on June 13, 1642, in four canoes with twenty-three men on board—eighteen natives and five Frenchmen. In addition to the difficulties of overland transport, the journey was dangerous by reason of enemies who seize the main roads every year and capture many prisoners. Being angry with the French, they had shortly before announced that if a Frenchman fell into their hands they would not only torture him, but would roast him alive over a slow fire as well. We travelled not without danger, fear, loss, and shipwreck, but thirty-five days after our departure, we arrived safe and sound at the residence of Three Rivers, returned thanks to God, spent twenty-five days partly there and partly at Quebec, and embarked again on August 7 for the Hurons.

On the second day of the journey, some of our men noticed recent tracks on the shore—whether made by friend or foe we knew not. Eustace Ahatsistari, a notable and experienced warrior, thinks them enemies. "However strong we may suppose them," he tells us, "there are no more than three canoes. We need have no fear." So we continue on our way. A mile further on, however, we meet them—seventy of them with twelve canoes concealed in the grass and woods. They suddenly surround us. In terror, the Hurons abandon the canoes and many take to the dense woods. We were left alone, four Frenchmen and a few others, Christians and catechumens, to the number of twelve or fourteen. Commending themselves to God, they stand on the defensive. But they were quickly outnumbered, and when a Frenchman, René Goupil, who was in the forefront of the fight, was taken with some Hurons, they no longer put up any resistance.

Barefoot as I was, I could not and would not escape. Moreover I refused to abandon a Frenchman and the Hurons, since some of those captured were unbaptized, and those who were free ran the risk of falling into the hands of the enemy who were combing the woods for them. I stood alone therefore, and voluntarily surrendered to the prisoners' guard, choosing to be companion in their peril as I had been on their journey. The guard was amazed at my action, and not without fear came up and placed me among them. I immediately heard the Frenchman's confession, instructed the Hurons in the faith, and baptized them; and as prisoners kept coming in, my work of instruction and baptism increased in proportion.

Guillaume Cousture, a brave young man, strong in body and fleet of foot—one of those laymen who serve God without any worldly interest—had escaped his pursuer's grasp when he looked back and saw I was not there. "I will not desert my dear Father," he decided, "for he is left forsaken in the hands of the enemy." So he returned at once to the savage foe, and gave himself up. Oh would that he had never taken such a decision! During the battle, he had slain one of their most prominent chiefs, and was therefore treated with the utmost cruelty. They stripped him naked, and like mad dogs ripped away his nails with their teeth, bit his fingers off, and pierced his right hand with a spear. He endured it all with invincible patience, filled with the thought of the nails that fastened our Savior. And now the executioners' first feeling of admiration for me yielded to ferocity. They turned on me with their fists and knotted sticks, left me half-dead on the ground, and a little later tore away my nails in the same way, and bit off my two forefingers which caused me incredible agony. They did likewise to René Goupil.

With the shouts of conquerors, they then set out to carry us captive into their territories, twenty-two of us, three being already dead. We suffered many hardships during this journey of thirty-eight days—hunger, intense heat, threats, blows, as well as the cruel pain of our unhealed wounds, which so putrefied that worms dropped off them. The enemy went even further. In cold blood, they inhumanly tore out our hair and beards, and with their nails, which are extremely sharp, they wounded us in the most tender and sensitive parts of the body. On the eighth day of our travel, we fell in with two hundred savages on their way to attack the French. These gave thanks to the sun, who directs the fortunes of war, so they believe, fired their guns to signal their joy, and forced us to disembark, whereupon they welcomed us with a rain of sticks. I being the last, and therefore more exposed to their beating, fell halfway along the road and thought I must die there, unable and unwilling as I was to rise. What I suffered is known only to One for whose love and in whose cause it is pleasing and glorious to suffer. They wanted, however, to take me into their country alive. So moved by cruel mercy, they carried me covered in blood from wounds—especially in the face— to a hill on which they had erected a stage. They now loaded me with a thousand insults and dealt me fresh blows on neck and body. They burned one of my fingers, crushed another under their teeth, and so twisted the bruised and torn sinews of the remainder, that although at present partially healed, they are crippled and deformed.

In the afternoon of the tenth day, we left the canoes to make the rest of the four days' journey on foot. Hunger was our constant companion. We went for three days without food, but on the fourth found some wild fruits. At last, on the eve of the Assumption of the most Blessed Virgin, we arrived at the first village of the Iroquois. They and the Huron slaves awaited us on either bank of the river, the Hurons to warn us to get away for otherwise we should be burned to death, the Iroquois to belabour us with sticks, fists, and stones aimed especially at my head, for they hate a head shaven and shorn. Two nails had been left me; these they now tore out with their teeth, and with their razor-sharp nails they ripped away the underlying flesh to the very bone. They then led us to a village situated on another hill. Before reaching it, we once more had to run the gauntlet between lines of youths armed with sticks. But we who knew how "He scourgeth every son whom He receiveth" made a free-will offering of ourselves to God, who was acting with fatherly sternness that He might be well-pleased in us, His sons. One by one we went forward: first, a Frenchman, stark naked, René in the middle, I in shirt and breeches last. Cruelly and long, "the wicked wrought upon my back," not only with sticks but with iron rods got from the Dutch. René, who was not very agile, received so many blows, particularly in the face, that nothing could be seen of him but the whites of his eyes, all the more impressive since he so much resembled one "as it were a leper and struck by God, having neither beauty nor comeliness." We had scarcely taken breath before they struck us three times with a heavy rod on the bare shoulders, and set about unsheathing their knives to chop off the rest of our fingers. They began with me, as being the most eminent and obviously respected by the French and Hurons. An old man and woman approach me; he orders her to cut off my thumb. She refuses at first, but after three or four threats, the old man compels her and she does his bidding. Thereupon, calling to mind the sacrifices I had offered Thee in Thy Church, I took hold of the amputated thumb with my other hand and offered it to Thee, my God, living and true, until on the advice of a companion I let the thumb drop, for fear they should put it in my mouth and force me to swallow it as they often do. I thank God they left me the one on my right hand, and so enabled me by this letter to beg my Fathers and brethren to offer petition for us in the holy Church of God, whose custom it is to pray "for the afflicted and for captives."

The following day, feast of the Blessed Virgin, they led us to another village five or six miles away. My barbarian escort robbed me of my shirt, and except for a rag which he could not deny to decency, he left me with nothing but a bit of sacking for which I begged to cover my shoulders. But bowed with frequent thrashings, they could not support the rough heavy weight, especially after a blazing sun had roasted my flesh as in an oven, so that the scorched skin of my neck, shoulders, and arms soon flaked off. At the entrance to the village they beat us again, striking us mainly on the bones of the legs. At night, we lay naked on the bare ground bound with chains, while they threw coals and glowing embers on our exposed bodies. To satisfy the curiosity of all, we were led all over the place. At the third village, we met four other Hurons newly captured and mutilated like ourselves. I managed to instruct and baptize them—two with the dew which I found quite abundant in the tall leaves of Turkish corn whose stalks they gave us to chew, the other two at a brook which we passed on our way to another village. At night, they led us into a cabin and ordered us to sing. We had to obey, but we sang "the canticles of the Lord in a strange land." From song they proceeded to torture, singling out René and me. They burned me with live coals, particularly on the breast, and then with thongs of bark bound me upright between two stakes so that I thought they were going to set fire to me. To show you however that if I bore the rest with strength and patience it was not my doing, but His "who giveth strength to the weary," I was left pretty well alone during this torture—and I wept. "I will glory in nothing save in my infirmities." I thank Thee, O good Jesus, for having learnt by some slight experience, what Thou didst consent to suffer for me on the Cross, where Thy most holy body was not even supported by cords, but hung on hands and feet transfixed with cruel nails. We spent the rest of the night skewered to the ground by stakes; and what did they not do or try to do to us?

But again I thank Thee, Lord, who kept me pure from the impure hands of those barbarians.

After this, René and I were left together in a kind of free slavery, and on Our Lady's birthday one of the chief Dutchmen from the colony about forty miles away came to treat for our ransom. He stayed several days, offered a large sum, but obtained nothing. René and I had been warned of danger, and went towards a hill to say our prayers. We made an offering of our lives to God and began the Rosary. We had reached the fourth decade when we met two young men who ordered us to return to the village. "This encounter does not promise well, especially in the circumstances," I said to René. "Let us commend ourselves to God and Our Lady." At the gate of the village, one of the two men draws a hatchet which he has kept hidden, and aims a blow at René's head. He fell half-dead, but remembered according to our pact to call upon the most holy Name of Jesus. Expecting a like blow, I bare my neck and fall on my knees, but after a time the barbarian bids me get up; he has no permission, he says, to kill me. I rise, and give the last absolution to my dear companion who was still breathing, and the barbarian finally put an end to his life with two further blows. He was not more than thirty-five years of age, a man of extraordinary simplicity and innocence of life, of invincible patience and perfect conformity to the will of God. Next day, at peril of my own life, I searched for his body to lay it in the earth. They had tied a rope round his neck, dragged him naked through the whole village, and then thrown him into the river at some distance away. I found him by the river bank, half-eaten by dogs. There, in the bed of a dry torrent, I cover him with stones, deciding to go back the following day with a pick-axe to make the burial more secure. I return to the spot with tools—but they have taken my brother away. I look for him everywhere. I wade waist-high into the river, groping with hands and feet for his body, but they assure me that the flood has carried it away. I hold funeral obsequies for him, singing the psalms and prayers appointed by the Church. Groaning and sighing, I mingle my tears with the torrent. When the snow melts at the coming of Spring, I get news of him. The young men of the country inform me that they have seen his bones on the bank of the river. I kissed them with reverence, and placing them with the head, as best I could I finally gave them burial.

11. The Missouri Mission

BLESSED PHILIPPINE DUCHESNE
To Sacred Heart nuns in France, A.D. 1822

I often long to be with you to profit by your holy recreations. I should prefer to be a mere listener, but you would tell me: "It is for you to do the talking, for you have crossed the sea and must have many a tale to tell us." But I am thoroughly rusty, and without wanting to displease you, I should often fall silent. While awaiting that meeting which I trust will be one day in heaven, I have put together some incidents to buy your prayers in return.

What pleases us most is the deputation sent by the Osage Indians to Bishop Du Bourg. The chief came to St. Louis to ask Monsignor to visit his tribe. His Lordship will go there next month with some traders from Missouri who have promised to help him in every possible way to win respect for his sacred character. The Bishop gave the Indian chief a crucifix which he accepted with respect. Later when he entered one of the stores in St. Louis the shopkeeper, anxious to see if the crucifix was treasured, offered to give in exchange a fine saddle, then liquor, and finally a large sum of money. Each time the chief refused, saying that never would he give away what he had received from the "one who speaks to the Author of Life."

Bishop Flaget has lost three of his missionaries who returned to Europe, one was the founder of the Daughters of Penitence and a saint. We have four children from Prairie de Chien, a month's journey from here. That is where the Councils between the Indians and the representatives of the Government are most often held. They carpet the place of assembly with beaver skins. The most skillful Indian is the speaker and always begins: "The Author of Life has made all things and He has made the earth for all men to enjoy." He concludes with a request for liquor, gunpowder, and bread.

Love of the "Blackrobes" is general among the Indians everywhere, even among the Sioux, a most savage tribe. A priest who has been among them and who often comes here tells me that they would supply all his needs were he willing to accept it, but that he does not want to be indebted to them for fear they ask him for fire-water, that is, brandy. One Indian was strikingly converted. As he lay on his death-bed he spoke of a previous illness during which he had thought he was dying, and he said aloud: "I then saw the Author of Life and He said to me, 'Go back, your hour is not yet!' But I know that this time I *shall* go to the Author of Life." Francis, a Christian Iroquois present, said to him: "The Author of Life probably sent you back so that you might have water poured on your head." The dying Sioux made answer: "Indeed, I think it was precisely for that I was told to return to life." Francis replied: "Do you want me to go and get a Blackrobe to pour water upon you?" The Sioux answered: "Go quickly. There is need of haste." The priest who came at once was quite satisfied with the dying man's answers and baptized him; a few moments later he died. He was solemnly buried by the priest, who also baptized the dead Sioux' son who was very ill. The priest was Father Acquaroni, a Lazarist from Rome, and one of our most zealous friends.

I am sending you a writing portfolio and some Indian slippers which will show you the handiwork of the natives. They give the names of animals to those who go among them, calling the pastor of St. Genevieve "the son of a white fish." A Canadian Iroquois who had been in Florissant returned home and died at a season when journeys are impossible. His father hollowed out a tree trunk with one of his weapons, put the body inside, and tied it to a tree. When Spring came, he was told by other Indians that the dead boy was crying out: "Let us go to Florissant!" The father then brought his son's body these eighteen hundred miles and gave the pastor of Florissant two hundred francs to bury him in consecrated ground.

I have been told that there is in this country a soil which has all the properties of soap and is used as such by the savages who wash and massage themselves with it and exchange it for gunpowder, necklaces, and blankets. Every householder here makes his own soap from ashes steeped for several days in water and then slowly filtered. They then mix it with oil and boil it for several days, and at the end they have a red and very good soap. As to plants and grains, the most common is Indian corn from which bread is made. We often eat this sort of bread, which many Americans prefer to that made from wheat, which grain also grows abundantly here. There are beans, pumpkins, cantaloupe, and watermelons. Potatoes are much in use; there are white, red, yellow, and bluish or purple ones, and sweet ones that taste just like strawberries, which grow wild here, as does a small fruit having rather the shape and taste of a lemon; it is called citron in English. Maize or Indian corn is eaten on the cob while it is tender.

My letter has often been interrupted for the love of God. May we have the happiness of making Him loved, and of loving Him ourselves with an effective and generous love.

12. Eskimos and Indians

ST. FRANCES XAVIER CABRINI
To some schoolchildren, New Orleans, May 31, 1904

A few weeks ago I was at Seattle, the capital of the state of Washington. This city has such a charming position that it might be called the garden of the United States. Indeed, here it is distinguished by the name of Queen City. It might very well also be called the City of Twenty Hills—the town in fact does spread over twenty hills. A most beautiful panorama crowns it. Whilst the snow-capped peaks of the Rocky Mountains on one side, and the Olympic Mountains on the other, remind us of the North Pole, the green hills bathed by the sea are perfumed with lemon and orange blossoms and rich with splendid vegetation. In February we actually gather strawberries. It is a continual Spring, though we are fifty degrees north latitude.

During my sojourn in Seattle I was asked to open a Mission in Alaska. The natives of Alaska are supposed to have come from Lapland. I should think it will be very interesting for the Sisters who are going there to visit their ice-huts. Their system of building is very simple. They need no architects or masons. With a few planks of wood which the sea-waves, guided by the hand of God, throw up in quantities on the coast of a country where there is perpetual snow and ice, these Eskimos build their roofs and walls, which are supported against the side of the mountain. Then they pour water over the huts, and this freezes at once. This operation is repeated until the walls attain a thickness that renders them inaccessible, even to icy winds. The Eskimos pass their lives in these huts, which are more like dens than houses, and they enter them by crawling through a low narrow opening.

In the summer, at 10 P.M. the sun is still shining, and in winter, at 3 P.M. it is dark night. Now and then, by a mirage similar to that seen in the African desert, one sees suspended in the air an entire city, which is supposed to be the far-away city of Petersburg. The Eskimos' manner of taking food is very strange. If you are invited by some great personage, such as the head of a tribe, you must not imagine you are going to eat a piece of salmon or roast codfish, in which these coasts abound. In front of the head of the family you see two plates, one with the dressed meats and the other empty. Now his work begins, and this must be very hard, for he chews all the food which is given to the guests. When this has been done, it is placed on plates and handed round accordingly. This ceremony over, all the guests eat of this well-prepared dish. The white people, however, have begun to build houses and villages there, so if any of you wish to join the Sisters who are going there, you need not live in ice-huts.

The journey from Seattle to Denver is very interesting. One passes through cities all so different from one another. In Utah I saw the lakes and the mountains of salt of a transparent milk color. But it is more interesting still to see the Indian Reserves. Though the Indians retain a few of their old habits, they are now more civilized owing to the progress of religion, especially through the apostolate of the Jesuit Fathers. There is much to be done yet, for there are still many superstitions among them. When an Indian dies, all the friends are called to weep over the corpse, whether they want to or not. They even have to chant their grief in a more or less monotonous strain like this: "You were very good, oh, oh, oh! You had a lovely house, ah, ah, ah!" You may imagine what the rest of the chant is like, and it continues throughout the dead of night. When the morning dawns, the Chief arrives, and they beg him to tell them if the dead man has gone to heaven or to hell. Then he commands them to fetch him a bowl of bread and water. They hold the strange belief that while the corpse is on earth it needs nothing, but if it goes to hell it has to be provided with bread and water, as these items are not to be found in hell. If the corpse is destined for heaven, it needs nothing, so it does not return to take bread and water. Naturally, the dead man does not return for its bread and water; consequently, the tribe concludes it has gone to heaven and makes merry over it, partaking of a great banquet.

The Indian woman has to work while the man quietly smokes opium. With this most powerful narcotic, the men make themselves drunk. The poor woman and mother of many little ones, who are too small to stand, is forced to tie her offspring round her waist in a sack, and in this unconventional way has to do her washing. If the baby cries, she moves it with a shrug of her shoulders and thus calms it. This is the way the Indian baby is fondled. How grateful we should be to Christianity, which has raised the dignity of woman, re-establishing her rights, unknown to the pagan nations. Until Mary Immaculate, the Woman *par excellence*, foretold by the prophets, Dawn of the Sun of Justice, had appeared on earth—what was woman? But Mary appeared, the new Eve, true Mother of the Living, and a new era arose for woman. She was no longer a slave but equal to man; no longer a servant, but mistress within her own walls; no longer the object of disdain and contempt, but raised to the dignity of mother and educator, on whose knee generations are built up. All this we owe to Mary.

13. Adventures in Barbary

ST. VINCENT DE PAUL
To a lawyer-friend, Avignon, July 24, 1607

Two years ago the favorable progress of my affairs might have led anyone to conclude that Fortune, contrary to my deserts, was only studying how to render me more enviable than imitable, but, alas! she did so merely to make me serve as an example of her inconstancy and fickleness, turning her favor to disfavor, her kindness to unkindness.

You might have known, Sir, for you were kept only too well informed of my doings, how I found, on my return from Bordeaux, that a will had been made in my favor by a kind old lady of Toulouse. Her property consisted of some movable goods and land which had been granted to her by the bipartite court of Castres, as compensation for a debt of three or four hundred crowns owed to her by a good-for-nothing, worthless scamp. In order to recover some of it, I set out for Toulouse with the intention of selling the property. I did so on the advice of my best friends, because I not only needed money to settle some debts which I had contracted, but also because I foresaw I was bound to undergo great expense in pursuance of a certain object which I must not even dare mention.

On my arrival, I learned that my fine fellow had decamped, because a warrant had been taken out for his arrest by my good old friend to whom he owed the money; I was told that he was doing very well at Marseille, and was quite well off. Whereupon my lawyer said (as indeed the nature of the case demanded) that I ought to go to Marseille, for he believed that if I had him arrested I might recover two or three hundred crowns. As I had no money to carry out his advice I sold the horse I had hired in Toulouse, intending to pay for it on my return, which has been so unfortunately delayed that I am deeply dishonoured at having left my affairs in such confusion. It would never have happened if God had given such a happy issue to my undertaking as appearances warranted.

Acting on this advice, then, I went to Marseille, captured my man there, had him thrown into prison, and settled with him for three hundred crowns, which he paid cash down. As I was about to return by land, I was persuaded by a gentleman, with whom I was lodging, to set sail with him for Narbonne, because the weather was favorable. I did so in order to arrive there sooner and spare expense, or, to put it more truly, never to reach there at all and to lose everything.

The wind was so favorable that it would have taken us in a day to Narbonne, 50 leagues distant, if God had not permitted three Turkish brigantines, which were cruising about in the Gulf of Lyons, on the look-out for ships from Beaucaire—where a fair was being held, which is looked upon as one of the finest in Christendom—to bear down on us, and attack us in such lively fashion that two or three of our men were killed and all the rest wounded, including myself, who received an arrow-wound that will serve me as a clock for the remainder of my life. We were forced to surrender to these ruffians, worse than tigers, who, in the first fury of their rage, cut our pilot into a hundred thousand pieces, because they had lost one of their own leaders, as well as four or five other scoundrels slain by our men. Then, after roughly bandaging our wounds, they put us in irons, pursued their course, committing a thousand robberies on the way, but releasing all who had surrendered without a fight, after plundering them. At last, laden with booty, at the end of seven or eight days, they made for Barbary, which is, without the authorization of the Grand Turk, a lair and den of thieves. On our arrival we were exposed for sale, with a proclamation to the effect that we had been captured on a Spanish vessel, because, were it not for this lie, we should have been released by the Consul whom the king maintains there to protect trade with France.

This is the way we were sold: stripping us stark naked they gave each of us a pair of drawers, a linen jacket, and a cap. They then marched us through the streets of Tunis, to which they had come expressly to sell us. After making us march five or six times through the city, they brought us back to the ship so that the merchants might see those who could eat heartily and those who could not, and thus show that our wounds were not mortal. They then brought us back to the market-place, to which the merchants came to examine us, just as one does when buying a horse or an ox. They made us open our mouths and show our teeth, felt our sides, examined our wounds, made us walk, trot, and run; they then made us carry loads and wrestle, that they might thus gauge the strength of each individual, besides a thousand other brutalities.

I was sold to a fisherman, who was very soon forced to part with me because I could not stand the sea. He sold me to an old man, a Stagirite physician and sovereign extractor of quintessences, a very humane and kindly man, who, as he told me, had labored for 50 years seeking to discover the philosopher's stone, but all in vain as far as the stone was concerned, though most successfully as regards another manner of transmuting metals. In proof whereof, I can assert that I have often seen him melt down equal quantities of gold and silver, first arranging them in thin layers, over which he put a layer of some powders, then another layer of the metals, and finally another layer of powders. He then put the lot into a melting-pot or goldsmith's crucible and placed them in a furnace for twenty-four hours. After which time he opened it and the silver had become gold. I have also seen him, and this very frequently, freeze, or fix, quicksilver into pure silver, which he sold to give alms to the poor. It was my duty to keep the furnaces going and, thanks be to God, this gave me as much pain as pleasure. He was very fond of me, and took pleasure in discoursing to me on alchemy, and still more on his religion, to which he bent all his efforts to win me, promising me abundant riches and all his knowledge.

God always wrought in me a firm conviction that I should one day escape through the constant prayers I offered up to Him and the Blessed Virgin Mary, to whose sole intercession I firmly believe I owe my deliverance. The hope and firm belief that I had of seeing you again, Sir, made me assiduous in begging him to teach me how to cure the gravel, which I daily saw him do in a miraculous manner. He did so, and even allowed me to prepare and administer the ingredients. Oh! how often have I since desired that I had been a slave before the death of your brother who was, with you, a co-Maecenas in doing good to me, and that I had known the secret which I now send you. Death would not have triumphed over him (at least in the way it did), even though it is said that man's days are reckoned in the sight of God. That, indeed, is true, not because God had reckoned the number of one's days as so many, but because the number had been reckoned in the sight of God since things have so fallen out; or, to put it more clearly, he did not die when he actually did because God had so foreseen it, or reckoned the number of his days to be so and so, but because God had foreseen his death and the number of his days to be what they were, since he died when he actually did.

I remained, then, with this old man from the month of September, 1605, until the following August, when he was taken away and carried off to the Grand Sultan that he might work for him; but all in vain, for he died of grief on the journey. He bequeathed me to one of his nephews, who at once resold me, after his uncle's death, because he had heard a rumor that M. de Brèves, the King's ambassador to Turkey, was coming, with true and formal patents from the Grand Turk, for the recovery of Christian slaves.

I was bought by a renegade Christian, from Nice in Savoy, a natural enemy, who carried me off to his *temat*, for such is the name given to land held in *metayer* from the Grand Sultan, for the people do not own anything; everything belongs to the Sultan. This man's *temat* was in the mountains where the country is excessively hot and sandy. One of his three wives (a Greek-Christian, but a schismatic) was a very intelligent woman, who liked me very much. Moreover, towards the end, another wife, a born Turk, was the instrument of God's boundless mercy in withdrawing her husband from apostasy, restoring him to the bosom of the Church, and of rescuing me from slavery. As she was curious to know our manner of life, she used to come daily to the fields where I was digging, and afterwards ordered me to sing the praises of my God. The remembrance of the *Quomodo cantabimus in terra aliena* of the captive children of Israel in Babylon made me begin, with tears in my eyes, the psalm *Super flumina Babylonis.* Then I sang the *Salve, Regina,* and several others. It was quite marvelous to see the delight she took in all this. She did not fail to tell her husband, in the evening, that he had done wrong in abandoning his religion, which she considered an extremely good one, from what I had told her of our God, as also from some of His praises which I had sung in her presence. She said that she had experienced such heavenly delight in hearing them that she did not believe the paradise of her fathers, for which she hoped, was so glorious, or gave her so much pleasure as she had experienced when I was praising my God; and she concluded by saying that it was really marvelous.

This other Caiaphas, or Balaam's ass, was the cause of her husband's saying to me, on the following day, that he was only waiting for an opportunity for us to make our escape to France, and that God would be glorified by what he would soon do. This short time lasted ten months, during which he encouraged me in vain hopes, which were indeed ultimately realized, for we escaped in a little skiff, and arrived at Aigues-Mortes on the fifteenth of June. Shortly afterwards we reached Avignon, where His Lordship the Vice-Legate, with tears in his eyes and a voice shaken with sobs, reconciled the renegade, in St. Peter's Church, to the honor of God and the edification of the onlookers. His Lordship has kept both of us near him, with the intention of bringing us to Rome, as soon as his term of office, which ends on St. John's day, has expired. He promised the penitent to have him admitted to the austere monastery of *Fate bene fratelli*, which the man had vowed to enter, and he has promised to provide me with a good benefice. He does me the honor of loving and tenderly cherishing me, on account of some secrets of alchemy which I have taught him, and which he values more highly, he says, than if I had given him a mountain of gold, because he has been working at alchemy all his life, and nothing affords him so much pleasure. As my Lord is aware that I am an ecclesiastic, he has ordered me to procure my letters of ordination, assuring me that he will provide well for me, and procure me a really good benefice. I was worrying how to procure a trustworthy messenger for this purpose, when a friend of mine, one of His Lordship's household, introduced me to Monsieur Canterelle, the bearer of this letter, who was setting out for Toulouse. I have requested him to be kind enough to push on to Dax, in order to present you with this letter and to procure my own letter of ordination, as well as those of my baccalaureate in theology, which I gained at Toulouse, and I beg you to let him have them. To this end, I am forwarding you a receipt.

I brought away with me two turquoises, which are naturally diamond-shaped, and I am sending you one with the request that you will as graciously accept it as I humbly offer it.

14. To Christian Mandarins

ST. ROBERT BELLARMINE
Rome, May 12, 1616

Father Nicholas Trigault, our Reverend Brother, caused us great joy when, on his return to us after so long a journey from the remote East, he informed us that in the vast Empire of China a door has begun to open for the admission of the faith of Jesus Christ, in which alone can be found certainty of eternal salvation. The entire city of Rome, head of all the kingdoms of the West, exulted at the news. So did the Sovereign Pontiff Paul V, who is the Father of all kings and Christian peoples that acknowledge the true God, King of Heaven and earth, and with him, we the Cardinals and Bishops, his assistants, greatly rejoiced, and also the whole Christian priesthood and people.

Long and sorely have we lamented that so great a multitude of men, endowed with such intelligence as are the people of the immense Empire of China, should have been all this time in ignorance of God, their Creator, and of His Son, Jesus Christ, who, according to the oracles of every prophet the world has known, gave Himself up to death for us in time that He might make us sharers of his glory throughout eternity. The devil, the perpetual enemy of the human race, who of old fell from Heaven and became the Prince of Darkness because of his pride, had, under pretense of preserving your Kingdom of China, closed the door of your salvation to the preachers of the Gospel.

Now, however, the grace of God has at last begun to dawn upon your country, and to convince you that the teaching of the Gospel does not take away earthly kingdoms but bestows a heavenly one. That is why I want to congratulate you, upon whom God has conferred so great a benefit, and that is why I am so glad at heart, knowing that I have now so many new brothers in our Lord.

But as faith in God the Father and His Divine Son does not by itself suffice for salvation, unless we also live soberly, justly, and piously in this world, I exhort you to run in the way of God's commandments without offense, abstaining from all injustice, impurity, lying, and deceit, abounding in every good work, making progress in holy virtues and especially in trustful love of God and real charity towards one another. If for the love of God you have to suffer any trouble or persecution, be glad and rejoice for your reward is very great in Heaven. This is the will of God, our Father, that our faith, hope, and charity should be proved by patience as gold is tried in the furnace. It would not be difficult for Him to free us at once from all tribulation and sorrow, but instead He permits His friends to suffer much in this world that He may crown them all the more gloriously in Heaven, and make them more like His only-begotten Son, who never ceased to do good and to suffer injury while He was on earth that He might teach us patience by His example.

Just as He humbled Himself, being made obedient even unto death, the death of the cross, and just as God the Father for that reason exalted Him to the throne of His glory, and gave Him a Name that is above all other names,... so, too, will the Son of God exalt us and make the body of our lowliness like the body of His glory, if we bear persecutions and adversities with steadfast patience of soul.

I need not say any more to you, for I know that my brothers of the Society of Jesus who are with you do not fail to teach and spur you on continually in the way of holiness. May God keep you safely in the Name of Christ our Redeemer, and let us pray for one another that one day we may all be together in heaven.

15. Europe, Help China!

BLESSED JOHN GABRIEL PERBOYRE
To a priest in Paris, Ho-Nan, August 22, 1837

When I left Paris, you kindly promised me the support of your prayers on condition that I wrote you a little letter from China. Charity has led you to fulfill daily your side of the contract; justice demands that I fulfill mine here and now.

At the moment I am sharing the company of two Chinese priests who are teaching me their language. Its genius is so different from the European tongue, and I am feeling rather happier in the study now than when I first embarked on it. It is really very beautiful when you know how to speak it well, and although full of aspirates, it sounds very sweet for all that. Every word is monosyllabic. Its many diphthongs make it harmonious, and five changes of pitch vary the pronunciation of its different vowels and transform it into music. To a Chinaman reading or recitation means singing. The characters of the alphabet are almost beyond reckoning; it is extremely difficult to master them all. With courage, however, and by following a definite plan, one can fairly quickly learn a good many of them. The missionaries who have not time to become scholars generally know sufficient to enable them to understand the books on religion. They apply themselves more to picking up spoken language since in practice that is so much more essential. There are in China some forty European and about eighty Chinese priests. This number of workmen is nothing like enough to cope with the Christians alone. In various provinces there are occasional conversions from among the pagans, but they make a scarcely perceptible difference to such a huge mass.

One young pagan was admitted into a room where I was seated. He took up his position in front of me and studied me with as close an attention as if he intended to paint my portrait; he then retired perfectly satisfied, so he said, at having seen a European nose. It was his heart's desire to behold this marvel at least once during his lifetime, because he had understood his father—who had seen our venerated confrère Monsieur Clet—to say that a European had a longer nose than a Chinaman. Mention of M. Clet reminds me to tell you that I congratulate myself upon tilling the portion of Our Lord's vineyard that he himself cultivated with such zeal and success. But can't you send us a whole squadron of Francis Xaviers for this China of ours which stands in such need of them? May God multiply our number, make us holy, and fill us with His Spirit!

The conversion of China however depends also on the prayers that the Christians of Europe offer for this country. *Pray for one another that you may be saved, for the unceasing prayer of a just man is of great avail* (Jas 5:16). If you see prayers going up to heaven on every side, multiplied more and more, more and more intensified, then you from afar are in a better position than we on the spot to judge whether the kingdom of God is at hand for this mighty nation. What consolation it would give the Church to see enter her fold a whole people as notable and attractive as the Chinese. Now if all the children would join hands and do violence to the Father of mercies, they would sooner or later obtain this great miracle in spite of the obstacles which seem to make it impossible. The members of the Association for the Propagation of the Faith have most happily made it their business to undertake this noble mission. Would that all their brethren in Jesus Christ could be fired with a similar zeal for the interests of our divine King, enlist in the same spiritual campaign, and take up the arms of prayer to carry on the warfare which will bring Satan's empire to ruin.

16. Straitened on Every Side

St. Théophane Vénard
To a priest-friend, May 10, 1860

Perhaps you may fancy I am dead, or that time has swept away our old friendship. I hope suppositions will disappear when you see this monstrous bit of paper—the only thing I can get—and on which I shall try to paint for you (as I have nothing but a brush) a description of our life here.

I write to you from Tonkin, and from a little dark hole, of which the only light is through the crack of a partially-opened door, which just enables me to trace these lines, and now and then to read a few pages of a book. For one must ever be on the watch. If the dog barks, or any stranger passes, the door is instantly closed, and I prepare to hide myself in a still lower hole, which has been excavated in my temporary retreat. This is the way I have lived for three months, sometimes alone, sometimes in company with my dear old friend, Mgr. Theurel. The convent which sheltered us before has been destroyed by the pagans, who got wind of our being there. We had just time to escape between two double walls about a foot wide. We saw through the chinks the band of persecutors, with the mayor at their head, garotting five or six of the oldest nuns, who had been left behind when the younger ones took flight. They beat these poor women with rods, and we heard them howling like very demons, threatening to kill and burn everybody and everything, unless they were given a large sum of money. This agreeable visit lasted for four hours, till they were invited by the principal people of the village to go and eat and get drunk with them. It was not till cock-crow that we could make our escape, and take refuge in a smoky dung-heap belonging to a pious old Christian widow, where we were joined by another missionary.

What do you think of our position, dear old friend? Three missionaries of whom one is a bishop, lying side by side, day and night, in a space about a yard and a half square, our only light and means of breathing being three holes, the size of a little finger, made in the mud wall, which our poor old woman is obliged to conceal by some faggots thrown down outside. Under our feet is a brick cellar, constructed in the dead of night with great skill by one of our catechists; in this cellar, there are three bamboo tubes which are cleverly contrived to open on to the borders of a neighboring lake with its fresh air.

You might ask, Why don't we go mad? Always shut up in the thickness of two walls, with a roof one can touch with one's hand, our companions spiders, rats, and toads, always obliged to speak in a low voice, "like the wind," as the Annamites say, receiving every day the most terrible news of the torture and death of our fellow-missionaries, and worse still, of their occasional apostasy under torture. It requires, I own, a special grace not to be utterly discouraged and cast down. As to our health, we are like poor plants in cellars. One of my brethren writes to me today to say that for eighteen months he has not seen the sun; he dates his letter "from the land of the moles." As for me, I live on without being too bilious; my weakness is my nerves. I need something strengthening such as wine, but we have barely enough to say Mass, so one must not think of it. Not many days ago I managed to pass into an adjoining house, and was very much astonished to find myself tottering like a drunken man. The fact was that I had lost the habit, and almost the power, of walking, and the daylight made me giddy.

As a result of the destruction of our College, upwards of 1200 young men are on the wide world, without homes or occupation; not daring to return to their families, and wandering from one Christian mission to another, till they almost inevitably fall into the hands of the persecutors. Scarcely one has yielded to the cruelty or blandishments of their tormentors, and the Church may indeed be proud of having engendered such noble confessors of the Faith. But you see how impossible it is for us, pastors of the flock, to console or break the bread of life to our poor suffering children. We are compelled to hide and leave our lambs to the wolves. Before this terrible persecution our mission was so flourishing. And now I feel like Jeremiah groaning over the ruins of Jerusalem. Will they ever be rebuilt?

But as for myself, dearest friend, I trust in God that I shall accomplish my course, and that finally, by the merits of our Lord, I shall share with His friends in the crown of the Just. I wrote to my father in June, 1859, but I fear the letter has never reached him. Send him this one, and ask him to redouble his prayers for his poor old missionary-son.

17. A True Son of Monsieur Vincent

BLESSED FRANCIS-REGIS CLET
To a priest in Paris, December 28, 1819

Since I have often heard tell in France of the dungeons and pitch black holes into which accused men are thrown until they are brought to trial, I feel in duty bound to send you a short account of Chinese prisons. If it serves no other purpose, it should make Christians blush with shame at being less humane than the Chinese in their treatment of the unhappy victims of man's vengeance, a treatment which is a sorry rehearsal of God's tribunal—and indeed they take precious little trouble to leave the judgment to Him. I am able to speak of it from certain knowledge, seeing that I have passed through twenty-seven prisons during my transfer from Ho-nan to Wuchangfu. Now nowhere was there either cell or dungeon, nowhere. The prison in which I am at this moment houses murderers, brigands, robbers, yet from dawn to dusk every one of them enjoys freedom to take a walk, to play games in a huge courtyard, and there to fill his lungs with the fresh air so necessary to health. I have seen a man who had poisoned his own mother—ghastly crime!—and he was at liberty in this open space until the day of his execution.

In order to give you a more precise idea of Chinese prisons, let me tell you they are on a pretty large scale; if you have seen one, you've seen a hundred. Now imagine a courtyard of greater or less length and proportionate width, and grouped round it fairly spacious rooms at ground level. This courtyard is swept daily and kept spotlessly clean, while the rooms in really large places may hold roughly twenty-five people. These rooms are called "cages" because they are encased from top to bottom in wooden poles the thickness of a man's leg intersected by laths the width of your thumb from bar to bar. They take this precaution to prevent prisoners from damaging the walls. The inner section forms a kind of long hall. It has one huge door flanked by a window on either side, and as the door is only closed during the night, it admits light to the vast living quarters. The prisoners sleep side by side on planks raised a foot from the ground to avoid damp. At the approach of winter, each is given a rush mat to protect him from the cold, and when summer comes, a fan to temper the heat. A lamp must burn all night in each room, and a superintendent who sleeps on a bed is specifically charged with the maintenance of order and must provide for the inmates' needs. In the courtyard four or five men take it in turn to beat an instrument, but after four or five days of it, the din does not prevent sleep. Each room is locked and the key entrusted to the mandarin of the prison. Outside the main gate there is a small lodge where a number of warders who relieve each other in rotation guard the gate, opening and closing it as need arises. The more eminent prisoners appoint one of themselves—someone with a good head on his shoulders—to quell the disputes inevitable among a mixed crowd devoid of discipline and morals. If however they get to blows the mandarin is warned, and along he comes with great gravity, orders that so many strokes of the bastinado be inflicted on the culprits, and then preaches his audience a little homily on keeping the peace.

I must not forget to tell you that Chinese compassion goes to the length of supplying prisoners during the hot season with endless cups of tea or some other refreshing drink, and in winter with tunics and cotton-lined trousers for the most destitute. In France, to show pity to the imprisoned is made the subject of sermons. Not out of charity but simply in order to seize the chance of reviling our holy religion, so-called philosophers raise loud voices in protest against the callousness, nay the inhumanity, with which prisoners are treated. And I, I hereby raise the voice of a dying man to contrast pagans and Christians. The preachers from their Christian pulpits call for the charity of the faithful on behalf of those in prison; and I, I call for Christianity. I call for the goodwill of the kings who govern, and the watchful care of magistrates, in favor of that mighty band of unfortunates who die a million deaths before actually meeting their end by final execution. The amelioration that kindly folk bring to prisoners is only temporary; it is the business of the State ministers, their simple duty, so to improve their lot as to enable them to face with patience and resignation the capital punishment which lies before them, to enable them to accept it as a means of satisfying divine justice and as giving them the right to the eternal happiness promised to penitent sinners.

In sending you this account of prisons in China, I have a purpose in mind. If our Reverend Father Superior General thinks it advisable, I should like it inserted in public news-sheets under this heading: "Extract of a letter from a Frenchman, apostolic missionary in China, imprisoned for the Faith in the prisons of Wuchangfu, capital of Hupeh."

Please suppress my name; I long and wish to have it written solely in the Book of Life.

18. The Road to Tonkin

ST. THÉOPHANE VÉNARD
To his family, Tonkin, June 23, 1854

You are the first to whom I write from Tonkin, and I take up my
pen to give you some details of our journey. M. Legrand and I
embarked at Macao on June 2nd towards evening. We thought
our Chinese captain would weigh anchor immediately. Not a bit
of it. A Chinaman will never do anything in a straightforward
way. They had to deliberate as to the voyage, consult the Devil,
take precautions against pirates, and so on. Whilst waiting, we
went to see a place where the English have a contraband trade in
opium. There were we, two poor European missionaries, among
a people who don't admire anything that comes from Europe,
and who are always ready to insult those who do not inspire them
with fear. We were thrust into a little hole where we could only
sit or lie down, breathing foul air and covered with vermin. Here
we had to stay day and night, the Chinese called us "Foreign
Devils," and amused themselves by examining all we had on, and
all that we did. We set sail at last in company with seventy other
vessels, and made all sail towards Hai-Nan, a large island, where
we remained several days. We did not dare land or show ourselves
in any way. On leaving Hai-Nan, the Chinese junks separated,
only a small number steering for Tonkin. Until then the sea had
been calm and beautiful; afterwards it came on to blow, and I
paid my usual tribute to the fishes in consequence. Two days later
we came in sight of Tonkin. I cannot tell you what I felt. I offered
myself again to God, begging Him to dispose of me as would be
most for His glory and honor, and I invoked my Mother Mary,
and my guardian angel, and the patron saints of Tonkin. The
general view of the country is magnificent; rich plains with grassy
hills, a luxuriant vegetation, such as one reads of in Robinson

Crusoe, and the whole backed by a magnificent range of snowy mountains. The mandarin of the Customs House came to inspect our vessel. We could see this august personage through the cracks of our prison, scarcely venturing to breathe the while, and most carefully abstaining from all noise and movement; but the old fox returned to the shore without having scented the nest. The next day a Christian boat came for us, and brought us to the flourishing Mission House of the Spanish Dominicans. We heard afterwards that if we had delayed our landing for a few hours only, the news of our death would have followed that of our arrival; for three royal ships, having heard a rumor of our coming, surrounded the Chinese junk, so that no escape would have been possible. Mgr. Hilarion Alcazar received us in his episcopal palace. Don't let the name mislead you. A bishop's residence here means a poor cabin, half of wood and half of mud, thatched with straw. We stayed there eight days, but I was ill all the time. An Ammonite doctor gave me some strengthening drug which enabled me at last to continue my journey. The Ammonites possess physicians of undeniable skill. The one who attended me could tell at once by the pulse the nature of my malady, and said it arose from a derangement of the liver. We bade goodbye to the cordial, frank, and noble Spanish hospitality, and started on the last stage of our journey. We went in a junk by night. One generally goes by night, for greater security: sometimes by water, on rivers or canals, with a continual change of boats: sometimes by land, like mighty lords in palanquins, or on the backs of slaves in a species of net or hammock, while the matting at the sides hides you from the passersby. Sometimes one can only go on foot, without shoes, in the little narrow paths between the rice-fields. If it be day time, one has a fair chance, but at night one must be content to walk "clippety-clop," falling into holes one moment, into rice-water the next, unable to find a firm footing anywhere; and often when you think you are going on swimmingly, your foot slips on the greasy damp soil, and you measure your length in the mud. Now don't you think this a very picturesque way of travelling? I assure you it gives rise to a host of comical adventures.

It was on the 13th of this month that we arrived at the scene of our future labors. I was introduced for the first time to my Vicar-Apostolic, the illustrious Mgr. Retord. Two other missionaries had also arrived on business. We were therefore six Europeans together—two bishops and four missionaries—a rare event in Tonkin. Very soon we felt as if we had known each other all our lives. We talked on every conceivable subject, and before we separated we sang together a whole heap of new and old songs and national hymns.

Persecution continues without respite in long-standing edicts, but the mandarins do not persecute so rigorously as in the past. As a result, there is a lull which enables Christian groups to organize. However, fresh rumors have begun to circulate, and although there is no new edict so far, many Christian groups have taken the precaution of pulling down their church building.

19. Vietnamese Doctor's Dilemma

BLESSED SIMON HOA
To Bishop Cuénot, October 20, 1839

My Lord,
Profound salutations a thousand thousand times over.

They are redoubling their search here, and fear is running high throughout the village by reason of the priest's presence.

I have made every possible effort to put new heart into the villagers. I have put each and every one of them in my debt, and even as far as the pagans in the surrounding district, there is no one whom I have not tried to win over by acts of kindness. In spite of it all, I am afraid we cannot conceal the Father much longer, and I do not know where to convey him in order to elude the spies during the present crisis.

Since the issuing of Edict 28 of the 8th Moon, my neighbors plague me and are creating untold difficulties for me. The mayor is the only man ready to help. Alas! I cast myself at your feet a thousand thousand times, imploring you to pray hard. Perhaps our Lord, infinitely kind and infinitely powerful as He is, will stretch out His hand in succor; otherwise, we shall not escape this time.

I believe that by the time this letter reaches you, all here will have already obeyed the edict which commands them to build pagodas to false gods. For my part, I am absolutely determined to do nothing of the kind. My doom then is henceforth sealed.

Pray for me, my Lord, that I may suffer courageously amid the general desertion.

What causes me constant distress is the realization that when I am captured and can no longer look after the Father, every one will turn his back on him—that is only too certain. Nevertheless, I cannot imitate the rest in disobeying our Lord, and so I am leaving the Father to his own resources; he fully realizes it and is deeply grieved, but what else can I do? He cannot very well bid me build a heathen altar to avoid arrest and death in order to stay and take care of him, and therefore the Father and I have already taken a final farewell of each other. Oh the anguish of it! The misery!

I entreat you once again to take pity on me and pray for me.

And please also be so good as to seize some opportunity of sending me a few words of encouragement to be my last consolation.

I make bold to beseech you, my Lord, to pray for me. I dare not add more.

With my profound respects,
Simon Hoa

[The mandarins' edict of execution runs:

The 21st year of Minh-Mang, the 13th of the 11th month.

We, Lam-Duy-Nghia, Le-Ba-Phu and Nguyen-Duc-Chinh, members of the Royal Council, must obey the King's orders.

Up to the present time, the religion of Jesus has been forbidden again and again. Now the man named Hoa, a citizen of this kingdom, has gone so far as to abet and harbor in his own house the European, De-La-Miet [i.e. Delamotte], one of the principal leaders of this religion; he has even constructed a secret cellar and a double wall in the house; furthermore, being afraid that all this should become known, he carried the criminal off to hide him elsewhere; and finally, while this European was lodged with Khiem, he paid him frequent visits and has allotted him domestics from his own house as servants: it is thus abundantly clear that his intention was to conceal him in every possible way. Under these circumstances, what other course is open but to inflict on him the penalty due to his crime? Therefore let the aforesaid Hoa be forthwith beheaded and his head set up for three days to serve as a warning to others.]

20. "Now I Begin to Be a Disciple"

ST. IGNATIUS OF ANTIOCH
To the Romans, A.D. 107

Ignatius, also called Theophorus, to the Church endowed with mercy through the Majesty of the Most High Father and of Jesus Christ His only Son, to the Church beloved and enlightened by the will of Him who has willed all things that have being in accordance with the faith and love we bear towards Jesus Christ our God; the same Church that holds its presidency in the territory of the Romans, worthy of God, worthy of dignity, worthy of every blessing, worthy of praise, worthy of credit, honored for purity, whose presidency is one of love, fulfilling the law of Christ and bearing the Father's name. This Church do I salute in the name of Jesus Christ, Son of the Father. To those who according to the flesh and the spirit are united by His every command, to those who one and all are filled with the love of God and purified from every shade of false opinion, I freely send my heartiest greetings in Christ Jesus our God.

Since I prayed to God that I might see your faces—the faces of His friends—He has granted my prayer, and even more than I asked. Bound as I am in Christ Jesus I hope to embrace you, if indeed it is His will that I should be deemed worthy to finish the course. A good beginning has been made. Only let me reach the goal, by God's grace, and claim my portion unhindered. Your love it is that I fear, lest it should do me an injury. It is easy enough for you to do whatever you want; but it is difficult for me to gain my God if you will not leave me alone.

I do not wish you to court the approval of men, but to please God, as indeed you do. Never again shall I have such an opportunity of attaining to God. Never, if you keep silence, will you be accredited with a more noble work. For if you say nothing at all about me, I shall be a word of God. But if you are enamored of my bodily presence, then once more I shall be a mere voice. Grant me only this: that I may be offered in sacrifice to God now while the altar is prepared. Then, as a choir united in love, you may sing to the Father in Christ Jesus, because God has deemed the Bishop of Syria worthy to be summoned from east to west, from sunrise to sunset. It is good to sink below the horizon of this world unto God, in order to rise again in Him.

You have never borne any man a grudge. You have taught others. It is my one desire that the things you have enjoined by your teaching should be observed inviolably. Only ask for me strength, both within and without, so that I may not merely talk, but also show a determined will—not merely be called a Christian, but also prove to be such. If I prove myself a Christian, then I can fittingly be called one; then am I an example of faith, though hidden from the world. Nothing that is seen is of any account. For Jesus Christ our God, now hidden in the Father, is the more clearly revealed. Christian belief, held in hatred by the world, is spread not only by persuasion but also by noble deeds.

I am writing to all the churches, and I protest to everyone that I die for God willingly, if only you do not hinder me. I implore you, do not proffer me an unseasonable kindness. Let the wild beasts have me, for through them my way to God lies open. I am God's wheat, and I am ground by the teeth of wild beasts that I may be found pure bread of Christ. Rather, entice the wild animals that they may become my tomb, and leave nothing at all of my body. Thus when I sleep in death I shall burden no one. Then shall I be truly a disciple of Jesus Christ when the world cannot see even my body. Beseech the Lord on my behalf, that through these instruments I may be found a sacrifice to God. I am not laying down laws for you as though I were Peter or Paul. They were Apostles; I am one condemned. They were free; I even now am a slave. But if I suffer, it is as a freedman of Christ, and in Him I shall rise again, free. Now that I am in bonds I am learning to cast aside all desires.

From Syria all the way to Rome I am fighting with wild beasts, by land and by sea, by day and by night, bound fast to ten leopards—for such are the soldiers of my bodyguard. When bribed, they become even worse. Through their unjust treatment of me, however, I am instructed the more, *yet am I not hereby justified*. Oh, I mean to *enjoy* those wild beasts that are prepared for me! And I pray that they will make short work of me. I will coax them with flattery to devour me without delay, and not treat me as some others whom they have been afraid to touch. But if they should be reluctant and unwilling, I will compel them by force.

Pardon me, but I know what is best for me. Now at last I begin to be a disciple! Let nothing visible or invisible hinder me, through jealousy, from attaining to Jesus Christ. Come fire, come cross, come whole herds of wild beasts, come drawing and quartering, scattering of bones, cutting off of limbs, crushing of the whole body, all the horrible blows of the devil—let all these things come upon me, if only I may be with Jesus Christ.

Neither the furthest bounds of the earth nor the kingdoms of this world would be of any advantage to me. It is more noble for me to die for Jesus Christ than hold sway over the uttermost ends of the earth. I seek Him who died for us. I desire Him who rose again on account of us. My birth to a new life is at hand. Bear with me, brethren. Do not come between me and life; do not desire my death; since I would belong to God, do not hand me over to the world; entice me not with earthly goods. Let me receive the pure light. Once I attain to it, I shall be a man. Suffer me to be an imitator of the passion of my God. The man in whom He dwells will understand my longing and will sympathize with me, knowing, as he must, what straits I am in.

The ruler of this world wishes to carry me off, and to deflect my purpose, which is set on God. Let none of you who are on my side aid him. Rather, become God's champions, through being mine. Do not have Jesus Christ on your lips and the world in your hearts. Let envy have no place in you. If, when I am with you, I should call for your help, do not believe me. Believe rather what I now write to you. I am writing to you as one living but longing to die. My earthly affections are crucified, and there is in me no fire of fleshly passion. But I have a fountain of living water which speaks within me saying, "Come to the Father." I take no delight in perishable food, nor in the pleasures of this life. My desire is for God's Bread, the flesh of Christ, born in former time of David's seed: and for drink I desire His Blood, a love-feast undefiled.

I desire to live no longer, as men think of living; and my desire will be fulfilled, if only you would wish it also. Do wish it, so that your wishes and mine may be accomplished. I entreat you in these few words. Believe me, Jesus Christ will make it clear to you that I speak truly, He, the unerring mouth of God, through whom the Father has spoken truly. Pray for me, that I may attain my end through the Holy Ghost. What I write to you does not accord with human feelings, but with the mind of God. If I suffer, you will have wished me well: if I am rejected, you will have hated me.

Remember in your prayers the Syrian Church, which, in my stead, is shepherded by God Himself. Jesus Christ alone will watch over it now, and your love. As for me, I blush to be counted amongst her members, for I am not worthy, being the least of them, and as one born out of due time. But through His mercy I am someone, if only I attain to God. My spirit salutes you, and so also does the charity of the Churches which received me, not merely as a passer-by, but in the name of Jesus Christ. And even the members of those Churches which are not on the road through which I passed in my bodily journeying escorted me on my way through each city.

I am writing this to you from Smyrna by the kind services of the Ephesians—may they obtain the blessings they deserve! Crocus, whose name is so dear to me, is with me now, along with many others. As to those who have preceded me for the glory of God from Syria to Rome, I trust that you have discovered them. Let them know that I am near. All are worthy of God and of you, and it is fitting that you should provide them with every comfort. I have written this letter to you the day before the ninth of the kalends of September. Farewell; be strengthened unto the end in the patient endurance of Jesus Christ.

The Christian
in the Home

21. Two Loves Built Two Cities

ST. THÉOPHANE VÉNARD
To his brothers, Paris, 1851

At Paris we are in the midst of two extremes of vice and virtue—the lowest, most degrading vice, and the most heroic virtue. In returning from Meudon, which is our little country house, I constantly pass through the Bois de Boulogne. It is a magnificent park, beautifully laid out with walks and drives, shaded by fine trees, and full of exquisite flowers. It is crowded with people on foot, in carriages, and on horseback. On leaving the park you pass through the Barrière de l'Etoile and its triumphal arch, to an avenue which leads to the Place de la Concorde. This is planted with trees and lined with fine houses and beautiful villas. There is an even greater crowd here than in the Bois. You see elegant dandies and beautiful ladies strutting like peacocks who need to go to school again to learn modesty, humility, and even commonsense. Everybody lounges about, their only object to see or be seen. Then comes the evening, when all seem to think it necessary to go to some theater or ball, winding up with ice and coffee in the Boulevards; the city is lit up all night and the world goes to bed when the sun is rising. I should never end were I to tell you how ridiculous human nature appears when left to itself. One gives himself the airs of a philosopher, another of a poet, this one has a passion for music, that one for picture galleries; every one talks politics and three quarters of them do not know what they are talking about. You ask me about the sights, the latest inventions, the balloons. Well, as to balloons, the ladies themselves are the most marvelous specimens! If man would but refer the glory of his inventions to God, they might bring a blessing; but we see nothing, hear of nothing but materialism and "Nature." God help both France and Europe. If ever you come here you will be as much struck as I at the dissipation of the place, the never-ending turmoil, the bustle, noise, unrest. How I hate these endless streets which tire my feet, eyes, and ears, where the world and its views reign supreme, and the one object of every living being seems to be pleasure and pleasure only. Do they find it? Well, perhaps those do who care for nothing but dissipation and jollity. But happiness? No; happiness is to be found only in the home and in the family circle where God is loved and honored, and everyone loves and helps and cares for the other. The great cry now is "the People." The word written up everywhere is "Fraternité." In Paris they have pretty well wiped out family life. To realize the true meaning of Brotherhood it should be written not on the walls, but in the heart. There is a beautiful give and take in the different relationships of life where all are united in one great love in Him who sacrificed His life for us, our Lord and Savior Jesus Christ. If only everyone could feel this, how perfect would be the harmony on earth.

I am very much struck with the young men I have met unconnected with the Seminary. They are such contradictory creatures. A good deal of pride with a good deal of generosity; a great love of independence with a certain submission; a great deal of impurity with a vestige of higher thoughts learned at their mother's knee; some courage and audacity, and yet more weakness and foolish yielding; an ardor for work by fits and starts but in general inconceivable idleness; a desultory way of living and acting without aim or purpose; in fact, the old strife between the spirit of evil and the spirit of good. There is another species, whom one sees all day long lounging in cafés and never alone, restless young men who walk in a wild sort of way, judging and criticizing everybody and everything. They neither respect nor esteem women. They want to know everything, hear everything, see everything. They talk for the sake of talking and their least sin is that of doing nothing. Their secret lives are more pitiable than their public ones. But there are exceptions. In the midst of this city real saints are found, but most of those who have eyes do not see them or know them. They are hidden from the crowd and known only to God, but thanks to Him, they are multiplying. Christianity is not dead, as the gentlemen of the Voltaire school like to think. I know some young men living in the world, in the very center of the greatest riches and luxury, yet humble, good, devout, charitable, reverent, seeking out the poor in their garrets, "religious as a woman," as the saying is. Their manners are simple and natural for they are thoroughly in earnest. They are bright, amiable, and courteous, with faces which prepossess one at first sight. All their lives are spent in doing good. I don't mean to say they don't commit faults sometimes, for human nature is frail; but their very failings increase their humility and make them lean more completely on the divine mercy. God be praised. All young men, more or less, may rank in one or other of these classes. It does not cost more to side with justice, but then one must have a conscience and reason calmly as to the object of life: in a word, serve and love God. Goodbye.

22. The Managing Mama

ST. JANE FRANCES DE CHANTAL
To Mademoiselle de Chantal, her daughter
Paris, April 13, 1620

God be blessed for having so wisely and so happily guided you in the preliminaries of your approaching marriage. May His divine goodness give you perfect peace. I assure you, my darling, the more matters progress the more I feel satisfied. M. de Toulonjon is, in my opinion, the kindest of men. He has come back as pleased as possible, and we have every reason to feel the same. Yes, my dear Françon, you have certainly given me great pleasure by showing me such complete trust, but on my part, God knows indeed how I have prayed and longed to see you happily settled, and how much more deeply I have felt your troubles than my own. Truly your contentment always comes first with me—of that there is no question. It was my love for you, you may be certain, that carried me away on this occasion, because I saw it was for your happiness. We undoubtedly owe it all to the goodness of our Lord, who has taken care of you and me and heard our prayers. The enclosed letter will show you how much his Lordship of Bourges also desires this marriage.

Well now, you must remain firm, and if apprehensions about this or that try to take hold of you, shut the door resolutely upon them, and do not entertain them under any pretext whatsoever. Be led in everything by reason and by my commonplace counsel. Believe me, my dear child, it is very good for you, and if you continue to follow it, you will find it is wise. Write out at length, as you promised me, all your impressions and feelings, and tell me whether God has united your heart to that of M. de Toulonjon. Such is my hope and overwhelming desire, and I trust that God will have thus blessed your first meeting. As for me, my darling, I repeat what I have already told you in all sincerity, namely, I thoroughly like him. The affection I feel towards him is warmer than I can express. In fact, none of our relatives and friends who are acquainted with him could be more satisfied than you and I.

M. de Toulonjon is very anxious about rings for you. He wants to send me here a large share of all the precious gems of Paris, so that I may purchase whatever I prefer for you. Actually I should prefer that you had none of them, for to speak quite frankly, my dearest daughter, ladies of quality no longer wear jewelry at Court. They leave that to the wives of the townsfolk; however, you must choose for yourself when you come. But I have no idea how to persuade M. de Toulonjon to share my views, for he has begged me as a mere beginning to send you pearls and earrings, and a vanity bag studded with diamonds which is all that ladies now carry with their gowns. Really, we must not let him have his own way in going to such extravagance; so intense is his desire to please you that he would go to any lengths to give you what you want. If ever a wife ought to be perfectly happy, it is you. However, you realize what discretion you will need on your part to restrain him. You would do wisely to show a little economy and spend your money on serviceable things rather than on frippery and ostentation. I feel I do not want my Françon to go in for that kind of thing; moreover, my reputation is involved since you are my daughter and, as such, it is your duty to be discreet and circumspect, and to order your life prudently and profitably.

Finally, you ought not to wear a wedding-dress; it is my earnest wish that your marriage should have no parade, and I say so without any qualification. M. de Toulonjon told me that you do not wish to be married during the month of May. Have you no qualms of conscience on the point? It is sheer superstition. However, much as he wishes it, I do not think May will be possible.

The more I see of him, the more I like him, and the more I realize that you and I should thank God for your happy engagement. Send him a very courteous warm letter, be completely frank and open with him, and show that you return his love, for you need no longer stand on ceremony with him. His servant is waiting downstairs for my letter. My one desire, my dearest Françon, is that you should love your betrothed with your whole heart. Goodbye, dearly beloved daughter; speak really candidly when you write to me.

23. How to Be Happy Though Married

ST. ROBERT BELLARMINE
To his niece, January 1614

I have received your letter and am extremely pleased to know that you are happy over the marriage arranged for you. You have much to be thankful for because you have found a partner of good family on both sides, of excellent character, distinguished by great prudence, and of suitable age, qualities seldom found in the one person. May God bless your marriage, and may you long enjoy deep peace and happiness with the husband His providence has given you. However, since human affairs here below are subject to vicissitude, I should like to make a few suggestions which you will find helpful, provided you remember them and put them in practice.

First of all, in everything that is not sin, do your utmost to be of one mind and heart with your husband, for difference of aim and outlook may lead to estrangement of soul.

Secondly, husband and wife should bear with each other, *supportantes invicem in caritate,* as St. Paul enjoins. Everyone has faults. If they are patiently endured, peace will reign happily, but if each little peccadillo is going to arouse friction and put the other out of temper, it will be impossible to live in harmony.

Thirdly, revere your father and mother-in-law in all sincerity, and obey them with the respect you would show towards your own parents.

Fourthly, your husband should be regarded as lord and master, and you must know that he is to be obeyed and honored as the head. Thus St. Peter tells us that Sarah, Abraham's wife, addressed him as Lord, not husband. St. Augustine also, in speaking of his mother St. Monica, recounts how she would remain meek and silent, returning no answer when her husband burst in storming and raging; although she knew perfectly well he was furiously angry, she refused to quarrel with him, until finally her humility and modesty won him over for God. And indeed when her neighbors came to complain that their husbands beat them, she would reply that no doubt they deserved it, they were probably trying to usurp his position as head of the house. She added that they should look upon matrimony as a deed of sale in which they were sold into servitude; as slaves, they should be humble and submissive. Even though husbands ought to look upon their wives not as slaves but as partners, nevertheless the wife should always regard her husband as master.

Fifthly, the wife must love her husband as if there were no other man in the world, in much the same way as the husband should love her as if no other woman existed.

Sixthly, if unmarried ladies have hitherto been free to gossip and giggle, amuse themselves and waste time peeping out of windows, once they are married all that sort of thing must cease. They are now bound to greater seriousness, modesty, discretion, and silence so as not to give their husbands the slightest sign of undue levity, and of course they must avoid idleness if they are to look after their homes.

Throughout your life it will be advisable, rather it will be necessary, to take every possible means to obtain a true love of our blessed Lord. Pray frequently with great earnestness, at least say your morning and night prayers, go to confession every week, and to Holy Communion at any rate on the principal feasts of the Church. While I think of it, let me advise you to be brief in the confessional, and discuss with your confessor only what concerns the well-being of your own soul. I know what I am talking about; I have had experience in directing people in religion and people in the world, as well as monks of various kinds.

May the Lord bless you together with your betrothed. Pray for me.

24. More Matrimonial Maxims

ST. VINCENT DE PAUL

To St. Louise de Marillac, between 1639 and 1641

The grace of our Lord be ever with you!

It would be well to continue the ordinary prayers, and to give a special subject for prayer to this good girl who is about to be married.

1st: The motives which a wife has for leading a devout life with her husband. On this point you will give her three authorities. First, that St. Paul says the husband is the head of the wife, and therefore she should have the same dependence on him as the members have on the head; (2) what the same St. Paul says to wives—namely, that they should obey their husbands; (3) that God says a wife should leave father and mother to follow her husband.

The second point is to know what is the meaning of a wife's leading a devout life with her husband. Now, this consists in her loving her husband more than anything else, except God; in the second place, in pleasing and obeying him in all things that are not sinful.

The third point is the means a wife should take to lead a devout life with her husband; (1) to ask this from God; (2) not to permit the least disesteem for him in her heart; (3) not to say or do anything that might displease him; (4) to propose to herself the example of some married woman who leads a good life with her husband; to have a devotion to honor the marriage of St. Joseph and the Blessed Virgin.

Your mind is too diffident. Be confident that our Lord's good pleasure will be accomplished in your son.

If I can, I shall go to La Chapelle tomorrow, or, if not, I will send someone else there.

Good-bye, Mademoiselle.

25. The Stray Sheep Returns

ST. THÉRÈSE OF LISIEUX
To her cousin, Carmel, July 16, 1894

Your letter has given me deep joy. The way in which our Lady has graciously fulfilled your every longing leaves me lost in wonderment. Even before your marriage she saw to it that the ideals of the partner to whom you were to be linked should exactly match your own. What happiness to feel yourself so perfectly understood, and above all to know that your union will last for ever, that when life is over, your love for the husband so dear to you will still endure.

All well! We have both bidden good-bye to the blissful days of our childhood, and now we face life's responsibilities. The path each of us treads is very different but it leads to precisely the same goal. You and I must have but one sole aim: to grow in holiness along the road that God in His goodness has mapped out for us.

I feel that I can talk quite openly to you, dear friend of my childhood. You understand the language of the Faith much better than the idiom of the world, and the Lord you received in your first Holy Communion has ever remained the Master of your heart; it is in Him that you love the noble soul henceforth completely one with your own, and it is because of him that your love is so tender and so strong. O how glorious our Faith is! Instead of restricting hearts, as the world fancies, it uplifts them and enlarges their capacity to love, to love with an almost infinite love since it will continue unbroken beyond our mortal life. Indeed, life has been given us simply to purchase our home in heaven, where we shall meet again the dear ones we have loved on earth.

Dear Céline, I had been asking our Lady of Mount Carmel to grant you the favor you have received at Lourdes. I am so pleased you are wearing the sacred scapular; it is a sure pledge of predestination, and it also unites you more closely to your little sisters at Carmel, doesn't it? You beg me, cousin mine, to pray for your dear husband. Do you imagine that I could possibly let you down? No; in my prayers, poor as they are, I could not pray for one without the other. I am asking our Lord to be as generous to you as He once was to the bridal pair at Cana. May He invariably change the water into wine! I mean, may He prolong His gift of happiness, and as far as possible sweeten the bitter trials you will meet with on your way. Trials! Fancy introducing that word into my letter—how could I?—at a moment when I realize that life for you is all sunshine. Forgive me, dear heart, and enjoy in peace that gladness God bestows without taking anxious care for the morrow. I feel certain that He has fresh favors and many consolations in store for you.

Dare I ask you, little cousin of mine, to give my respects and greetings to M. Pottier? I cannot help looking upon him also as my cousin. I am leaving you, darling Céline, but remain always deeply united in affection, and it will be a lifelong pleasure to call myself

> Your little sister in our Lord,
> Thérèse of the Child Jesus

26. On Divorce

ST. JEROME
c. A.D. 394

Jerome to Amandus, his brother-priest, holy and acceptable to the Lord.

I found subjoined to your letter a short paper containing the words: Ask him (that is, me) whether a woman whose husband is an adulterer and a Sodomist and who has left him and been forced to marry another man, may be admitted to communion with the Church while the husband from whom she separated is still alive. Must she do penance for her fault?

As I read this, there flashed across my mind that phrase of the psalm: *To make excuses in sins* (Ps 140). Human as we are, we are all indulgent towards our own faults, and what we do of our own accord we attribute to a necessity of nature. It is as though a young man were to say: "My body is too much for me, the fire of nature kindles my passions, the way I am made simply demands sex-experience." Or again, as if a murderer offered the excuse: "I was in want, I needed food, I had nothing to cover me; if I shed another's blood, it was to save myself from perishing of cold and hunger." Give that sister, then, who is inquiring of me about her predicament, not my ruling but the Apostle's. *Do you not know, brethren (for I speak to them that know law), that the Law has dominion over a man as long as he lives?* he asks. *For the married woman is bound by the Law while her husband is alive; but if her husband die, she is set free from the law of the husband. Therefore while her husband is alive, she will be called an adulteress if she be with another man* (Rom 7). And in another place: *A woman is bound as long as her husband is alive, but if her husband dies, she is free. Let her marry whom she pleases, only let it be in the Lord* (1 Cor 7:39). Thus the Apostle has cut away all pleas with his clear statement that a wife who remarries during her husband's lifetime is an adulteress. You need not tell me tales about an assailant's physical violence, a mother's wheedling, a father's heavy hand, or about the swarm of relatives, the trickery and insolence of servants, the losses to household property. As long as her husband lives, even though he may be an adulterer, a homosexual, a man stained with every crime and divorced by his wife because of his misdeeds, he still ranks as her husband and she may not marry another. It is not the Apostle who decides this on his own authority; it is Christ speaking through him. Paul is simply echoing the words of Christ, who tells us in the Gospel: *Whoever puts away his wife, save on account of immorality, causes her to commit adultery; and he who marries a woman who has been put away, commits adultery* (Mt 5:32). Notice what He says: *He who marries a woman who has been put away, commits adultery.* Whether she has parted from her husband or whether he has parted from her, whoever marries her is an adulterer. That explains why the Apostles, as soon as they realize the heavy burden of matrimony, exclaim: *If the case of a man with his wife is so, it is not expedient to marry.* Our Lord answers them: *Let him accept it who can* (Mt 19:10, 12), and holding up the example of the three eunuchs, He immediately shows the blessedness of virginity, which is not fettered by any bond of the flesh.

I have not been able to make out exactly what she means when she speaks of being forced to take a husband. In what way was she forced? Did the man assemble a crowd and overpower her against her will? If she was thus victimized, why did she not afterwards repudiate her assailant? If she reads the books of Moses she will find that if violence is offered to a betrothed maiden within the city, and she does not cry out, she must accept the punishment of an adulteress; if she is attacked in the field, she is clear of guilt and her ravisher alone will be called to account. If this sister of yours, then, who according to her own report has been forced into a second union, wishes to receive the Body of Christ and not to be branded an adulteress, she must do penance. At least from the moment she embarks upon a different course of life, all further marital relations with her second husband must cease. It would be more correct to call him adulterer than husband. If she finds this difficult and is unable to desert a man to whom she has given her love, if sensual pleasure takes preference over our Lord, let her note the Apostle's declaration: *You cannot drink the cup of the Lord and the cup of devils. You cannot be partakers of the table of the Lord, and of the table of devils* (1 Cor 10:21). And he says again: *What fellowship has light with darkness? What harmony is there between Christ and Belial?* (2 Cor 6:14,15).

Therefore I beg you to comfort her and urge her to seek salvation. Flesh that is diseased must be cut away and cauterized. It is not the treatment but the wound that is to blame if the surgeon shows a merciful severity which spares by not sparing and is cruel only to be kind.

27. The P.O.W. Reclaims His Wife

ST. LEO THE GREAT
March 458

Leo, Bishop, to Nicetas, Bishop of Aquileia, greeting.

Upon his return to us, my son Adeodatus deacon of our See presented your request, beloved brother. You ask for a ruling from our Apostolic See concerning matters which may well seem extremely difficult to decide. In our search for a solution of present problems, however, we must be careful to put religious principles first; it is to them we should chiefly look for the healing of the wounds inflicted by the ravages of war.

You tell me that as a result of military defeat and the very serious inroads made by enemy forces, homes have been disrupted, husbands carried away into captivity, and wives left without resources. Assuming that their own menfolk have either been killed or are never likely to escape from their captors' hands, the women, driven by loneliness, have taken other husbands. Now however that by God's help conditions have improved and prisoners thought dead have returned home, it is not surprising if your Reverence is in some doubt as to what we should decree regarding women who have remarried. We know the Scriptural saying, *A wife is joined to her husband by God* (Prv 19:14); and again we know the precept, *What God has joined together, let no man put asunder* (Mt 19:6). We must therefore maintain that lawful marriage contracts should be renewed, and once the evils attendant upon war are remedied, that which was his by right must be restored to every man, the greatest care being taken to ensure that each recover his own possession.

Nevertheless no blame is to be attached to any man for taking the place of the husband who was presumed dead; he must on no account be treated as the violator of another's rights. Many things formerly the property of those taken captive may have likewise passed into other ownership, and yet it is merely strict justice that such property be restored to them on their return. If this principle is duly honored in the case of slaves or land, as also of houses and goods, how much more should it be observed when it comes to the restoration of the ties of wedlock, in order that the rupture inevitably caused by war may be set right by the healing hand of peace?

Therefore, when men returning from long captivity prove so constant in their love for their wives that they wish to renew the marital relationship, whatever necessity occasioned in the past should be overlooked without assigning any blame whatever, but the women must be restored as fidelity demands. If, however, there be any so enslaved by passion for their second husbands that they prefer to stay with them rather than return to their rightful partners, they deserve to be publicly branded: let them be excluded from the Church's communion. In a matter that might have been excused and remedied by an equitable pardon, they have preferred to defile themselves with adultery, thus making it quite plain that their one desire was sinful self-indulgence.

The women then must return to their former status by cheerfully resuming their married obligations, but they must not be regarded as having forfeited their honor in any way, as if their need had arisen from evil desire; for as those who refuse to go back to their husbands are to be accounted reprobate, so it is fitting that they who return to a love entered upon with the blessing of God should be judged worthy of all praise.

28. To an Expectant Mother

ST. FRANCIS DE SALES
To a spiritual daughter, September 29, 1620

It does not surprise me in the least to learn that you feel somewhat dull-witted and heavy-hearted: after all, you are with child. When your delicate frame is heavy with its burden, weakened by its task, indisposed by all manner of pains, you cannot expect to find your heart as animated, vigorous, and ready to act as it used to be, but all that in no way prejudices the activity of the apex of the soul; it remains as pleasing to God as if you were brimming over with all the cheerfulness in the world. In fact, it is far more pleasing because it demands so much more effort and struggle. However, the doer derives little pleasure from it, because the soul's activity lies beyond the feelings, and so does not afford the same emotional delight.

Dear child, we must not be hard on ourselves, or exact more than we have to give. When body and strength are impaired, we can only ask the will to make acts of submission and acceptance of the travail, and add holy aspirations uniting our will with God's. These are made in the apex of the soul. As for our outward behavior, we must plan what we have to do and do it as best we can, and leave it at that, even though we have performed the task grudgingly and with tired and heavy heart. If we are to rise above this depression, dejection, and despondency of soul, and turn it to use in God's service, we must face it, accept it, and realize the worth of holy self-abasement. In this way, you will transmute the lead of your heaviness of spirit into gold, a gold purer far than any of your gayest, most light-hearted sallies. Well, then, be patient with yourself. See to it that your higher self puts up with your lower. Make a frequent offering of the tiny creature to our Creator's eternal glory, since He has chosen you to cooperate with Him in forming your child. But take the greatest care of your health: don't put yourself out or force yourself to pray at present. You must treat yourself with the utmost gentleness. If it tires you to kneel, sit down; if you can't pray for half an hour, pray for a quarter, or simply half that again.

Dearest daughter, at Annecy we possess a Capuchin artist who, as you may imagine, paints pictures solely for God and the adornment of His house. When at work, he has to concentrate so closely that he cannot paint and pray at the same time. This worries and distresses his mind, yet in spite of it, he sets to work with a will for the sake of the honor that it must bring our Lord, and in the hope that his pictures will prompt many worshippers to praise God and bless His goodness.

Now, dear daughter, the babe being formed in your womb is to be a living representation of the divine Majesty, but as long as your vigor and physical strength are employed on the work, your spirits will inevitably droop and grow weary, and you will be unable to perform your daily duties with your usual zest and cheerfulness. Endure your lassitude and low spirits lovingly, and think of the honor God is to receive from your finished work, for it is your own reproduction which will find a place in the eternal temple of the heavenly Jerusalem, and will there give everlasting joy to the eyes of God and angels and men. The saints will hymn God's praises for what you have achieved, and you will join your voice to theirs when you behold it. So be patient with the feeling of drowsiness and dullness, and hold fast to our Lord's holy will, who has thus ordained things in His eternal wisdom.

To conclude, I cannot express all that my mind formulates and desires for your spiritual perfection; I tell you, your soul is to be found in the center of mine, since such has been and is God's will. God in His goodness grant that both yours and mine may be in perfect accord with His all-holy, all-wise ordinances. May He shower His blessings upon you and yours, especially upon your dearly loved husband.

Prayer for an Expectant Mother

Eternal God, Father of infinite goodness, who hast ordained marriage to increase the human race here below and re-people the heavenly City above, and hast destined woman to be the principal agent in the task, it is Thy will that fruitfulness should bring proof of Thy blessing. Look upon me now, bowed down in adoration before the face of Thy Majesty to thank Thee for the conception of the child who is Thy gift to my body. But, Lord, since Thou hast acted thus in Thy lovingkindness, stretch out the arms of Thy providence and bring to perfection the work Thou hast begun. Impart to my childbearing something of Thine own divine excellence, and by Thy never-failing assistance, help me to bear this babe, the result of Thy creative power, until the hour is ripe to bring the child to birth. Then, O God of my life, come to my aid, with Thy holy hand support my weakness and receive the fruit of my womb; preserve the infant who is Thine by creation until the sacrament of baptism lays him in the bosom of your bride, the Church, and makes him Thine too by redemption.

Saviour of my soul, who on earth showed such tenderness towards the little ones gathered into Thine embrace, receive yet another, I pray, and adopt him into Thy sacred sonship. When he belongs to Thee and can call Thee Father, then shall Thy name be hallowed in him, and Thy kingdom come. Therefore, O Redeemer of the world, I vow, dedicate, and consecrate my child with all my heart to obedience to Thy law, to love of Thy service, and the service of Thy love.

And inasmuch as Thy just wrath subjected the mother of the human race with all her sinful posterity to much pain and sorrow in childbirth, I accept at Thy hands, O Lord, whatever travail may be mine in that hour. I make but one petition. By the sacred joy with which Thine innocent Mother gave birth, be gracious to me in my hour of pain, poor and unworthy sinner that I am, and bless me and the child Thou hast bestowed upon me, with the blessing of Thine everlasting love. With complete trust in Thy goodness, I ask this gift in all humility.

And you, most holy Virgin-Mother, my Lady and incomparable Mistress, peerless boast of womankind, open wide your protecting arms and receive into the motherly lap of your sovereign courtesy my desires and supplications, so that your Son in His mercy may deign to grant my prayer. Most lovable of all creatures, by the virginal love you cherished for St. Joseph, your husband most dear, by the infinite merits of your Son's birth, by the sacred womb that bore Him and the breasts that gave Him suck, I entreat of you to obtain for me what I ask.

Holy angels of God, appointed to guard me and the child I bear, defend and govern us, so that under your protection we may one day attain to the glory which is your delight, and in your company praise and bless the Lord and Master of us all, who liveth and reigneth for ever and ever. Amen.

29. Infant Baptism

ST. AUGUSTINE
A.D. 408

To Boniface, his fellow-Bishop, Augustine sends greetings in the Lord.

You ask me whether parents do harm to their baptized children when they try to restore them to health by offering sacrifice to demons. And, supposing the act does them no harm, how then can their parents' faith be of any real value to them at baptism, if their aberration from it causes them no injury? This is my answer.

When a child has received his first birth from those who are impelled by natural instincts, and is afterwards regenerated by those who are impelled by spiritual desire, so great is the power of this saving sacrament of Baptism in the sacred structure of the Body of Christ, that the child cannot be caught in the toils of another's sin to which his own will gave no consent. *Both the soul of the father is mine*, we are told, *and the soul of the son is mine. The soul that sinneth, the same shall die* (Ez 18:4). The son himself does not sin, you see, when without his knowledge the parents or some other person resort to rites of diabolical worship on his behalf. On the other hand, however, it was from Adam that the child derived that guilt which was to be cancelled by the grace of this sacrament, seeing that he was not as yet a soul having an independent existence. He was not, so to say, a distinct soul, to whom the text, *Both the soul of the father is mine, and the soul of the son is mine* could be applied. Now that he is a human being in his own right, however, quite other from him who begot him, he is not involved in the guilt of another's sin committed without his consent. At the time when it was incurred, the son derived his guilt from being one with him and one in him from whom he derived it. But one person does not derive guilt from another when each is living his own personal life. When each does so, *The soul that sinneth, the same shall die* applies equally to either.

But the possibility of the child's being regenerated through the agency of another's will when presented for the sacred rite is the work of the Spirit alone who regenerates the child thus presented. For it is not written, Unless a man be born again of the will of his parents, or of the faith of those who offer him or administer the rite, but, *Unless a man be born again of water and the Holy Ghost* (Jn 3:5). It is, then, by water, the visible outward sign of grace, and by the Spirit—who produces the inward gift of grace which cancels the bond of sin and restores God's gift to human nature—that the man born solely of Adam in the first place, is afterwards re-born solely in Christ. Now the Spirit who regenerates is possessed in common both by the parents who present the child and by the little one thus born again. Hence in virtue of their participation in one and the same Spirit, the desire of those who offer him does benefit the child.

Do not be disquieted because some bring their little ones for baptism, not indeed in the belief that they will be regenerated by spiritual grace to life everlasting, but because they suppose that by this means the children will retain or recover bodily health. It will be no hindrance to their spiritual regeneration that this is not the intention of those who present them for baptism. The point is that the sponsors take the necessary steps and pronounce the sacramental words without which the infant cannot be consecrated to God. The Holy Spirit, however, who dwells in the saints, who dwells I mean in those who have been fused together by the flame of love to form the one silver-winged dove, sometimes accomplishes His work through the ministry of those that are not merely ignorant but culpably unworthy of such a charge. In fact the infants are presented to receive the spiritual grace not so much by those in whose arms they are held (although if they themselves are faithful believers, they too take part in the act), as by the whole society of saints and believers. For they are rightly regarded as being offered by all who take pleasure in their baptism, and whose holy and united love assists them in receiving the grace of the Holy Spirit. Thus all is done by the whole Mother Church which subsists in the saints, because she is the mother of each and every one of them. For if the sacrament of Christian Baptism, being always one and the same, is valid even when administered by heretics, how much more must we believe that within the Catholic Church what is merely straw may be of service in bringing the grains of wheat to the winnowing-floor, where they are to be prepared for incorporation in the heap of good corn?

You consider the last query in your list the most difficult, because of the scrupulous care you always take to avoid anything untruthful. "If I set a child before you," you say, "and ask: 'When this child is grown up, will he lead a good clean life? Or possibly prove a thief?,'" no doubt you will reply, "I don't know." If I go on: "Child as he is, are his thoughts good or evil?," you will likewise reply, "I don't know." If then you do not venture to make any positive statement either about his future behavior or about his thoughts at that very moment, what are his parents doing when they present their children for baptism? They answer as sponsors in their name, and declare that the little ones are performing an act which their tender age is incapable of understanding. Even supposing they could understand, we have no means of ascertaining their thoughts. We ask the sponsors: Does he believe in God?, and though at that age the child does not even know there is a God, they reply: He does believe; and in the same way they make answer throughout. Now I am surprised that in such matters the parents can so confidently answer in the child's name that he is undertaking something so supremely excellent as what the minister of baptism demands, and yet at that very time, were I to ask: "Will the child now being baptized lead a good clean life when he grows up, or will he turn out a thief?" I doubt whether any one would dare to answer, "He will or he will not" with the same confidence as the sponsor now assures me that the child believes in God and is seeking after Him. And you conclude by saying: "I beg you to have the kindness to reply briefly to these difficulties. Please do not merely quote traditional custom, but satisfy me with a reasoned argument."

Well, I shall do the best I can to answer you, and may our Lord prosper my attempt!

Now in everyday speech we often say as Easter approaches, "Tomorrow, or the day after, is the Lord's Passion," although He suffered so many years ago and His Passion was enacted once and for all. And on Easter Day itself we say, "Today the Lord rose again," although all those years have passed since His resurrection. No one is so stupid as to accuse us of falsehood when we speak in this way, simply because the day so called corresponds with the actual one according to the calendar, and an event is said to happen here and now which in fact took place long ago but is being sacramentally commemorated on that day. And yet, not only through all the special rites of Easter, but every day, is He not offered up in sacrifice before our congregations; so that anyone who, being questioned about it, declares that He is offered in sacrifice, is telling the strict truth? If the sacraments bore no resemblance at all to those realities of which they are the sacred signs, they would not be sacraments. Just as, according to a certain mode of being, the sacrament of Christ's Body is the Body of Christ, and the sacrament of Christ's Blood is the Blood of Christ, so also the sacrament of faith is faith. Now, believing means precisely that—to have faith. Accordingly, when the infant who has not yet the ability to exercise faith is said to believe, this reply means that he has faith because of the sacrament of faith. That is why the Apostle says of this same sacrament of Baptism: *We are buried together with Christ by baptism into death* (Rom 6:4). He does not say: "We have signified our burial." No; he says outright: *We are buried.* In fact he has given the sacrament of so great a sacred mystery the very name of the mystery itself.

Therefore the infant, even though he may not yet possess that faith which depends on the consent of those who exercise it, nevertheless becomes a believer because he receives the sacrament of that faith. When he grows up to man's understanding he will not repeat the sacrament, but will grasp its implications and readily adjust his mind to the truth contained in it. As long as he is unable to do this, the sacrament will avail for his protection against the forces of the adversary, and should he depart this life before attaining to the use of reason, such will be its power that he will be delivered by the Church's love commending him to God through this sacrament, from that condemnation which through one man entered into the world.

I have answered your questions in a way that might not convince a man of less intelligence than yourself, or one intent on picking holes in an argument. But it is possibly more than enough, I think, to satisfy a man of keen and peaceable mind. And I have not urged the fact of long-established custom, but have tried to meet you with reasoned principles in support of a custom fraught with such blessings.

30. A Son Dies

ST. FRANCIS DE SALES
To a close friend, Anneçy, June 1615

Now that I have received your letter and your message which was duly transmitted to me, I am thoroughly acquainted with the capacity of that heart of yours, especially with its warmth and its power to love and attach itself to whatever it holds dear. This explains why you speak so frequently to our Lord about your beloved dead son; it is this too which prompts your desire to ascertain what has become of him.

Now you really must repress these yearnings, my dear Mother, for they spring from far too excessive and passionate a love. When you catch your mind unawares trifling with such things, you must there and then, even if it means praying aloud, return to our Lord's side with these or similar words: "O Lord, how sweet is your providence, how gracious your mercy! Ah, happy indeed is the child who has been enfolded in your fatherly arms. Held there, he can experience nothing but good, wherever he may be."

Yes, you must take the greatest care not to go beyond that in order to dwell on paradise or purgatory—thanks be to God, there are no grounds whatever for considering any other place. Recall your mind in this way and turn at once to acts of love of our crucified Lord.

When you commend your child to the divine Majesty, simply say to Him: "Lord, I commend to You the offspring of my womb, yes, but even more truly the child sprung from the depths of Your mercy; born of my blood, true, but reborn from Yours." And leave it at that. For if you allow your soul to harp on the theme, it will never want to leave a subject so well-suited to its grasp, and so acceptable to its lower and natural emotions. The result will be that under pretext of prayer and devotion, it will run to waste in a good deal of self-indulgence and purely natural consolations, and so rob you of the time you should consecrate to the supernatural and sovereign purpose of your love. There is no question about it: we simply must check these outbursts of natural feeling whose only effect is to upset our mind and distract our heart.

Come then, dear Mother, whom I cherish with a truly filial affection, let us keep our conscious thoughts firmly under control in our hearts, concentrated upon the task of loving God as we love no one else, and let us never allow them to wander at will in speculations as to what is taking place in this world or beyond the grave. But once we have apportioned to creatures their due share of affection and kindness, let us refer everything to the supreme love, overmastering all else, that we owe to the Creator, and let us unite ourselves to His divine will.

31. The Unwanted Child

St. Teresa of Avila
To her nephew, Avila, December 15, 1581

May the grace of the Holy Spirit be with you, my son. I received your letter, and, though it made me very happy to hear of the good fortune which our Lord has bestowed on you, your own very natural grief caused me fresh grief too. As I wrote to you in great detail about my brother's death—God rest his soul!—I will not renew your grief still further.

May God be ever praised for having shown you the great favor of bestowing a wife on you whom you will find so great a comfort. My warm congratulations: it is a very great joy to me to know you are so happy. Diego Juarez told me more than either you or my brother did about the qualities of Señora Doña Maria and the other good things that had happened to you. Considering you are so far away, your letters are very brief. It was a great mercy of God that you fell on your feet and made such a speedy marriage, for, as you began to go your own way when you were so young, you might have given us a lot of trouble. That makes me realize how much I love you, for, though I am very grieved at the offense you committed against God, the little girl is so like you that I cannot help taking her to my heart and loving her dearly. For so tiny a child, she is extraordinarily like Teresa in her patience.

May God make her His servant, for the fault is not hers. You must not neglect to see she is well brought up—and if she stays where she is now, she will not be when she grows older. It will be best if her aunt brings her up till we see what God is making of her. As God has given you the means, you can send money for her upkeep here, and it can be invested for her. By the time she is twelve, the Lord will ordain what is to be done with her, and it is a great thing that she should be brought up to be good. The income will then be available for whatever purpose it may be needed. She certainly deserves all this, for she is a nice child and, tiny though she is, she never likes leaving here.

We should not need to apply to you for any money for this purpose, were it not that our house here is in sore straits just now. For Francisco de Salcedo died—God rest his soul!—and left us a legacy which is too small to provide for our dinner—and we have not enough for supper either—and thereupon almost all our other alms came to an end at once. As time goes on we shall do better, but so far we have had nothing more, so we are suffering severely. At the moment I am expecting my sister and her daughter here. You would be very sorry for them if you saw how needy they are. I am particularly sorry for Doña Beatriz, who wants to be a nun but has no money to give. It would be a very great charity to send them something, if you are able to: however little it is, it will mean a great deal to them. The person who needs no money is myself, but will you pray God to enable me to fulfil His will in everything, and to make you all very holy for me, for everything but holiness soon comes to an end.

All the nuns in this house send you their very best remembrances: we all commend you to God. You bear the name of a good father, my son, so see to it that your deeds are good too. I kiss the hands of you all many times, and I will say no more.

32. To the Father of a Family

ST. PLACID RICCARDI
To his brother, Easter 1906

You are now living in a city, and it is most necessary to guide and guard your children. There is no need for me to press the point, you know it better than I: school, companions, play, amusements, books, all these and more call for the exercise of much thought and wise solicitude in those who have undertaken the tremendous responsibility of parenthood. But it is worthwhile, worth it all, for, underneath everything, there lies the sacred ideal of *the family*. Even if fathers and mothers must feel something akin to despair at being called to account for an unworthy child, what of their joy at possessing children who are thoroughly good and deeply religious, who do not attach too much importance to brains, success, money-making, and suchlike. Parents cannot take this lesson too seriously to heart, especially mothers who are chiefly responsible for their children's upbringing. Society is suffering acutely because of the lack of truly Christian mothers. Since society is based on the family, its very shape and fate is largely in the hands of women. If they were given a thorough Christian education and well-grounded in Christian principles, the whole of society would rise regenerated in newness of life.

Again for the sake of the whole family, I recommend what I have said before regarding evening prayer—let it be short but never omitted. This will satisfy your conscience, and at the same time provide a salutary lesson for your guests. In these days of miserable unbelief, a Christian must show a certain amount of social and religious courage. He need not sound a trumpet about it, I grant you, and to force your own views on those unhappy people who do not understand would certainly be undesirable; but though your guests should not feel constrained to join in the prayers, neither should their presence make any difference nor hinder them. Let us live and let live. We know the duties of hospitality.

May God pour down every blessing on you, your family, your children. He who emptied Himself with such generosity so as to enrich men and comfort them in every need will not do less for one who loves and serves Him from the depths of his being. Wait patiently for His consolation. But remember it always pleases God when we come before Him as suppliants. He loves us to ask, pray, beseech, to the point of importunity. That is what beggars do, and that is what we also must do. For after all, are we not simply beggars before Him? What else can we claim to be? Our poverty and misery are immense, our need extreme. True, necessity forces us; we have to look after our everyday affairs, but in the final analysis there is only one sure refuge, God. Heaven help us! If we had to rely on man's aid alone, we should fare badly indeed. It is little use expecting anything from the mighty ones of this world—for the most part, they leave the poor to their poverty, and mean and ungenerous as they are, turn a deaf ear to the cry of those who are weak and helpless. But the Heart of God invites all to put it to the proof. The more He gives, the more He desires to give. He loves to see the trust which makes us persist in knocking unceasingly.

Ask for a miracle if you will, Sebastiane *mio*, but be sure you submit your petition entirely to God's will. Beyond all doubt, He does listen to our prayers and is ready to console us, but He sees things in a different way. He views them as a whole, we merely in part; He in the light of eternity, we in time only; He puts the well-being of the soul before that of the body, looks to our eternal salvation even at the cost of this life. You love your little Tommy, but God loves him far more; you long to do everything you can for his good, but God desires and aims at that good much more. Listen, Sebastian. Reason should dominate pain, for our Redeemer has sanctified pain and by so doing has given us Christians a right way of facing it. For us, pain does not come to hurt and destroy but to raise to the heights. None of God's works happen by chance, they have all been arranged by Divine Wisdom, God has His reasons for everything that comes to pass. If God were not God, if He had never revealed Himself, we might not know what to make of it. But knowing that He is infinite Goodness all diffusive of itself, that according to His will His mercy is poured out upon all His works, we can rest content, at peace even under affliction. This thought should suffice for you.

I have no need to tell you where to find a rock of refuge and true strength in this fresh onslaught of the storm; the date of this letter will make my meaning clear. He who rose in glory from the tomb declared: *I am the resurrection and the life.* The hope of a believer stretches from time to eternity. I wish a most happy Easter to you and yours; they are joyful wishes for blessings of consolation and peace, that blessed peace of our Lord's first greeting to His Apostles after His resurrection. That sums up everything. Where there is peace, there is God. And what more can we desire? Do we not find all in Him? Make this your prayer for me, and I shall be satisfied.

33. The Education of a Little Girl

St. Jerome
To the child's mother, A.D. 403

You are the daughter of a mixed marriage, but as for Paula—why, her parents are none other than yourself and my dear Toxentius.

Who would have credited the fact that in answer to a mother's promise a Christian granddaughter should have been granted to Albinus, a pagan high-priest, that her grandfather should listen with delight to the little one babbling Christ's Alleluia, and in his old age pillow on his breast a child vowed to God? The man who is surrounded by a crowd of Christian children and grand-children is pretty well already a candidate for the faith. Yes, he may spit on this letter of mine and hold it up to ridicule, call me a blockhead and a fool, but his son-in-law did precisely the same thing before he too received the faith. Christians are made, not born. I tell you this, Laeta, most devoted daughter in Christ, to teach you not to despair of your father's salvation. The same faith that has earned you a child may win over your father also, and you may one day rejoice over the blessedness of your entire household. Remember God's assurance: *Things that are impossible with men are possible with God* (Lk 18:27).

And now I am going to do as you ask, and teach you as her mother how to educate our precious little Paula. This is how a soul must be brought up that is to become the temple of God. In her upbringing, nothing must reach her ears or cross her lips that is not based on God's holy fear. Her nurses and governesses must be unworldly, strangers to society, not women who will pick up vicious habits and, what is worse, teach them to the child. Provide her with an alphabet made of boxwood or ivory and see that each letter is given its correct name. Let these be her play-things so that even her games may teach her something. And not only should she grasp the right order of the letters and get them by heart in a singsong rhyme, but you should constantly shuffle them, putting the last letters in the middle and the middle ones at the beginning so that she recognizes them by sight as well as by sound. As soon as she begins to draw her pencil over her paper, guide her tiny fingers while her hand is still unsteady by laying your hand over hers, and make her confine her efforts to the lines already ruled and not stray beyond them. Promise her a prize for good spelling and encourage her with small presents such as children of her age love. Let her have little friends to keep her up to the mark and provoke her to make greater effort when she is rather slow to respond, but coax her by praise to keep her wits awake. Then she will be proud of herself when she does better than others and blush when they do better than she does. Above all be careful that she does not take a dislike to her lessons, otherwise the aversion contracted in childhood may persist in later years. The very words she learns little by little to put together should not be taken at random but deliberately chosen and collected, so that while she is practicing something else, her memory will also benefit. You must take care, moreover, that some fool of a woman does not get the child into the habit of using baby-talk, or of wasting her time disporting herself in costly finery. The one will ruin her conversation and the other her character. She must not learn in early years what she will afterwards have to unlearn. Much of the eloquence of the Gracchi is ascribed to the way their mother spoke to them from their infancy. Hortensius became an orator while still in his father's arms. Early impressions are not easily eradicated from the mind. Once wool has been dyed purple, can anyone restore it to its former coloring? A brand-new jar long retains the taste and smell of what is first poured into it. Greek history relates that Alexander, the mightiest of kings and lord of the world, never succeeded in freeing himself from faults of manner and gait that as a small boy he had picked up from his tutor Leonides. It is easy to imitate what is evil, and if you cannot emulate people's virtues you are quick enough to copy their imperfections.

When the child visits her grandfather let her climb on his knee, throw her arms round his neck, and sing Alleluia in his ear whether he likes it or not. Her grandmother will kiss and caress her, her smiles show that she recognizes her father, and she will be such a pet that the possession of the rosebud will be a joy to the whole family. Tell her at once who her other grandmother is, and who her aunt; tell her of her true Sovereign in whose army she, His little recruit, is being trained to serve.

You may reply: How shall I be able to observe all these injunctions—I, a woman of the world living in Rome among these crowds of people? Well, then, do not undertake a task which is beyond you. When your little one can do without you, send her to her grandmother. Give up this most precious gem for Mary's chamber, and place her in the cradle where the Infant Jesus cried. Let her be brought up in the monastery and join the choirs of nuns. If you will send your tiny Paula, I promise myself to be both teacher and foster-father to her. Old as I am, I shall carry her pick-a-back on my shoulders and train her stammering speech. Far more glorious than that of the worldly philosopher shall my task be, for I shall instruct, not a Macedonian king to die one day of Babylonian poison, but a handmaid and bride of Christ to be prepared for the kingdom of heaven.

34. From a Four-Year-Old

St. Thérèse of Lisieux
To her sister's friend, April 4, 1877

I have never met you but all the same I love you very much. Pauline told me to write to you, she is holding me on her knees because I don't know how to use a proper pen by myself, she wants me to tell you I am a little lazybones, but that isn't true because I work hard all day playing pranks on my sisters, poor pets, and lastly I'm a little rogue who never stops laughing. Byebye, darling Louise, I send you a big fat kiss, give the Visitation a good hug for me, I mean Sister Marie Aloysia and Sister Louise de Gonzaga because I don't know any of the others.

35. Off to School

ST. THÉOPHANE VÉNARD
To his little brother, Montmorillon, 1847

Well, how do you like school? Are you finding the lessons hard? Horrid? Cheer up! You are only at the bottom of the ladder so far. You will soon climb a few rungs and look back on what you've already done. Have you met fellows you like? Are you having a good time together? Tell me all about it. Poor little chap, you are often in my thoughts, and I wish I were there with you, especially during the first few weeks at school.

It is half past six in the evening and the wind is whistling through the chinks of the door. It is bitter weather, isn't it? My heart goes out to you, old boy. I bet your paws and poor little toes are all over chilblains, as mine used to be, and the tip of your nose blue with cold. Am I right? Heigh-ho! That's a schoolboy's life. We go to learn how to put up with things. But let's stop talking about winter and wish each other a very, very happy New Year and heaven some day, though not just yet, I hope. I have no desire to see my young brother off there so soon. I remember long ago how you used to look forward to New Year's Day simply for all the gifts and goodies it brought. And now all the presents and candies have disappeared and only school remains. Oh, dear me! Never mind; you will be glad one of these days that you learned your lessons. They will fit you better to do what God wants you to do, so as to win heaven at the end of it all. For that alone must be the object of all we do. Work hard, work steadily, not for praise or honor or prizes, but simply to please God. Don't forget to say your prayers; obey your teachers because God has set them over you, be kind and affectionate towards your companions, and then everybody will like you and you will be thoroughly happy.

36. Latin without Tears

ST. THOMAS MORE
To his children, September 3, 1522

The Bristol merchant brought me your letters the day after he left you, with which I was extremely delighted. Nothing can come from your workshop, however rude and unfinished, that will not give me more pleasure than the most accurate thing another can write. There was not one of your letters that did not please me extremely; but, to confess ingenuously what I feel, the letter of my son John pleased me best, both because it was longer than the others, and because he seems to have given to it more labor and study. For he not only put out his matter prettily and composed in fairly polished language, but he plays with me both pleasantly and cleverly, and turns my jokes on myself wittily enough. And this he does not only merrily, but with due moderation, showing that he does not forget that he is joking with his father, and that he is cautious not to give offence at the same time that he is eager to give delight.

Now I expect from each of you a letter almost every day. I will not admit excuses—John makes none—such as want of time, sudden departure of the letter-carrier, or want of something to write about. No one hinders you from writing, but on the contrary all are urging you to do it. And that you may not keep the letter-carrier waiting, why not anticipate his coming, and have your letters written and sealed, ready for anyone to take? How can subject be wanting when you write to me, since I am glad to hear of your studies or of your games, and you will please me most if, when there is nothing to write about, you write about that nothing at great length. Nothing can be easier for you since you are girls, loquacious by nature, who have always a world to say about nothing at all.

But whether you write serious matters or the merest trifles, it is my wish that you write everything diligently and thoughtfully. It will be no harm if you first write the whole in English, for then you will have much less trouble in turning it into Latin; not having to look for the matter, your mind will be intent only on the language. That, however, I leave to your own choice, whereas I strictly enjoin you that whatever you have composed you carefully examine before writing it out clean; and in this examination first scrutinize the whole sentence and then every part of it. Thus if any inaccuracies have escaped you, you will easily detect them. Correct these, write out the whole letter again, and even then examine it once more, for sometimes in rewriting, faults slip in again that one had expunged. By this diligence, your little trifles will become serious matters; for while there is nothing so neat and witty that will not be made insipid by silly and inconsiderate loquacity, so also there is nothing in itself so insipid, that you cannot season it with grace and wit if you give a little thought to it. Farewell, my dear children.

37. Go to the Jesuits

ST. TERESA OF AVILA
To her brother, A.D. 1576

I should not like you to forget this, so I am putting it down here. Unless you begin now and take great trouble with those boys, I am very much afraid they may get friendly with some stuck-up set in Avila. So you must send them to the Company at once— I am writing to the Rector, as you will hear when you go there—and if good Francisco de Salcedo and Master Daza agree, let them wear college caps. One of Rodrigo's daughter's six children is a boy, which is fortunate for him: they have always kept him to his studies and he is now at Salamanca. A son of Don Diego de Aguila did what I am recommending to you. In any case you will hear there what is usual. Pray God my brother's boys may not grow up to think too much of themselves.

You will not be able to see much of Francisco de Salcedo, or of the Master, unless you go to their houses, for they live a long way from Peralvarez; but you ought to be alone with them for talks like these. Do not forget that you should not fix on any particular confessor just now, and you should have as few servants in your house as you can manage with. It is better to engage more than to have to get rid of some. I am writing to Valladolid to get the page to come; but, even if the boys have to go without one for a few days, there are two of them, and they can go together, so it does not much matter. But I am writing to have him sent to you.

You are inclined to think a great deal of your prestige—you have already demonstrated that. You must mortify yourself in this respect, and not listen to everybody, but follow the advice of these two in everything, and also of Father Muñoz, of the Company, if you think well, though the other two are sufficient in serious matters, and you can abide by what they say. Remember you may begin things without realizing at first that you are doing harm and that you will gain more in the eyes of God, and indeed in the eyes of the world, by keeping back your money for almsgiving, and your children will gain too.

I should not favor your buying a mule just yet. Get a little pony which will be useful for journeys and also for use at home. There is no reason at present why those boys of yours should not go on foot: let them keep to their studies.

38. A Christian School

ST. JOHN BOSCO
To the Salesians in Turin, Rome, May 10, 1884

Whether near or far I am always thinking of you, and I have only one desire—to see you happy here and hereafter. It is this thought, this desire, which prompts me to write you this letter. The distance that separates us distresses me; not to have you within sight or reach pains me beyond anything you can imagine. Had I been able, I should have penned these lines a week ago, but endless occupations have hindered me. Although I shall be returning to you within a few days, I should like to anticipate my arrival by a letter since I cannot come for the moment in person. These are the words of one who loves you tenderly in Christ Jesus and has a right to speak to you with a father's freedom. You will allow me, won't you? Give me your full attention and put into practice what I am going to tell you.

I have assured you that you are the one continual object of my thoughts. Now one evening lately I had gone up to my room and was preparing for bed. I was saying the prayers taught me by my beloved little mother when suddenly—whether I fell asleep or was carried away by a distraction I don't know—I seemed to see two former pupils of the Oratory standing in front of me. One of the pair came up, greeted me affectionately, and exclaimed:

"Don Bosco! Do you recognize me?"

"Yes, I know you all right," I replied.

"And do you still remember me?" the other asked.

"Yes, and every one of your contemporaries. You are Valfrè, and belonged to the Oratory before 1870."

"Tell me," Valfrè continued, "would you like me to show you the youngsters who were in the Oratory in my days?"

"If you could, I assure you it would please me enormously," I told him.

Thereupon Valfrè showed me all the young people looking just as they did at that date, the same height, the same age. I seemed to be present in the old Oratory at recreation time. The scene was full of life, full of movement, full of joy. One was racing, another jumping, another playing leapfrog. Here games were in full swing, there boxing and football. In one corner, a knot of boys press round a priest, hanging on his words as he tells a story; in another, a young cleric is the center of a group of little fellows playing at shop and up to tricks of all kinds. Here, there, and everywhere, singing and laughter; on all sides clerics and priests, and around them boys making a merry hullabaloo. It was quite clear that between boys and masters there was an exchange of perfect cordiality and trust. I was charmed by it, and Valfrè said to me: "Notice how a close family spirit carries with it affection, and affection engenders confidence. It is this that opens hearts. The boys then chat freely and without constraint to masters, staff, and Superiors; they tell the plain truth both in the confessional and out of it, and show themselves ready for every order since they feel sure everything is done for their well-being."

At this point, another of my former pupils, whose beard by now was completely white, came up to me and asked: "Don Bosco, now would you like to see the boys of the Oratory today?" The speaker was Joseph Buzzetti.

"Yes," I replied, "because it is now over a month since I saw them." And he showed me them. I saw the Oratory and all those at recreation. No longer however did I hear peals of merriment and bursts of song; gone were the bustle and liveliness of the former scene. The manner and looks of many betrayed tedium and boredom, sulkiness and distrust, which went to my heart. I saw, it is true, many who were running and playing, rushing about heedlessly and happily, but not a few were standing alone leaning against the pillars, haunted by uneasy thoughts. I saw some on the staircases, in the corridors, and on the balconies overlooking the garden in order to escape from the general recreation; others were walking slowly in groups exchanging remarks in undertones and darting sly, sharp glances in all directions. They smiled, yes, but the look that accompanied the smile was such as to make one not merely suspect but feel pretty certain that St. Aloysius would have blushed to be found among them. And even the boys who were playing showed quite obviously that their hearts were not in the game.

"Have you had a good look at the boys?" Joseph asked.

"I am looking at them," I told him with a sigh.

"How different from what we were once upon a time," my old pupil exclaimed.

"Altogether too different. This whole recreation is repugnant to the boys."

"This is at the bottom of all the coldness of so many towards approaching the Sacraments, their 'couldn't-care-less' attitude towards religious practices in church and elsewhere, and their deliberate refusal to settle down in a place where Providence loads them with every gift for health of body, soul, and mind. This explains the lack of correspondence to their calling, this explains the ingratitude to Superiors, this explains the resentment and discontent with all their deplorable consequences."

"I understand, quite understand," I answered. "But how can we put fresh life into these beloved boys of mine, to make them regain the old cheerfulness, joy, and frank confidence?"

"By love!"

"By love? But aren't my boys sufficiently loved? You know whether I love them. You know how much I have suffered and borne for them in the course of a good forty years, and how much I shall go on suffering and enduring. What weariness, what humiliations, what opposition, what persecution in order to provide them with bread, a roof, teachers, and especially to procure the salvation of their souls. Why, I have done all that was in me for the boys who are the love of my whole life."

"I am not referring to that just now."

"To what do you refer then? To those who are taking my place? To the directors, prefects, masters, assistants? Can't you see how completely devoted they are to study and work? Don't they lavish their best years on these boys whom divine Providence has put in their charge?"

"I do see it, I acknowledge it to be a fact. But that is not enough; something further is required."

"What is still lacking?"

"That the boys should not only be loved but that they themselves should realize it."

"But haven't they eyes in their heads, haven't they any intelligence? Can't they see that whatever is done is simply done for love of them?"

"No, I repeat, that is not enough."

"What do you demand then?"

"They must not only recognize that affection underlies everything that suits them, when their youthful likes and dislikes are humored, but they must learn to see the same affection behind those very things that go against the grain: discipline, study, self-denial. They must bring themselves to accept them promptly and cheerfully."

"Could you explain more fully?"

"Watch the boys at recreation."

I had already watched them and so I answered: "And what precisely is there to notice?"

"Have you been educating boys for so many years and you don't see what I'm getting at? Look more carefully. Where are the Salesians we knew?"

I did look, and I observed that very few priests and clerics were mixing with the boys, and still fewer were taking part in their games. The Superiors were no longer the soul of recreation. The majority of them were chatting among themselves without bothering about what the pupils were doing; others surveyed the scene but paid no attention to the boys; yet others looked on in an absentminded kind of way, and failed to notice whether anything was amiss. Very occasionally someone spoke a word of reproof in a threatening tone. A certain Salesian Father would have liked to join a particular group of boys, but I saw that they were studiously avoiding both masters and Superiors. My friend then resumed:

"In the old days of the Oratory, weren't the masters always among the boys, above all during recreation? Do you remember those happy years? Weren't they simply heavenly? We always look back to those days with emotion because the masters ruled by love and we kept nothing from them."

"I agree; to me it was pure joy. The boys used to crowd round me eagerly, listening for every word and filled with anxiety to pay attention to my advice and put it into practice. But nowadays you must realize how endless interviews, business of every kind, and the state of my health all make it impossible for me."

"Granted; but if you cannot do it in person, why don't your Salesian sons follow your example? Why don't you demand, go further and insist, that they treat the boys as you treated them?"

"I do, I'm for ever repeating it. But nowadays many, far too many, seem to have no conception of spending themselves as we once did."

"They neglect the little things and thus lose the great—the very reward of their own work. If the masters accept what appeals to the boys, the boys will accept what appeals to the Superiors; and then their task will become easy. The result of this change in the Oratory is that many of the boys place no trust in those in authority. In the olden days, all hearts were open to the Superiors so that the boys loved them and obeyed promptly. Now, however, Superiors are regarded as nothing more than Superiors; they are no longer fathers, brothers, friends. Consequently you will find more fear than love. Now if you want to create one mind and one heart, for the love of God you must break down that fatal barrier of distrust and open the door to cordial confidence. Obedience will then guide the pupil as a mother guides her little one, and the peace and joy that was once ours will reign throughout the Oratory."

"Very well, what can we do to overthrow these barriers?"

"Build up a close family spirit with the boys especially at recreation. Without the family spirit, affection doesn't make itself felt, and if it doesn't make itself felt, there will be no mutual understanding. Anyone who would be loved must show love. Jesus Christ made Himself little with the little ones and shared our weakness. Study the perfect Pattern of the family spirit! A master seen only in the teacher's desk remains a master and no more, but let him recreate with the boys and he becomes a brother. The priest seen only in the pulpit is doing, you would say, neither more nor less than his duty, but let him speak a word at recreation and he becomes a friend. How many changes of heart spring from a few chance words spoken in a boy's ear at play! One who is conscious of affection will return it, and one who is loved can get all he wants especially from boys. This mutual trust sets up an electric current between boys and those placed over them. Hearts are opened, make known their needs, and lay bare their faults. This affection prompts them to bring to Superiors their strivings, their trials, their hurt feelings, their troubles, failings, and negligences. Our Lord did not crush the bruised reed nor quench the smoking wick. There you have your model. Imitate Him, and no longer will there be anyone among you who works out of vainglory or punishes simply to vindicate injured self-love; no one will avoid the charge of supervision because he jealously fears that another will put him in the shade; no one will grumble about others because he is out to gain the affection and admiration of the boys to the exclusion of the other Superiors—actually, all he will get for his trouble is lip-homage and contempt; no one will let himself be captivated by a favorite and pass over the rest of the class so as to give him special honor; no one will put his own convenience first, and treat as of no consequence the very strict duty of supervising; no one for fear of being unpopular will omit to correct those in need of correction. Where true love is the guiding principle, no one wants anything but the glory of God and the salvation of souls. It is when this love grows weak that things begin to go wrong. Why do they want to substitute cold regimentation for the warmth of affection? Why are those in authority departing from the observance which Don Bosco gave them? Why are they gradually discarding their practice of forestalling disorders with wise vigilance, in favor of a system of promulgating rules which as far as officials are concerned may be far more convenient and less exacting? If enforced by the rod, such rules merely enkindle hatred and feed resentment; if allowed to go by default, they give rise to disrespect for authority and engender grave abuses. Restore love and the constraint will vanish and the load of deadly secrets along with it. Only in cases of immorality must Superiors be inexorable. It is better to run the risk of driving an innocent boy from the house than to retain a scoundrel. The assistants should make it a most strict duty of conscience to report to Superiors anything of this kind which they know to be offensive to God."

"And what is the principal way," I then asked him, "to ensure that the family spirit, mutual love, and complete trust should prevail?"

"The exact observance of the rules of the house."

"And nothing more?"

"The best dish at a meal is that of good cheer."

As my old pupil finished speaking thus, and I stood watching that recreation filled with displeasure, I felt myself slowly overcome with intense and increasing weariness. The oppression grew to such a pitch that unable to resist any longer, I shook myself and woke up.

I found myself standing near my bed. My legs were so swollen and painful that I could not remain on my feet. It was very late so I went to bed determined to write and tell my beloved sons all about it.

I would far rather not have these dreams because they tire me so. Next day I felt utterly exhausted and could not get to bed quickly enough that evening. But hardly was I in bed when the dream began again. Before me was the playground with the boys who are at present in the Oratory, and the same former pupil. I made haste to address the latter: "I shall tell my Salesian sons what you have said to me, but what am I to tell the boys of the Oratory?"

"Tell them," he answered, "they must realize how the Superiors, masters, and assistants wear themselves out, how it is for their sakes that they study, otherwise they would never submit to a life of such sacrifice. Tell them they must remember that humility is the source of all peace, and they must learn how to bear with one another's failings, since perfection is to be found nowhere in this world but in heaven alone. They must stop grumbling because this cools affection, and above all they should take care to live in God's holy grace. Anyone who is not at peace with God is not at peace with himself, nor at peace with others."

"You mean to tell me that some of my boys are not at peace with God?"

"There you have the primary cause of the poisoned atmosphere for which a remedy must be found—other causes you know yourself; I need not name them. No one ought to feel constraint if he has nothing to hide; such a one has no fear of secrets coming to light which would redound to his shame and disgrace. On the other hand, if his soul is not at peace with God, a boy remains tortured, troubled, rebellious, irritated by trifles, everything seems to him to go wrong, and because he has no affection for those over him, he imagines they have none for him."

"But, my dear fellow, don't you see how the boys of the Oratory frequent Confession and Communion?"

"True, they often go to Confession, but the thing fundamentally lacking in the boys who go is a firm purpose of amendment. They always mention the same old sins, the same dangerous occasions, the same bad habits, the same acts of disobedience, the same neglect of duty. So it goes on month after month and year after year, and some continue like this to the very top of the school. These are Confessions of little or no value. They bring no peace, and were a boy to be summoned before the judgment seat of God in such a state, it might go hard with him."

"And are there many of them in the Oratory?"

"Few in comparison with the number in the house. There they are!" And he pointed them out to me.

I looked and saw those boys one by one, but in those few I saw things which filled my heart with bitter sorrow. I don't want to put these things down on paper. When I return, I intend to tell them in detail to each one concerned. Here I can only say that it is high time to pray and make stern resolutions; to prove our determination by deed rather than word, and show that there are Comollos, Dominic Savios, Besuccos, and Siccardis still living among us.

Finally I asked my friend: "Have you anything more to tell me?"

"Drum it into them, little and great, that they must always remember they are sons of our Lady, Help of Christians. She it is who has gathered them together so as to remove them from the dangers of the world and enable them to live in brotherly love, and so glorify God and herself by an upright life. She it is who provides them with daily food and education, grants them countless graces and even miracles. Remind them that they are now on the eve of the feast of their holy Mother. With her help the barriers of distrust, raised by diabolical craft between boys and Superiors, and used by the devil to ruin certain souls, must be demolished."

"And shall we manage to tear them down?"

Yes, undoubtedly, provided that old and young are ready to put up with a certain amount of self-denial for love of Mary, and to put into practice what I have pointed out to you."

All this time my eyes were on my boys, and at sight of those whom I saw heading for eternal perdition, I felt my heart almost bursting so that I woke up. I saw many other very important things which I should still like to tell you, but I have no time and it would not be fitting.

One more word. Shall I tell you what this poor old man who has spent his whole life on his beloved boys would ask of you? Simply this: so far as may be, bring back the happy days of the first Oratory. They were days of sympathy and Christian trust between the boys and those in authority, days of friendliness and forbearance towards one another for love of our Lord, days of frankness, simplicity, and candor, days of love and true joy for all. You can give me the comfort and hope I need, by promising to fulfil all I would have you do for your own spiritual welfare. You do not sufficiently realize your happy lot, sheltered as you are in the Oratory. In the sight of God, I declare a boy has only to enter a Salesian house for our Lady to take him at once under her special protection. So let us all be of one mind. The love of those who rule and the love of those who obey must make the spirit of St. Francis de Sales reign in our midst. O my dear sons, the time is approaching when I must leave you and depart to eternity. *(Secretary's note:* At this point Don Bosco stopped dictating; his eyes filled with tears not of grief but of unutterable tenderness which betrayed itself in his look and in the sound of his voice: after a few moments he resumed.) I long to leave you, then, my priests, my clerics, my dearest boys, in whatever way the Lord desires.

And now, the Holy Father whom I saw on Friday, May 9th, sends you his blessing with all his heart. The feast of our Lady, Help of Christians, will find me with you before the statue of our most loving Mother. I want this great festival celebrated with all solemnity, and Don Lazzero and Don Marchisio are to see to it that we enjoy it in the refectory as well. The feast of our Lady Help of Christians must be the prelude to the eternal feast which we shall celebrate unitedly one day in heaven.

39. Pocket-Money for Meg

ST. THOMAS MORE
To his eldest daughter, September 11, 1522

You ask for money, my dear Margaret, with too much bashfulness and timidity, since you are asking from a father who is eager to give, and since you have written me a letter such that I would not only repay each line of it with a golden philippine, as Alexander did the verses of Cherilos, but if my means were as great as my desire I would reward each syllable with two gold ounces. As it is, I send only what you have asked, but would have added more, only that as I am eager to give, so am I desirous to be asked and coaxed. So the sooner you spend this money well, and the sooner you ask for more, the more you will be sure of pleasing your father.

I happened this evening to be in the company of his Lordship, John, Bishop of Exeter, a man of deep learning and of a wide reputation for holiness. Whilst we were talking, I took out from my desk a paper that bore on our business and by accident your letter appeared. He took it into his hand with pleasure and examined it. When he saw from the signature that it was the letter of a lady, he was induced by the novelty of the thing to read it more eagerly. When he had finished, he said he would never have believed it to have been your work unless I had assured him of the fact, and he began to praise it in the highest terms (why should I hide what he said?) for its pure Latinity, its correctness, its erudition, and its expressions of tender affection. Seeing how delighted he was, I showed him your speech. He read it, as also your poems, but although he praised you most effusively, yet his countenance showed that his words were all too poor to express what he felt. He took out at once from his pocket a portague* which you will find enclosed in this letter. I tried in every possible way to decline it, but was unable to refuse to take it to send to you as a pledge and token of his goodwill towards you. This hindered me from showing him the letters of your sisters, for I feared that it would seem as though I had shown them to obtain for the others too a gift which it annoyed me to have to accept for you. But, as I have said, he is so good that it is a happiness to be able to please him. Write to thank him with the greatest care and delicacy. You will one day be glad to have given pleasure to such a man. Farewell.

---

* A Portuguese gold coin.

40. Counsels to a Student

ST. THOMAS AQUINAS
To a disciple, c. 1270

You have asked me, John, most dear to me in Christ, how you should set about studying in order to build up a rich store of knowledge. This is the advice I give you on the subject.

1. Do not plunge straight into the sea, but rather enter it by way of little streams, because it is wise to work upward from the easier to the more difficult. This, then, is what I would teach you, and you must learn.
2. I would have you slow to speak, and slow to betake yourself to the parlor.
3. Cherish purity of conscience.
4. Never omit your times of prayer.
5. Love to stay in your own cell if you want to gain admission to God's wine-cellar.
6. Show a cheerful face to all.
7. Never pry into other people's business.
8. Do not become over-familiar with anyone, because familiarity breeds contempt and gives a pretext for neglecting serious work.
9. Take care not to interfere in the words and actions of outsiders.
10. Do not waste time in useless talking.
11. Be sure to follow in the footsteps of good and holy men.
12. Do not concentrate on the personality of the speaker, but treasure up in your mind anything profitable he may happen to say.
13. See that you thoroughly grasp whatever you read and hear.
14. Check up on doubtful points.
15. And do your best to hoard up whatever you can in that

little book-case of your mind; you want to fill it as full as possible.

16. Do not concern yourself with things beyond your competence.

By following this path, you will throw out leaves and bear serviceable fruit in the vineyard of the Lord of Hosts all the days of your life. If you stick to these counsels, you will reach the goal of your desires. Farewell.

41. What, Women Too?

ST. THOMAS MORE
To his children's tutor, May 22, 1518 [?]

I have received your letter, my dear Gonell, elegant as your letters always are, and full of affection. Your devotion to my children I perceive from your letter, your diligence from theirs. Every one of their letters gave me pleasure, but I was particularly pleased because I notice that Elizabeth shows a gentleness and self-command in the absence of her mother which some children would not show in her presence. Let her realize that such conduct delights me more than all the letters I could receive put together. Though I prefer learning coupled with virtue to all the treasures of kings, yet renown for learning when not united to a good life is nothing but glittering and notorious infamy, especially in a woman. Since erudition in women is a novelty and a reproach to masculine sloth, many will gladly attack it and impute to scholarship what is really the fault of nature, thinking from the vices of the learned to get their own ignorance esteemed as virtue. On the other hand, if a woman (and with you as their teacher, this is my desire and hope for all my daughters) should add to eminent virtue even moderate intellectual ability, I believe she will profit more truly than if she had acquired the riches of Croesus and the beauty of Helen. I do not say this because it will redound to her glory, though glory follows virtue as a shadow does a body, but because the reward of wisdom is too solid to be lost like riches or to decay like beauty, since it depends on the inward consciousness of what is right, and not on the gossip of human beings, than which nothing is more foolish or mischievous.

Among all the benefits that learning bestows on men, there is none more excellent than this, that by study we are taught to seek in that very study not praise, but utility. Such has been the teaching of the most learned men, especially of philosophers, who are the guides of human life. Therefore, my dear Gonell, since we must take this road, I have often begged not you only, who out of your affection for my children would do it of your own accord, nor only my wife, who is sufficiently urged by her motherly love for them, but I have begged all my friends to warn my children to avoid the precipices of pride and haughtiness, and to walk in the pleasant meadows of modesty; not to be dazzled at the sight of gold; not to grieve if they lack what they mistakenly admire in others; not to think more of themselves for gaudy trappings, nor less for the want of them; neither to deform by neglect the beauty that nature has bestowed on them, nor try to heighten it by artifice; to put virtue in the first place, learning in the second; and in their studies to esteem most whatever may teach them piety towards God, charity to all, and Christian humility in themselves. By such means, they will receive from God the reward of an innocent life, and in the assured expectation of death will view it without dread. And meanwhile, in the solid joy which is theirs, they will neither be elated by the empty praise of men, nor dejected by evil tongues. These I consider the genuine fruits of learning, and though I admit that all men of learning do not possess them, I would maintain that those who devote themselves to study with such aims in view will easily attain their goal and become perfect.

Nor do I think that the harvest will be much affected whether it be man or woman who sows the field. They both have the same human nature which reason differentiates from that of beasts; both, therefore, are equally suited for those studies which cultivate the intellect and, like land well-ploughed, yield a crop after the seed of good principles has been planted. If it be true that the soil of woman's brain is poor and more apt to bear bracken than corn—by so saying, many prevent women from study—I think, on the contrary, that a woman's mind is on that account all the more diligently to be cultivated, that nature's defect may be redressed by industry. This was the opinion of the ancients, of those who were most prudent as well as most holy. Not to speak of the rest, St. Jerome and St. Augustine not only exhorted excellent matrons and most noble virgins to study, but also, in order to assist them, diligently explained the abstruse meanings of holy Scripture, and wrote for tender girls letters replete with so much erudition that nowadays old men who call themselves professors of sacred science can scarcely read them correctly, much less understand them. Do you, my learned Gonell, have the kindness to see that my daughters thoroughly learn these works of those holy men. From them they will learn in particular the end they should propose to themselves in their studies, and the fruit of their endeavors, namely, the testimony of God and a good conscience. Thus peace and calm will reign in their hearts, and they will be disturbed neither by exaggerated praise nor by the stupidity of those illiterate men who despise learning.

I fancy I hear you object that these precepts, though true, are beyond the capacity of my young daughters, since you will scarcely find a man, however old and advanced in learning, whose mind is so fixed and firm as not to be tickled sometimes with desire of glory. But, dear Gonell, in order to banish this plague of vainglory far from my children, I do ask you and their mother and all their friends to sing this song to them, go on singing it, drive it into their heads, that vainglory is despicable and to be spit upon, and that there is nothing more sublime than the humble modesty so often praised by Christ. To this purpose nothing will more conduce than to read to them the lessons of the ancient Fathers who, they know, cannot be angry with them; and as they honor them for their sanctity, they must needs be much moved by their authority. If, besides their reading of Sallust, you will read something of this nature to Margaret and Elizabeth, as being more advanced than John and Cecily, you will bind me and them still more to you. Thus you will make my children who are dear to me first by nature, even dearer by learning and virtue, and dearest of all by reason of their advance in wisdom and an upright life. Farewell.

42. The Art of Selection

St. Basil
To his nephews, c. A.D. 371

A man of my age who has seen a good deal of life has had his fair share of the ups and downs of fortune which teach us many things. Since, then, I am experienced in human affairs, I feel qualified to point out to you who are setting out on the venture of life a well-beaten path. So if you listen attentively to my words, you will take your place in the second rank of those whom Hesiod praises. "The noblest kind of man," he says, as you may remember, "sees at a glance what is best. He is good who follows the advice of others. But the man incapable of either is of no use to himself or anybody else." Now day after day, you are to sit at the feet of tutors, and come into contact with illustrious men of old through the writings they have left behind. This is the piece of advice I have come to give you: Do not hand yourselves over to them absolutely. Do not surrender your mind as if it were a ship's rudder answering to control. No; take what suits you, and learn to discard the rest.

Young men, you and I set little store by earthly existence. Things that merely improve this life have no true value for us; they are not what we call "the real thing." Good family, athletic valor, a handsome face, tall stature, men's esteem, dominion over others—none of these are important in our eyes or a petition fit for prayer; it is not our way to pay court to those who can boast them. Our ideals soar far above all that. Everything we do, we do as a preparation for the life to come. We weigh all in the light of that life, and consider it our duty to love and strive with might and main to attain whatever will help us reach it; whatever does not lead to it, we rightly put aside as worthless. As soldiers however drill and exercise themselves in mock fights, so we may train ourselves by studying profane literature before turning to the sacred Scriptures. But we must read with discernment.

It becomes us to descend into the arena of life by the path of virtue, and since this is the constant theme of the poet's song, of the historian, and above all of the philosopher, it is this aspect of their writings we must keep in view. All Homer's poetry lauds the man of upright life, and almost all wise men of renown have set forth their praise of duty fulfilled. It is for us to respond to their injunctions, to accept those narratives which contain principles of moral beauty, and illustrate their lessons by our deeds. A certain ruffian, for instance, reviled Pericles; Pericles took no notice of him whatever. All day long, the one showered abuse without restraint, the other turned a completely deaf ear. When evening came and darkness fell and the man began to take himself off, Pericles escorted him with a lighted torch in order not to profess a philosophy that he never put into practice. Again, Euclid of Megara provoked someone to anger. The man threatened, indeed took an oath, to kill him. By contrast Euclid likewise took an oath to come to terms with him and conciliate his wrath. If only a man in the grip of anger would recall an example such as this!

Or again, there was a man who struck Socrates, son of Sophroniscus, full in the face, dealing him blow upon blow. Socrates offered no resistance; he allowed the drunkard's anger free rein. Within a short time his face was swollen and livid from bruises. When at last his assailant gave over, Socrates simply wrote on his forehead, as an artist engraves his name on a statue: "So-and-so did this." That was his sole retaliation. Surely it is well for us in our generation to imitate such models. For this story of Socrates is akin to the command that if someone strike us on the right cheek, we should turn to him the other also, and never attempt to take revenge, just as Pericles and Euclid carry out the precept: "Submit patiently to those who injure you, and gently endure their anger," and similarly, "Pray for your enemies, bless them and curse them not."

To be sure, we may possibly learn these lessons more perfectly from our own Scriptures, but knowledge can accrue from all sides like tributaries flowing into the broadening stream. For that reason the poet rightly considered the expression "to store up little by little" applied to growth in knowledge rather than to the amassing of gold. Accordingly when Bias was about to set out for Egypt, to the question what course he proposed to follow that would give his father most pleasure, the son replied: "I shall lay in provision for old age." By calling virtue "provision" he has carefully defined it, as one who would indicate its value to human life. But as for myself, were you to quote to me the proverbial old age of Tithonus or even of Methusalah, the oldest man in all history who attained, so they say, a thousand years save thirty, were you to pile up the years of mortal man and add them all together, why, I should laugh as at the babbling of babes when I consider Eternity—Eternity, everlasting and ageless, that human thought can never grasp or encircle, any more than it can assign any end to an immortal soul. It is in view then of Eternity that I would urge you to acquire the provision spoken of; leave no stone unturned if it is going to help you by any means at all to attain your goal.

43. The Sorrow of His Mother

ST. BERNARD
To the Countess de Blois, c. A.D. 1152

I am sorry your son has behaved badly towards you. I deplore as much the conduct of the son as the wrongs of his mother. Yet, after all, such conduct is excusable in a young son. Youth is ever prone to such faults and is itself an excuse for them. Do you not realize that "all the thoughts and imaginations of a man's heart are bent towards evil from youth?" You may be sure that the merits and alms of his father will bring about a change for the better in him. You must offer more and more vows and prayers to God for him, because, even though at the moment his conduct towards you is not what it should be, yet nevertheless a mother ought not and cannot lose her maternal affection for her children. "Can a mother ever forget the son she bore in her womb?" asks the Prophet, and he adds: "even if she were to forget, I will not be forgetful of thee." The young man has so many excellent qualities that we must offer prayers and tears to the Lord, that God may enable him (as I am sure he will) to emulate the goodness of his father. He must be treated with gentleness and kindly forbearance, because by such treatment he will be more encouraged to do good than if he were exasperated by nagging and scolding. I am sure that by these means we will soon be able to rejoice over a happy change in him. There is nothing I desire more than that he should change for the better. I wish I could find his conduct towards others as irreproachable as I have always found it towards myself, for I have never known him anything but most ready and willing to do all I wished. May God reward him for this! But, as you have asked me to do, I am always remonstrating with him about his conduct towards you, and I shall continue to do so.

44. The Anger of His Father

St. Alphonsus Liguori
To his father, Don Giuseppe de Liguori, October 1737

I beg you for pity's sake to show a little more charity towards your son. He came to see me this morning at Naples and burst into tears in front of me, tears which he could not restrain because he was so weighed down by grief. Good heavens above! Do you want to drive him to desperation, or provoke him to throw himself down a well or do something equally mad? I do implore you not to treat him to black looks at table and to give him some assistance, since the poor boy is now married, cut off from Naples, and without comfort of any kind. Do be careful not to precipitate any foolhardy action on his part, and now that he is sick, you should give him some special proof of kindness. Remember that he is your son, and not some mongrel or other, and surely far dearer as such than property or wealth. You may be certain of this: if you practice love within your own family, God will help you ouside it. What do you intend to do about the state of affairs? What is done is done. So has it been foreseen from all eternity. Who is to blame? I recommend you to God at Mass every morning, and I hope that the Blessed Virgin will come to your assistance. Asking you for your blessing.

45. A Fraternal Admonition

St. Aloysius Gonzaga
To his brother Rodolfo, Milan, March 17, 1590

The Peace of Christ. The desire I have always had for your spiritual welfare makes me write herein (as the Lord bids me) what in the same Lord I think very useful and expedient for the securing and establishing of that salvation. And this is, that before you go to Germany, during this holy season of Lent, between now and Easter, Your Lordship should bring yourself to make a general confession at least dating from that which I know you made five years ago in Mantua, up to the present time. For thus you get the certainty (so far as one ever can in this life) that none of those offenses against His Divine Majesty remain upon your soul, which perhaps were left behind by the more or less furtive and secret confessions that you made during the time when through human respect you were not daring to profess yourself Christ's servant. This will, I think, be all the easier because you have already overcome and removed the main difficulty. So nothing now remains but the fruit of hope and the very certain pledge of the grace of God which can be taken for granted from the means that I accordingly recommend to Your Lordship so strongly, so strongly for this end. I put before you two means in particular which occur to me.

One is, to have within you always that supreme esteem of the grace of God—oh, just as I could never say enough to express even the least part of it, so no one else can make us fully understand it save the blessed God. So I leave it to Him to teach it to you. Only I will say that, even as God is above all created things, honors, possessions, and anything else you like, so (were it possible) must be the esteem that we have within us of His Divine Majesty, above every other esteem or notion.

The second means is to cooperate with the degree of that grace, putting forth good works not only before God but also before men. And since it seems that to commend religion is the suitable business owed to God by a "Religious," I will now descend to a few special points, which you can attend to according to the measure of grace that the Lord shall deign to communicate to you.

Among them, the first is to commend yourself to God in the morning with some such prayer as is the Daily Exercise or some other prayer in which you could also think of some one of the points which you can find in the Daily Exercise placed at the end of the little book I send you, compiled by order of Monsignor Cardinal Borromeo of happy memory; and since there are in it other suggestions that you can read there, I will not enlarge on this further save to recommend Mass to you, according to our compact.

Next, I would not like you ever to go to bed at night without first seeing in yourself whether you are conscious of offense against God, so that if you feel guilty of mortal sin, from which God preserve you, you may resolve to cancel it so soon as possible by means of the sacrament of Penance. You must recall that this is always necessary if you have to be sorry for anything, but you must never, for that, wait for a fixed time such as Easter, because no one can promise you that you will live till then.

Next, "to put forth good works before men," I recommend to you the respect you owe to your relatives and superiors. Wholly because of the sense of obligation I feel myself, and not because I think you really need it, I commend to you the reverence that you owe to the Lady Marchioness your Mother—just *as* mother, and, *such* a mother!

Further, you know, as being the head of your brothers, how right it is that you should keep them united, and act so that they may ever have reason to be glad of this union. About your vassals I will merely say that God has put them in a special and individual manner into your safe keeping, perhaps to convey to you the special and spiritual care that Your Lordship must have of them, seeing in the Providence of God towards yourself the way in which you ought to provide for them.

Now I finish. And since the execution of what I have commended to you must come rather from God's grace than from your own efforts or my recommendation, therefore I offer and promise you that in my prayers, such as they are, I will always keep you commended in the sight of His Divine Majesty, and may He keep you and guide you to that happy end to which His elect do come.

46. A Sisterly Touch

St. Bernadette
To Jean-Marie, her brother, July 1, 1876

Cousin Nicholau has told me in her letter that you expect your discharge from the army this year. Do give me some idea of what you intend to do. You must realize that although miles away, I'm as much interested in your doings as if I were on the spot. Any question I ask is not, you may be sure, prompted by mere curiosity, my dear one. As our dear father and mother have left us, I feel it my duty as your eldest sister to watch over you.

I admit that at the moment I feel acute anxiety over your future and Pierre's too. I pray every day that our Lord and our blessed Lady will guide your decision. Above all else, I strongly advise you to be very faithful to your obligations as a Christian. That is where you will find strength and light in all your troubles and difficulties. I know that soldiers have a lot to endure, and to endure in silence. If upon rising they would only take the trouble to say to our Lord every morning this tiny phrase: "My God, I desire to do and to endure everything today for love of Thee," what glory they would heap up for eternity! Why, a soldier who did that and was as loyal as possible to his Christian duties would earn as much reward as any cloistered monk!

47. These Brothers!

St. Catherine dei Ricci
To her father, Pierfrancesco dei Ricci, November 15, 1543

May the Divine Majesty grant you patience and give peace to your troubled soul! May you be enlightened to see what is best to be done, and have the grace to do it. I have received a letter from Ridolfo, begging me to plead his cause with you, and forward you the letter he has written to you. I understand only too well your displeasure against him and the serious faults of which he is guilty. But, Father, I beg you to be patient and prudent. He has acted very wrongly and disobeyed both God and you, his loving father, who have spent so much care upon him. In spite of all that, I beseech you for the love of God to forgive him. If you have cursed him—and he deserved it—now restore him to your blessing. Since the harm is done, there is nothing to be gained by making bad worse and driving him to despair. Justice may be on your side, and the world may tell you to be firm in asserting your rights, but I believe that it is by showing mercy you will please our Lord. When Mother thinks the moment has come, Ridolfo will, I know, ask your pardon. I implore you to grant it when he asks. Tell him the truth gently, promise to help him if he behaves himself, and threaten to withdraw your help should he misconduct himself. As long as he is afraid to approach you or speak to you, medicine will be precious little use to him. He fully acknowledges that you are in the right and is very humble and most anxious to atone by his future conduct for the offense he has given you. The sooner you forgive him, the more quickly he will recover from his illness. You are the person to restore him to health of soul and body. Speak to your son again. Do not refuse me, Father! If I am truly your daughter and you love me as much as you profess, you will grant me what I ask. I thank you with all my heart for your affection: may our Lord reward you!

48. A Sop to Aunt Castorina

St. Jerome
To his mother's sister, Castorina, A.D.374

Every one who hates his brother is a murderer (1 John 3:15). This is the plain statement of John, apostle and evangelist—and well indeed might he say so. It is only too true that murder often springs from hatred. Although his sword may never yet have struck a blow, the hater is already at heart a murderer. Pray, why all this preamble, you ask? Simply to urge that you and I bury old resentments and prepare a pure heart for God to dwell in. *Be angry*, so David tells us, *and sin not* (Ps 4:5). The Apostle explains this verse in more precise detail: *Do not let the sun go down upon your anger* (Eph 4:26). Tell me, how are we two going to face the Day of Judgment? The sun is witness that it has gone down upon our anger not one day but for many a long year. *If thou art offering thy gift at the altar,* our Lord says in the

Gospel, *and there rememberest that thy brother has anything against thee, leave thy gift before the altar and go first to be reconciled to thy brother, and then come and offer thy gift* (Mt 5:23). Woe to me, vile wretch! Must I say, Woe to you also? For so many years, we have either brought no gift to the altar, or have brought it while we still nursed our groundless grievances. How did we ever make our own the daily petition, *Forgive us our debts, as we also forgive our debtors* (Mt 6:12) when heart and tongue were at such variance, entreaty so inconsistent with conduct? Therefore I am now renewing the request I made to you in my previous letter of a year ago. Let us both preserve that peace which was our Lord's legacy to us, and may Christ look with pleasure upon my desire and your intention. Soon harmony restored or harmony ruptured will receive reward or penalty before His tribunal. Very well; if you now rebuff me, which God forbid, the guilt will not be on my head. Once you have read it, this letter of mine will secure my acquittal.

49. And a Sop to Uncle Gregory

ST. BASIL
To Gregory, his uncle, A.D. 371

I have kept silence. But am I to be silent always? How should I bear to condemn myself any longer to this most grievous punishment of silence, neither sending myself nor receiving greeting? Having endured steadfastly in this dour determination until now, I think I have the right to make the prophet's words my own: *I have endured like a woman in travail* (Is 42:14), longing ever for meeting or message, ever disappointed on account of my sins. No other explanation can I devise for what is happening; I cannot but be convinced that I am paying full penalty for my past sins in this estrangement from your charity—if indeed it is not impious to use the word "estrangement" of you in anyone's regard, and still more so with reference to ourself, to whom you have stood from the beginning as a father.

But now my sin, like some thick clinging cloud, has hidden all that from me. For when I consider that nothing of good has been accomplished by events except that they have caused me pain, how can I in all fairness fail to attribute present conditions to my own ill-doing? However, if my sins are responsible for this state of affairs, let me see an end of vexations at last; if there was some wise dispensation, its purpose has been plentifully achieved. The sentence indeed has been no short one. Unable then to contain myself further, I have taken the initiative in speaking freely, entreating you to be mindful both of us and of yourself, you who have shown for us all our life long a solicitude beyond the claims of kin.

I charge you then *by whatever is of pressing appeal in Christ, of fellowship in the Spirit, of tender compassion, fulfill* our desire (Phil 2:1-2). Raise up the downcast here and now, and give more cheerful prospects a chance, yourself leading others towards the best rather than following someone else towards what is not right (cf Ti 1:11). For never was there trait of body deemed so proper to a man as peace and gentleness are characteristic of your soul.

Therefore, whether it be by your presence, or by letter, or by an invitation to meet you, or by any other means you may choose, afford us relief. Indeed, our prayer is that your Reverence would appear in person in our Church, and heal both us and the people alike simply by the sight of you and by your charitable words. If this is possible it will be the best course, but if you prefer some other we are ready to agree. All we ask is that you be persuaded to let us know for certain what recommends itself to your prudence.

50. Making the Choice

St. Théophane Vénard
To his brother Eusebius, August 3, 1851

You are now of an age to choose your future career; an age when people begin to think for themselves, and when certain convictions are formed in the mind and influence the conduct. In your intercourse with men, you will encounter much prejudice, many strange ideas and perversions of the truth, for society in Europe has become thoroughly corrupt. I do not mean to say that there were not plenty of bad people in olden times just as there are now, for man is ever the same. But formerly there were certain social canons and conventions that none but the really profligate disregarded. Religion was the accepted foundation of society, and God gives life to nations as well as to individuals. Now all these safeguards are removed or ignored, as you will realize when you grow older.

Well, you are wondering about your future. Pray simply, humbly, and fervently to know God's will, and your path will be made clear. Then you must follow the inspiration divine Mercy puts into your heart. Some say: "I will be a priest," or "a soldier," and they add: "Oh, such and such studies are not necessary for this or that profession." This is the reasoning of pure idlers. Others go on about piety: "Piety! It's only for priests and nuns. God does not expect so much from us!" *(How do you know?)* These are the arguments of cold and calculating natures. Now I want you to say to yourself: "I am, above all, a man, a rational being, created to know, love, serve, and glorify God. I come from God. I go to God. I belong to God. My body is His. My mind is His. My heart is His. I shall be judged according to my deeds, according to the way I have corresponded with the grace given me. Well, then, by God's help, I shall use this body, this mind, and this heart as much as I possibly can for His greater glory, honor, and love." Life well-employed consists in this: A faithful correspondence to grace and a good use of the talents we have been given. This rule of life applies equally to all.

But you want to know, "What does God ask of *me?*" Humility, prayer, obedience to His divine commands and to the voice of our mother the Church, and complete self-surrender to His divine providence. You tell me that your hopes, your tastes, the secret inspiration of grace draw you strongly towards the priesthood. May God's holy Name be praised! If our Lord calls you, you must respond. One day the child Samuel heard a voice crying aloud, "Samuel, Samuel!" "Here I am, Lord," he replied. If you think our Lord has called you, then like Samuel you must answer: "Here I am, Lord. What wilt Thou have me to do? With the help of Thy grace, I will do all Thou dost appoint, for I know that grace will never be withheld." You are the child of our divine Lord and His blessed Mother, the child of His love, the sheep of His pasture; have confidence in God. Never forget that God is in everything, little as well as great. He ought to be the one motive of your thoughts, words, and actions. A great future stretches before you, a high vocation. Anchored on God's infinite mercy, repeat humbly yet with complete trust the words of St. Paul: *I press on towards the goal, to the prize of God's heavenly call in Christ Jesus* (Phil 3:14). O Eusebius, you are at the grandest moment of your life! Shall I tell you why? Because you are at an age of strong passions, of hard struggles, of mighty victories. Our Lord "looks" upon a young man and "loves" him. That young man is yourself. Courage, be worthy of your Master! Perhaps you and I shall find ourselves soldiers of the same regiment, travellers on the same road, bound for the same destination. May His holy will, not ours, be done! Leave your future in His hands, in the heart of Jesus made man. Remember that He too was once a young man, for Jesus Christ is the God-child, the God-youth, the God-man, the God of all ages.

Try to fulfil each day's task steadily and cheerfully. Be merry, really merry. The life of a true Christian should be a perpetual jubilee, a prelude to the festivals of eternity. I am going to ask you to do one thing for me. For a few minutes every day, read and meditate upon one or two verses of St. John's Gospel, chapters 14-17. That is our Lord's parting sermon to man, and every letter is a precious pearl. Pray daily in the words of Solomon for wisdom and understanding: "God of my fathers and Lord of mercy, who hast made all things with Thy word, give me wisdom that sitteth by Thy throne. For I am Thy servant and the son of Thy handmaid, a weak man of few days upon the earth, and falling short the understanding of judgment. Send wisdom out of Thy holy heaven that she may be with me and labor with me, that I may know what is acceptable before Thee—and do it. Amen."

The Christian
in the Church

51. The Runaway Prince

ST. STANISLAUS KOSTKA
To a friend, A.D.1567

My best wishes to you. Thanks be to God and to the intercession of the Virgin Mother of God, I have got halfway safe and sound. Jesus and my Virgin Mother have given me plenty of crosses on the road. Close to Vienna two of my servants *(aulici mei)* overtook me. As soon as I recognized them, I hid myself in a wood hard by, and thus escaped their onset. After climbing a number of hills, and passing through many a wood, when I was refreshing my wearied body with some bread by the side of a clear stream, I heard the tramp of a horse. I got up and looked at the rider. It was Paul! His steed was covered with foam, and his face was hotter than the sun. You can fancy, Ernest, how frightened I was.

All chance of flight was gone because of the rate at which he was riding. So I stood still. And plucking up courage, I went to the horseman, and just like a pilgrim begged respectfully for an alms. He asked about his brother, described his dress and his height to me, and said he was very like myself in appearance. I replied that in the early morning he had gone along this road. Without waiting a moment he put spurs to his horse, threw me some money, and went off at a gallop. As soon as I had thanked the Holy Virgin, my Mother Mary, I betook myself to a cave nearby to avoid being pursued. After staying there a short time, I resumed my journey.

Let me tell you another misfortune and of what crosses Jesus my Lord made me a present, and learn from this to join me in praising him. My brother had paid the guards at the gates of the towns and villages to look out for his runaway Stanislaus, to cross-question and examine me, and he had given them a full description of me. This was a great trouble to me, but I chanced to meet one of the Society of Jesus, who was on his way, by order of his superiors, from Vienna to Dillingen. He recognized me, and I told him the reason of my journey, of my disguise, and of my brother's pursuit, and I explained to him the difficulties I had to encounter at the gates of the various towns. Accordingly to evade the two first posts he took me in a carriage. He would have driven me the whole way to Dillingen, if my desire to be unknown and to suffer for my Jesus had not stood in the way.

At length, after going through so many troubles, I reached Dillingen, where I was most kindly received by the Fathers of the Society, and was presented to the Reverend Father Provincial, from whom I received the favor I so much desired of being accepted. O Ernest, if you knew how happy I am! I find a heaven in the midst of saucepans and brooms. I beg you when you get this letter to pray that my Jesus may deign to show His love to me by manifold crosses and afflictions, and to keep me as His sinful little servant among His holy ones. And may you, Ernest, be faithful to your holy vocation. I shall not forget you *ad limina apostolorum*.

52. Loss and Gain

ST. BERNARD
To the parents of a future monk, A.D. 1131

If God is making your son His own, as well as yours, so that he may become even richer, even more noble, even more distinguished and, what is better than all this, so that from being a sinner he may become a saint, what do either he or you lose? But he must prepare himself for the kingdom which has been prepared for him from the beginning of the world. He must spend the short time which remains of his life on earth with us in order to scrape off the filth of secular life and shake off the dust of the world, so as to be fit to enter the heavenly mansion. If you love him you will surely rejoice because he is going to the Father, and such a Father! It is true that he is going to God, but you are not losing him, on the contrary, through him you are gaining many sons. All of us at Clairvaux or of Clairvaux will receive him as a brother and you as our parents.

Knowing that he is tender and delicate perhaps you are afraid for his health under the harshness of our life. But this is the sort of fear of which the Psalm speaks when it says: "Fear unmans them where they have no cause to fear." Have comfort, do not worry, I shall look after him like a father and he will be to me a son until the Father of mercies, the God of all consolation, shall receive him from my hands. Do not be sad about your Geoffrey or shed any tears on his account, for he is going quickly to joy and not to sorrow. I will be for him both a mother and a father, both a brother and a sister. I will make the crooked path straight for him and the rough places smooth. I will temper and arrange all things that his soul may advance and his body not suffer. He will serve the Lord with joy and gladness, "his song will be of the Lord's, for great is the glory of the Lord."

53. To an Obstreperous Mother

ST. IGNATIUS LOYOLA
To the mother of a novice, Rome, January 28, 1554

The sovereign grace and eternal love of Christ our Lord be always with us to our help and favor.

I have received a letter from Your Ladyship dated the twelfth of this month in which you show a desire that your son, Ottaviano, should be moved to Naples, for the sake of your health which you think would be improved by seeing him.

I think Your Ladyship will already have understood that in anything in which I can serve and comfort you without going against the will of God our Lord, I shall be most ready to do. In this matter, however, it is not fitting that anyone of my profession should show himself more ready to please men than God, a thing which should be alien not only to religious but even to any secular person. Now because I think it would be against the divine will to put that young man in danger, I cannot consent to have him brought to Naples now until he is more resolute and Your Ladyship calmer and more content with your son's choice. I cannot think that for the bodily or spiritual health of Your Ladyship the presence of your son is necessary; because, to believe this, would be not only a slur on Your Ladyship but also on God's high Majesty, for it would then appear that God had no other way of healing Your Ladyship in body and soul than our falling into disorder and committing sin, for at this time to bring Your Ladyship and your son together would be to bring him into temptation.

You should remember that you are not the first mother whose son has become a religious and that no earthly father or mother has so much part in their children as God has, who has both created them and redeemed them with the blood of His only begotten Son. Thus we must accept God's holy will and Your Ladyship's consolation depends on this acceptance more than on the visit of your son.

For the rest, in whatever I can give satisfaction and happiness to Your Ladyship according to God, I shall always do so; and so much the more willingly, as the more Christlike and patient do I learn is your submission to the will of God our Lord.

May His divine and sovereign goodness grant us all grace always to know His holy will and to follow it out perfectly.

54. A Well-Deserved Snub

ST. BERNARD
To a layman, A.D. *1150*

I have never met you, but I have heard of you. You have the reputation of being a wise man and you enjoy a respected position in the world. But my dear son Peter, to whom you seem to be well known and related by blood, has asked me to write to you or, I should say, to write back to you. For you have written to him, and I could wish that your letter had been creditable to yourself and profitable for him. This is not the case, for you have had the audacity to try and dissuade a soldier of Christ from the service of his Lord. I tell you, there is one who will see and judge this. Are not your own sins enough for you that you must saddle yourself with the sins of another by doing your best to entice a repentant young man back to his follies and thus, in your hard and unrepentant heart, to lay up wrath for yourself on that day of wrath? As though the devil were not tempting Peter enough without the help of you who are supposed to be a Christian and his friend and leader. You have behaved towards him like another serpent, but he has not yielded to you like another Eve. He was shaken but not overthrown by what you wrote, for he is founded upon a firm rock.

I shall not return evil for evil, on the contrary I shall try to overcome evil with good by praying for you, by desiring better dispositions for you, and by trying to impart them with my letter. First of all, so that you may be in very truth as wise as people say you are, I send you to the Wise Man saying: "Suffer him to do good who may, and thou thyself, when thou mayest, do good." You have the time to do good, but for how long will you have it? How much of life is there left to you, especially now that you are an old man? "For what is life but a vapor which appeareth for a little while, and afterwards shall vanish away?" If you are truly wise then that curse will not come upon you: "Never yet did I see a fool secure in his possessions but I prophesied disaster, there and then, for his fair prospects." The truly wise man did well to call the falsely wise fools, for the wisdom of this world is foolishness with God. "Ah, if you would but take thought, learn your lesson, and pay heed to your final end." If only you were wise in the things of God, if only you had a true estimation of the things of this world and paid more heed to the depths beneath you, surely then you would dread what is beneath you, crave for the heights above you, and scorn what lies to your hand! My mind, or rather my soul, suggests much that I might say to you. But until I know from your answer how you have taken what I have already said, I will refrain from adding anything more. I do not wish to become burdensome to one with whom I hope to be on friendly terms in future, and whom I would gladly help to salvation if he would permit me. Although she has done nothing to deserve it, I greet your dear wife in Christ.

55. A Priest in the Family

BLESSED JOHN GABRIEL PERBOYRE
To his father, Paris, 1821

No, you are not mistaken; the thought of you is ever in my mind, just as that of Mother is, and since I received your letter scarcely half an hour has passed without my thoughts straying in your direction. Your letter gave me such happiness. I have been making up my mind to write for ages; I admit I have been rather careless over letter-writing.

I spoke to Uncle about my little brother Anthony. I doubt whether you will do any harm by sending the boy to stay with him for some time in order to get a good grounding in the rudiments of the sciences, both sacred and profane. But I do implore you, dearest Father, to take the greatest care never to influence him, either by word or in any way whatsoever, to enter upon the ecclesiastical state. Were he to decide upon it without a very special vocation, above all, were he to take it up as a career from purely human motives of self-interest, he would be guilty of a dreadful sacrilege, and for you as well as for himself the step would prove the most deplorable disaster. All I want is that he should learn to live as a good Christian, without idolizing the god of material good things as I did for fifteen years. Alive as I am to the fact that you spend much trouble and anxiety in preserving the purity of all your children, yet I often feel terribly worried about his innocence. You have to let him out of your sight frequently, I know, and for the greater part of the time he is mixing with servants and evil-tongued workmen whose mouths are filled with indecent gossip, and as you know better than I, such folk are not quite as restrained in your absence as in your presence, however much you lecture them from time to time on the fear of God.

I send you and Mother a kiss.

56. Another Salome

ST. VINCENT DE PAUL
To St. Louise de Marillac, A.D. 1636

The grace of our Lord be ever with you!

I have never seen such a woman as you are for taking certain things tragically. You say your son's choice is a manifestation of God's justice on you. You really did wrong to entertain such ideas, and still worse to give expression to them. I have often begged you before not to talk like that. In the name of God, Mademoiselle, correct this fault and learn, once and for all, that bitter thoughts proceed from the Evil One, and sweet and gentle thoughts from our Lord.

Remember, too, that the faults of children are not always imputed to their parents, especially when they have had them instructed and given good example, as, thank God, you have done. Moreover, our Lord, in His wondrous Providence, allows children to break the hearts of devout fathers and mothers. Abraham's was broken by Ishmael, Isaac's by Esau, Jacob's by most of his children, David's by Absalom, Solomon's by Roboam, and the Son of God's by Judas.

I may tell you that your son told Fr. de la Salle that he was embracing this state of life only because it was your wish, that he would rather die than do so, and that he would take Minor Orders to please you. Now, is that a vocation? I think he would rather die himself than desire your death. However that may be, whether this comes from nature or the devil, his will is not free in its choice of such an important matter, and you ought not to desire it. Some time ago a good youth of this city took the sub-diaconate in a similar state of mind, and he has not been able to go on to the other Orders; do you wish to expose your son to the same danger? Let him be guided by God; He is his Father, more than you are his mother; and He loves him more than you do. Leave Him to settle it. He can call him some other time, if such be His will, or give him some employment conducive to his salvation. I remember a priest who was here, who was ordained in a similar anxiety of mind; God knows where he is now.

I request you to make your prayer on the wife of Zebedee and her children, to whom our Lord said, when she was eager to settle her sons, "You know not what you ask."

57. No, Not Yet

ST. TERESA OF AVILA
To some young ladies of Avila, Valladolid, December 1580 [?]

Jesus!

May the grace of the Holy Spirit be in your souls and keep you steadfast in your good desires. It seems to me, Señoras, that Francis Suarez's daughter, Doña Mariana, is more courageous than you, for she has borne with her parents' displeasure nearly six years, confined to a small village most of the time. She would give much to be able to go to confession at St. Giles's as you do. It is not so easy as you think to take the habit against your parents' wishes, for though you may be resolved to do so now, I doubt whether you are so holy as not to feel unhappy afterwards at being in disgrace with your father. The best way is to pray about the matter to our Lord and leave it to Him. He can change hearts and find means to bring it about. When you least expect it, He will so order it that every one will be satisfied; therefore we must live in hope. His judgments differ from ours.

Be content with the assurance that a place is being kept for you, and leave yourselves in God's hands so that His will may be done in you. This is perfection: the rest is possibly only a temptation. May His Majesty dispose of the matter as He sees best. If it depended solely on my wish I should agree to yours at once, but as I have said, there are many things to be considered. May His Majesty have you in His keeping and make you as holy as I beg of Him.

58. Appeal to the Pope

ST. THÉRÈSE OF LISIEUX
To her sister Pauline, November 20, 1887

God is making me undergo plenty of trials before opening the door of Carmel. I am going to tell you how the visit to the Pope went. O Pauline, if you could have read my heart, you would have found it full of confidence. I believe I have done what God asked of me, and now nothing remains but prayer.

The Bishop was not present, M. L'Abbé Révérony took his place. To form any idea of the audience, you would have had to be there.

The Pope was seated high up on a grand chair; M. Révérony stood close beside him, scrutinizing the pilgrims as they filed past the Pope after kissing his foot, and passing comments on some of them. You may imagine how madly my heart went pit-a-pat as I saw my turn approach, but I was not going to come away without having spoken to the Pope. I did speak, but I didn't say all I had to say because M. Révérony wouldn't give me time. He interrupted me. "Most Holy Father," he said, "this is a child who wants to enter Carmel at fifteen years of age, but her Superiors have the matter in hand at the moment...." I should have liked to go into detail about it all, but I was not given the chance. The Holy Father simply said to me: "If it is God's will, you will enter." Then I was made to pass on into the next room. O Pauline, I can't tell you how I felt. It was as if I had been crushed to powder. I felt utterly forsaken, and in addition I am so far away, so far away. As I write this letter I could cry my heart out, it is ready to burst. Never mind; God cannot try me above my strength. He has given me the courage necessary to bear this last trial. Oh, it is a terrific one but, Pauline, I am the Child Jesus' little ball; if He wants to smash His toy He is quite free to do it.

Yes; I want absolutely everything that He wants.

I've by no means written all I intended to say. I can't put these things on paper, I'd have to tell you by word of mouth, and anyway, you won't read my letter till three days hence. Pauline, I have no one but God, God alone, alone. Goodbye, Pauline darling, I can't tell you any more. I'm afraid Papa may come along and ask to read my letter—and that's impossible.

> Pray for your little girl,
> Thérésita

59. The Sacerdotal Dignity

ST. JOHN CHRYSOSTOM
To his friend Basil, c. A.D. 386

The priestly office discharges its task on earth, it is true, but it takes its rank in fact among the things of heaven; and with very good reason. This position has been assigned to it by no mortal man, no angel, no archangel, no other created power; it has been instituted by the Holy Spirit Himself. He it is who lifts us out of our flesh-bound condition here below, to the sublime work of the ministry of angels. Therefore a priest must be as pure as if he were already standing in heaven amid the angelic hosts.

How awe-inspiring was the pomp prior to the New Covenant of grace! It was designed to awaken fear: the High Priest's little bells, the pomegranates, the precious stones of breastplate and ephod, the diadem, the mitre, the long linen garment, the plate of gold, the Holy of Holies, and the great silence that reigned over all (see Ex 28). But when one considers the mysteries of the law of grace, all this display, magnificent and terrifying as it was, appears positively paltry, and even in such things as these we realize the truth of that comment on the Old Law: *For though the former ministration was glorified, yet in this regard it is with-*

out glory, because of the surpassing glory of the latter (2 Cor 3:10).
Now turn and look upon our Lord, a holocaust stretched upon
the altar, the sacrificing priest bowed low in supplication over the
Victim, all the faithful imbued with this precious Blood—do you
feel that your feet are planted on earth among mortals, or are you
not rather uplifted to the very heavens? Once every material
thought has been cast out of your mind, are you not gazing with
naked soul and pure heart upon the heavenly glory which sur-
rounds you? O the wonder of it! O love of God! He who is
seated on high at the Father's right hand, allows Himself at that
moment to be grasped by men's hands, gives Himself to any who
are prepared to welcome and show Him love. This is what takes
place according to the eyes of faith. Are such marvels worthy only
of contempt in your estimation? Are they of such a nature that
any Tom, Dick, or Harry may tread them underfoot?

I would ask you to realize the preeminence of our sacred mysteries by considering a further prodigy. Picture to yourself Elias
encircled by a vast throng, the victim laid on the stones, everyone and everything motionless and silent save for the Prophet's
voice rising up in prayer. Suddenly fire rushes from heaven and
devours the holocaust (1 Kgs 18). Truly stupendous! One's very
soul is terror-stricken. And now transfer your minds to the celebration of our own mysteries. What do you see? I shall not call
them marvels for they utterly transcend all marvels. The priest
stands, summoning not quenchable fire but the Holy Ghost
Himself. He makes prolonged supplication, not that a flame may
descend from on high to consume the offerings, but that the
grace which issues upon the sacrifice may spread and set every
soul present ablaze, making them brighter than silver purified by
fire. Who but a lunatic raving mad and completely out of his
mind could despise this tremendous mystery? Do you not realize
that the human soul would be incapable of supporting this sacri-
ficial fire from on high; we should all be instantly reduced to

ashes were it not for the all-sustaining power of God's grace?

In a word, if you contemplate the depth of this mystery, that a man composed of mere flesh and blood should thus be able to draw near to that blessed and immortal nature, you will be able to form some idea of the sovereign power the grace of the Holy Spirit confers upon priests. It is by their hands that these wonders, and others of equal importance, are wrought for our glory and our salvation. Beings whose mortal condition and existence are bound up with the earth have been commissioned to conduct the affairs of heaven, have been invested with an authority that God has given neither to angels nor archangels. Never has He said to them: *Whatever you bind on earth shall be bound also in heaven, and whatever you loose on earth shall be loosed also in heaven* (Mt 18:18).

Temporal princes too have power to bind, but they may bind bodies only, whereas the bonds spoken of here constrict the very soul and forge the links in heaven. Thus everything the priest does here below, God ratifies up above, and the Master confirms the judgment of the servant. What else has God bestowed on priests if not infinite authority in the very heavens? *Whose sins you shall forgive, they are forgiven them,* He tells them, *and whose sins you shall retain, they are retained* (Jn 20:23). Could any power be greater than that? The Father has given all judgment to the Son (Jn 5:22); and I see the Son Himself transmit this privilege in its entirety to His priests. As if they were already raised to the ranks of the blessed, superior to mortal lot, and no longer enslaved by human passions, they have been invested with this tremendous authority. It would be transparent folly to treat with disdain so great a power, for without it we cannot obtain either salvation or the good things promised us.

If, then, no man can enter into the Kingdom of God unless he be born again of water and the Spirit (Jn 3:5), and if, again, he who does not eat the flesh of the Son of Man and drink His blood (Jn 6:53) is excluded from eternal life; if, I say, only consecrated hands—the hands of the priest—enable us to fulfill the conditions, well, then, without their help how can we escape the fire of hell or win the crown prepared for us? To priests has been entrusted the spiritual travail of bringing forth souls; yes, they have to give us birth to grace by baptism; through them we put on Christ Jesus, we are buried together with the Son of God, and we become members of our divine Head. Consequently we should revere priests above princes and kings, honor them even more than father and mother. Our parents begot us by blood and the will of the flesh (John 1:13), but priests make us children of God; blessed regeneration, true freedom, and adoption according to grace.

60. On Turning a Deaf Ear

ST. VINCENT DE PAUL
To a priest of the mission, A.D. 1646 or 1649

I know the state of anxiety in which you have been placed by the letter which your father wrote to you urging you to come to his assistance. Accordingly, I think I am bound to tell you what I think of it:

1st: That it is no small evil to break the bond by which you have bound yourself to God in the Company;

2nd: That, by losing your vocation, you will deprive God of the valuable services He expects from you;

3rd: That you will be responsible before the throne of his justice for the good which you will not do, and which, nevertheless, you might have done by remaining in the state in which you now are;

4th: That you will risk your salvation in the society of your relations, and perhaps be no comfort to them, any more than others were who left us on this pretext; for God did not permit it, because, if He had wished them to be better, there are other ways of effecting it;

5th: That our Lord, knowing the evil that results from the frequentation of the society of relations in the case of those who have left them to follow Him, did not wish, as the Gospel tells us, that one of His disciples should go simply to bury his father, or another to sell his possessions, in order to give them to the poor;

6th: That you would give bad example to your confrères, and be a source of grief to the Company, owing to the loss of one of its children, whom it loves and has reared with the greatest care.

That, Sir, is what I wish you to reflect on before God.

The motive you may have for withdrawal lies in the need of your father. But it is essential to know what are the circumstances, according to the casuists, which oblige children to leave a community. As for myself, I think it is only when fathers or mothers are suffering from natural causes and not from their condition in life, as, for instance, when they are very old or when, owing to some other natural drawback, they cannot earn a livelihood. Now, that does not hold true of your father, who is only forty or forty-five years old at most, and who is feeling quite well, is able to work, and is, as a matter of fact, working. Otherwise, he would not have married again, as he did quite recently, and to a young woman eighteen years old, and one of the most beautiful girls in the city. He tells me so himself, in order that I may give her an introduction to the Princess de Longueville whose son she wishes to nurse. I quite believe he is not too well off; but who is there who is not suffering from the present state of public misery? Furthermore, it is not his actual state of distress which obliges him to recall you, for it is not in fact very great; it is merely that which he apprehends, through want of a little confidence in God, although he has wanted nothing up to the present, and has reason to hope that God's goodness will not abandon him in future.

You may perhaps persuade yourself that it is by your means that God wishes, as a matter of fact, to help him in his need, and that it is on that account that His Providence is now presenting you with a cure of souls to the value of six hundred livres through the intervention of this same good man. But you will see that this is not so, if you just consider two things: first, that God, having called you to a state of life which honors that of His Son on earth and which is so useful to your neighbor, cannot wish at the present moment to remove you from this state in order to send you back to look after a family which is living in the world, which is only seeking its own comfort, which will continually worry you by asking for what you may, or may not, have, and which will burden you with trouble and annoyances, if you cannot assist it to its own satisfaction and yours; and in the second place, it is incredible that your father has been promised a cure to the value of 600 livres a year for you, because those of the diocese of Bruges are the poorest in the Kingdom. But even if this were so, how much would remain after subtracting your maintenance?

I am not telling you this because I fear the temptation may prevail over you; no, I know your fidelity towards God; but in order that you may write once for all to your father and tell him the reasons why you should follow God's will, rather than his. Believe me, Sir, his natural disposition is of such a kind as will give you very little repose when you are near him, any more than it now does when you are far away from him. The trouble he has been causing your poor sister, who is with Mademoiselle Le Gras, is unimaginable. He wants her to leave the service of God and of His poor, as if he were to receive some considerable help from her. You know he is naturally restless, and, indeed, to such an extent, that whatever he has displeases him, and whatever he has not excites violent desires. Finally, I think the greatest good you could do him is to pray to God for him, preserving for yourself that one thing which is necessary, which will one day be your reward, and which will even, on your account, bring down God's blessings on your relations. That is what I pray for with all my heart.

61. Before Mass

BLESSED JOHN OF AVILA
To a priest, c. A.D. 1560

You wish to know what is the best preparation to make before offering the most Holy Sacrament of the Body and Blood of our Lord Jesus Christ, and the most profitable considerations to bear in mind during the celebration. You ask this because you fear lest, for want of due dispositions, that which ought to bring great blessings to your soul should injure it instead. Men's bodies, as you know, are of very various temperaments, and there is just as great a dissimilarity in the constitution of their minds, for God bestows very diverse gifts upon different individuals. He does not lead all by the same path, therefore it is impossible to specify any particular devotion as the most suitable during Mass. What our Creator and Redeemer puts into the heart and what moves it most to piety is the best. These things are not matters of faith, and there is no certain rule about them, and if anyone has reason to think that his dispositions and preparation for this Mystery are instigated by God, there is no reason to change from them until our Lord should inspire him so to do. This should be ascertained by laying the matter before some experienced person and following his advice. Some have no special attraction for any one form of devotion at this time, and they, too, ought to consult someone as to their interior dispositions, so as to know whether they should allow themselves to be led by motives of love or fear, of sadness or joy; and how to apply the remedies most suitable to their needs. From what you have told me about yourself, I consider that you have made progress in virtue, and that it would be best for you to practice considerations likely to excite in you fervent love and reverence. For this purpose, I know of nothing better than to meditate on the fact that our Lord, with whom we are to treat, is both God and man, and to think over the reasons for which He comes down upon the altar. Surely such a stroke of love should be enough to awaken anyone from the slumber of indifference. Let such a one reflect upon this Mystery and say to himself: "It is God Almighty who will come down upon the altar at the words of consecration; I shall hold Him in my hands, and converse with Him, and receive Him into my breast." If only we remember this, and if, by the help of God's Holy Spirit, it penetrate our soul, it will suffice, and more than suffice, to enable us, frail mortals as we are, to perform this sacred duty as we ought.

Who can help being inflamed by love on thinking that he is about to receive the Infinite Goodness within his breast? Who would not tremble with reverential fear in that Presence, before which the powers of heaven are awed? Who would not resolve never to offend Him, but to praise and serve Him evermore? Is it possible for anyone not to be confounded and overwhelmed with grief at having sinned against that great Lord whom he bears in his hands? Can the Christian fail to trust such a pledge, or can he want for strength to walk the way of penance through the desert of this world, nourished by such food? In short, such considerations, by God's help, entirely change and possess the soul, and draw it out of itself; at one time, by feelings of reverence, at another, by love, and yet again, by the strong emotion caused by the realization of Christ's presence. Although these thoughts do not inevitably produce this result, yet unless the heart hardens itself into stone against their influence, they strongly conduce to it. Let your mind then dwell on such reflections; listen to the cry: *Behold, the Bridegroom cometh* (Mt 25:6), your God cometh! Retire into the secrecy of your own heart, and open it to receive what is wont to come from so powerful a Light. Beseech this same Lord that, as He has deigned to place Himself within your hands, He will give you the further grace to esteem, and venerate, and love Him as you should. Beg Him fervently not to permit you to be in the presence of His Majesty but with reverence, and fear, and love. Endeavour constantly to have a fitting sense of our Lord's presence, even should you contemplate no other part of this Mystery.

Think how men, when they have due respect for the king, stand before him with gravity and reverence even though they be silent. Better still, picture in your mind how the highest in the court of heaven behave in the presence of the Infinite Majesty. See how they tremble at the remembrance of their own littleness, and burn with the fire of love, so that they appear to be consumed in its furnace. Imagine yourself in the company of these, who are so reverent and so fervent in God's service, and being in such society and standing before so great a King, strive to feel as you should at such a time, even though you meditate on no other point. I wish to show you how it is one thing to be able to speak fitly to the king, and another to know how to conduct yourself becomingly in his presence, although you may have simply to stand by in silence. This is that union with our Lord which should keep you as closely united to Him during Mass as you are in the interior of your heart when alone with Him in your cell, and which will prevent your being distracted by the words you have to pronounce. You must, however, pay fitting attention to the Liturgy, while accustoming yourself at the same time to keep your mind fixed on God's presence. O great God, what should not be your feelings when you hold in your hands Him who elected our Lady and enriched her with celestial graces to fit her to minister to the God made man! Compare her hands, her arms, her eyes, with your own. The very thought should cover you with confusion. What stringent obligations do such benefits lay upon you! What care must you not take to keep yourself wholly for Him who honors you in such a way as to place Himself in your hands, and comes into them when you pronounce the words of consecration!

These, Reverend Father, are no mere words, nor lifeless thoughts, but they are arrows shot from the strong bow of God Himself, which pierce and wholly transform the heart, so that when Mass is over, the mind ponders on our Lord's words: *Scitis quid fecerim vobis?—Know you what I have done to you?* (Jn 13:12). Would that it were possible for a man to understand what our Lord has done for us in that hour, and to taste Him with the palate of the soul. Oh that man had scales that could rightly weigh this benefit! How happy would he be even in this world! When Mass is over, he would feel a loathing for all creatures, their society would be a torment to him, while his only joy would be to remember what the Lord had done to him, until he should say Mass again next day.

If God should ever give you this light, you will realize what shame and sorrow you ought to feel on approaching the altar without it, but he whom it has never illuminated knows not the torture of losing it. Besides the consideration of *who* it is that comes down upon the altar, you may also meditate on *why* He comes, and you will see a semblance of the love shown in our Lord's Incarnation, Nativity, Life, and Death, and how these mysteries are renewed in the Holy Sacrifice of the altar. If you could enter into the very Heart of our Lord, and if He would deign to show you that the reason of His coming down upon the altar is an impassioned and strong affection, which will brook no separation between the Lover and His beloved, your soul would faint away before the very sight of such a marvel. The mind is greatly moved by realizing Christ's presence on the altar, but when it further reflects that He comes to us because His affection for us is like that of the betrothed for his bride, which will not allow him to pass a single day without seeing and conversing with her, the Christian wishes he had a thousand hearts wherewith to make a fitting return for such love. He longs to cry out with St. Augustine: "*Domine, quid tibi sum, quia jubes me diligere te? Quid tibi sum?* Lord, what am I to Thee, that Thou shouldst bid me love Thee? What am I to Thee?" Why dost Thou so fervently desire to see and to embrace me? *Thou,* who dost dwell in heaven in company with those who understand so well how Thou shouldst be served and loved, dost come to *me,* who only know how to offend Thee or to render Thee slack service. Canst not Thou, then, O my Lord, be happy without me, that my love should draw Thee down to me? Oh, blessed mayst Thou be, who being what Thou art, hast yet set Thy heart upon such a creature as me! Can it be that Thou, King as Thou art, dost come here and dost place Thyself in my hands, and seem to say: "I died once for thy sake and I come to thee now to show thee that I do not repent of it, but on the contrary that, if there were need, I would give my life for thee a second time?" Who could remain unmoved by such love? Who could hide himself, O Lord, from Thy burning Heart, which warms our own by its very presence, and is like a mighty furnace, throwing out sparks of fire on all around it? Such a Lord as this, dear Reverend Father, visits us from heaven, and we, wretches as we are, hold intercourse with Him and receive Him within our breasts!

Let us now conclude our discourse on this great Mystery, so worthy of being meditated on and understood. Let us beg our Lord that as He has already done us one favor, He will grant us a second, for unless we appreciate His blessings, and thank, and serve Him for them as He deserves, they will benefit us little. Rather, as St. Bernard says of an ungrateful man: "*Eo ipso pessimus, quo optimus*—The greater his gain ought to be, the greater is his loss." Let us watch over our conduct during the day, for fear that Christ should punish our faults when we are at the altar. Let us ever bear in mind the thought: "I have received our Lord and sat at His table; tomorrow I shall do the same." By this means we shall avoid sin and have the courage to do what is right, for our Lord is accustomed to reward at the altar what is done away from the altar.

To conclude, I would remind you how, when Jesus was the guest of Simon the Pharisee, He complained that His host gave Him no water for His feet, and did not kiss His face, to show us that when He enters our house He would have us wash His feet with tears for our sins and manifest our love as the kiss of peace. May our Lord bestow on you both for yourself and for your neighbors this peace, which is born of perfect love, and may you grieve both for your own sins against God and those which other men commit against Him. I pray that you may enjoy this peace one day in heaven, and also that you may hold God's interests dearer than your own, because of the greater love you bear Him. I beg of you, for His sake, that if there be anything in this letter which requires amending you will correct it for me, and thank God for any good it may contain, and I ask you to remember me when you are at His altar.

62. Pulpit Howlers

ST. ROBERT BELLARMINE
To Cardinal Antoniano, March 7, 1603

My preacher, in a sermon of his on the text, *Super cathedram Moysis,* etc., so exalted priests that he made them out to be greater and higher in dignity than the Virgin Mother, than Christ, than God Himself. His proofs were very wonderful. A priest, he said, blesses the consecrated Host in which is Christ, but he whose dignity is less is blessed by him whose dignity is greater, *ergo* a priest is greater than Christ. Again, God creates creatures but a priest creates God Himself, *ergo* a priest is greater than God, and if he is greater than Christ and God, much greater must he be than the Blessed Virgin!

I was very much afraid that I would have to put a stop to his preaching after this exploit, but, when I pointed out to him in my room what unheard-of nonsense he had been talking, he edified me by his humility and obedience, expressing himself ready to do whatever I should bid him. So I told him that, on the following day, he must go into the pulpit and declare that the statements which he had made in his sermon were slips of the tongue due to rhetorical exaggeration. This he did most thoroughly, and I took the opportunity to give him a good, brotherly reproof, putting him in mind of the rule of St. Francis about simplicity in preaching. Then, to sweeten the medicine, I sent him some trout.

I must not detain your Lordship any longer. Enough to have made known to you something of our weal and our woe.

63. The Circumspect Priest

St. John Chrysostom
To his friend Basil, A.D. *386*

If the watchman see the sword coming, the Lord tells us, *and sound not the trumpet: and the people look not to themselves, and the sword come, and cut off a soul from among them: he indeed is taken away in his iniquity, but I will require his blood at the hands of the watchman* (Ez 33:6). If that is so, pray do not force me to lay myself open to so inexorable a judgment. For we are discussing, not military command or State administration, but duties which demand the qualities of an angel. The soul of a priest should be purer than the sun's rays if the Holy Spirit is not to leave him to his own resources. He must be able to say: *I live, now not I; but Christ liveth in me* (Gal 2:20).

Monks who choose a life of solitude, far from the city with its streets and tumultuous crowds, who live in unbroken enjoyment of safe anchorage, are nevertheless careful not to rely on the protection such a mode of life affords. They take numberless other precautions. They cut themselves off on all sides and strive with might and main to control their every word and action so as to enable them to stand before God with as much confidence and purity as frail human beings are capable of. I ask you then, what effort and fervor is demanded of a priest if he is to keep his soul free from all stain, and preserve the full radiance of its spiritual beauty?

Much greater virtue is required of the priest than of the monk, and the need is all the greater in so far as the priest is necessarily more exposed to influences which must defile him unless he forbids them access to his soul by constant alertness and stern resolution. For it is a fact that delicate features, grace of movement, a set poise, a soft voice, cosmetics used to good effect on eyes and skin, masses of hair skilfully tinted, handsome clothes, plenty of gold and sparkling gems are capable of working havoc with a man's passions unless he has disciplined himself by severe self-restraint.

It need cause no surprise if this kind of thing upsets a man, but it is more than surprising, it is positively incredible, that the devil's malice should be able to reach his soul and bring it to rack and ruin by precisely opposite means. Yet there are those who have avoided the one trap only to be caught in a vastly different one. For a careless slut with unkempt hair and slouching gait, clad in dirty rags, vulgar, ill-bred, coarse of speech, living a life of misery and scorn, friendless and forsaken by all, has begun by rousing a man's pity and ended by dragging him to utter perdition.

Since, then, wealth and want, adornment and neglect, elegance and boorishness, in a word, all that I have already enumerated, excite war in the heart of the man who meets them and ensnare him on all sides, how can he enjoy peace of mind in the centre of so many ambushes? Where is he to find a place of rest—I shall not say to avoid yielding to violence, because that is not over-difficult—but to protect his soul from the turmoil of impure thoughts?

I shall not pause here to dwell on the compliments paid to priests; they may engender untold trouble. Those from women can bring disaster. As for the tributes men offer, unless a priest can keep a level head, they may drag him in two contrary directions: to servile flattery or to stupid self-conceit. He is forced to fawn upon the flatterers, their adulation turns his head, he thereupon adopts a high and mighty attitude towards all beneath himself in rank, and is thus sucked into the whirlpool of arrogant pride. I will not enlarge upon the subject; only through long experience does one gain real insight into the magnitude of the evil.

Do you not shudder to admit a soul like mine to so sacred a ministry, to raise to the priestly dignity one clad in foul garments, a man whom Christ has excluded from the banquet of guests? A priest's soul should be resplendent with light, like a torch illuminating the whole world, while mine is so obscured by the dark mist rising from an impure conscience that, being always dispirited, it never dares to look its divine Master confidently in the face. Priests are the salt of the earth, but who would tolerate for long my lack of wisdom, my total incapacity for good? Who, indeed, but you alone, you who have for so long cherished me with a love that knows no bounds.

64. Prudence a Cardinal Virtue

St. Francis Xavier
To a fellow-Jesuit, Goa, March 1549

First and foremost be mindful of yourself and of your relations with God and your conscience, because on these depend your power of being much use to your neighbor. Do not forget to make the particular examination of conscience at least once a day, if you cannot make it twice. Let your own conscience be your care and concern much more than anybody else's, for if a man is not solicitous to be good and holy himself, how is he going to make other people such?

Be quick and eager for lowly and obscure tasks, so that you may learn to be humble and ever to grow in humility. To this end, see that you and no other teach the prayers to the children. Visit the poor in the hospital, and exhort them to go to confession and Holy Communion, hearing them yourself when you can, and help them in their temporal needs also by putting in a good word for them with those in authority. Do the same for those in jail, and try to get them to make a general confession of their whole past lives, as many of them never go to confession. In all your dealings, conversations, and friendships with others, so conduct yourself as if they might one day be your enemies. Use such prudence with this wicked world and you will live always at peace within your soul, and so have greater fruition of God. Be pleasant and cheerful with all and sundry. Avoid stiffness and surliness, for a gloomy face will deter many from approaching you and profiting by your counsel. So, let your looks and words speak welcome to every comer, and if you have to admonish somebody, do it with love and graciously, giving no reason whatever for him to think that you find his company distasteful.

Preach as often as ever you can, but take particular care never in your sermons to denounce any man who holds a public charge, for there is danger that such people may become worse instead of better if reprehended from the pulpit. The place to admonish them is privately in their own houses or in the confessional, when you have become friends with them. The better friends you are, the straighter you can talk, but while you are only on nodding terms be slow to scold. Deliver your strictures with a pleasant front, and in gentle, loving words rather than harshly. If you rebuke important or rich persons in good round terms, I am afraid they only lose patience and turn hostile.

Should you come across a man who wants to unburden in confession a conscience laden with a long accumulation of sin, you must in the first place make him carefully examine his conscience for two or three days beforehand. Hear his confession, and then as a general rule defer absolution for an equal time. During these three days, give him some points from the first week of the *Spiritual Exercises*, teach him the method of prayer, and urge him to stir up a true and heartfelt detestation of his sins by undertaking some voluntary penance, such as fasting or taking the discipline. If penitents possess anything to which they have no right, see that they restore their ill-gotten gains, resume friendly relations with neighbors not in their good books, and withdraw from occasions of fleshly and other sins of their addiction. Make sure that they do these things before you absolve them, because they are very ready with promises in confession, but very slow afterwards to carry them out. Some people suffer no remorse of conscience because they haven't got a conscience. When you find the penitents obliged to make restitution but unable to do so because those they wronged are unknown to them or dead, tell them to give the whole sum to the Confraternity of Mercy, unless indeed you know of deserving cases on whom the alms might safely be conferred. Not all the poor are deserving and cadgers are to be found among them sunk in vice and sin. The Brothers of Mercy know these gentry well, so whatever alms you have to distribute, give them to the Brothers for people in real need. Another advantage of this is that when it becomes known that you have no help to give except spiritual, you will not be approached by those seeking only for money. But take care not to frighten away by stern rigor poor sinners who are trying to lay bare the shocking state of their souls. Speak to them rather of the great mercy of God, and make easy for them what is at best a difficult task. Be especially gentle with those who from weakness of age or sex have not the courage to confess the ugly things they have done. Put heart into them as well as ever you can. Tell them that whatever they have to say will be no news to you, for you have knowledge of much graver sins. Make everything as easy as possible for them. Sometimes, in such cases, as I know from experience, people are helped by your telling them in general terms about your own lamentable past. Teach them what is right and what is wrong. Treat of sudden death which takes men off sadly unprepared, and touch on some point of the Passion, by way of a colloquy between a sinner and God.

Finally, and above all else, take care of yourself and never forget that you are a member of the Society of Jesus. May God our Lord be with you, and may He abide with us also who are here. Farewell.

65. True and False Zeal

St. Vincent de Paul
To Father Peter Escart, Saint-Lazare-les-Paris, July 25, 1640

The grace of our Lord be ever with you!

I very humbly beg your pardon for delaying so long to reply to your letter and I promise, with God's help, to amend.

Your letter afforded me such consolation as I cannot express, seeing the zeal which our Lord has given you for your own advancement in perfection, and also for that of the Company. Continue, Sir, in the name of our Lord, to implore this grace from His Divine Goodness, and to labor to acquire it with a will: *For the time is short* and we have a long way still to go (1 Kgs 19:7). Oh! Father Escart, whom I love more tenderly than I do myself, how gladly do I offer up this same prayer to God for both of us! But alas! so great is my wretchedness that I ever remain in the dust of my imperfections, and, instead of my sixty years being, as they should, a more powerful stimulus to labor for the amendment of my miserable life yet I know not how it is, I advance less than ever. Your prayers, Father Escart, my dear friend, will help me to do so, as will those of the many holy souls whom you see at Anneçy. I beg you to say a Mass for me, at the tomb of our blessed Father, for this intention.

I do not know if it is the sight of my own wretchedness that leads me to say what I am now about to write to you; but I mean to do so in the sight of God and in the spirit of simplicity in which, as it seems to me, I reflected on the matter, this morning, before God.

I shall therefore tell you, Sir, that it seems to me your zeal for the advancement of the Company is always accompanied by some asperity, which even turns to bitterness. All that you tell me about certain individuals and all that you call cowardice and sensuality in them leads me to see this, and especially the spirit in which you say it. *O Mon Dieu!* Sir, one must be very much on one's guard against that. In the case of the virtues, it is easy, Sir, to pass from defect to excess, from being just to being rigorous and rashly zealous. It is said that good wine easily turns to vinegar, and that health in the highest degree is a sign of approaching illness. It is true that zeal is the soul of the virtues; but, surely, Sir, it must be, as St. Paul says, according to knowledge;

and that means, according to experimental knowledge; and as young people, as a rule, have not this experimental knowledge, their zeal runs to excess, especially in the case of those who are naturally severe. Oh, Sir, one must be very much on one's guard against that, and mistrustful of most of the movements and sallies of the mind, when one is young and possesses such a temperament. Martha complained of the holy idleness and holy self-indulgence of her dear sister Mary Magdalen, and considered the latter was behaving badly because she did not busy herself, as she herself was doing, in attending on our Lord. You and I would, perhaps, have felt the same, if we had been there; and yet, *O the depth of the riches of the wisdom and of the knowledge of God! How incomprehensible are his judgments!* (Rom 11:33). Behold our Lord saying the idleness and self-indulgence of Magdalen were more pleasing to Him than the indiscreet zeal of Martha! You may, perhaps, tell me that there is a difference between listening, like Magdalen, to our Lord, and listening, as we do, to our own little weaknesses. Ah! Sir, how do we know but that it is our Lord Himself who has inspired the two persons of whom you write with the idea of going on a journey, and also of taking those little comforts which you mention? I am perfectly certain of one thing, Sir, and that is, *For those who love God all things work together unto good* (Rom 8:28), and I have no doubt whatever that these very same persons really do love God. How, otherwise, would they have left their parents, friends, possessions, and all the natural satisfactions which they had in them, in order to go seek the poor sheep that have gone astray among those mountains, if they did not love God? And if the love of God is in their hearts, should we not think that God inspires them to do what they do, and leave undone what they leave undone, and that all they do and leave undone is for the best! In the name of God, Sir, let us enter into these really true sentiments and practices, and let us fear lest the evil spirit may be leading us from our excessive zeal to be wanting in respect for our superiors and charity for our equals. For, Sir, that is, as a rule, what our less discreet zeal terminates in, and that is the advantage which the evil spirit gets out of it. Hence I beg you, Sir, in the name of our Lord, to labor together with me to rid ourselves of such manifestations of zeal and, especially, of those which injure respect, esteem, and charity. And because it seems to me that the evil spirit has these designs on you and me, let us study to humble our minds to give a good interpretation to our neighbor's behavior, and to bear with him in his little weaknesses.

Yes, but if I put up with him, then good-bye to our little rules; not one of them will be observed in future. And "You know, moreover," as you may say to me, "you told me to see that they are observed."

In reply to the first difficulty, namely, the ruin of the observance of rule, I say we should be quite satisfied with acquainting the Superior, with all the respect and reverence that is his due, of the breaches of rule one observes, and the inconveniences that may thereby ensue, and then wait until our Lord provides a remedy either at the next visitation, at which one should mention the failings of the community in general, and of each individual in particular, even of the Superior himself, and especially any want of attention in having the rules observed; and, indeed, one may acquaint the Superior-General with them, after which one should remain tranquil, in the hope that our Lord may provide a remedy for them, either by a change of officers, or because those persons may themselves change in the course of a retreat, as the result of mental prayer, in which God will give them light and strength to remedy such failings. In short, one should commit the matter to divine Providence, and be at rest.

As for the second objection, which is, that it is your duty to see that the rule is observed, I may say, Sir, that that is quite true; however, this is to be understood in the sense that one should act in the way I have referred to, that is, the matter should be mentioned to the Superior, in a spirit of humility, gentleness, respect, and charity and, after that, if there be no remedy, then the Superior-General should be informed. And that indeed is what you have done, but in a spirit of haste, severity, and even bitterness; we should always suspect, Sir, such a spirit in everything we do; for *the Lord is not in the earthquake,* but in a spirit of gentleness (1 Kgs 19:11). But if, after all that, things go on as before, well then, we must remain at peace; and that, Sir, is what I beg you to do.

I hope, at the end of this autumn, to pay you a visit, and we shall then talk it over more fully, as also the journey you suggest to me. In the meantime, Sir, I beg our Lord to be the joy and peace of your heart.

And now, Sir, I must conclude, and I shall just say I love you more tenderly than I do myself, and that I am perfectly confident that, after you have honored in a special manner, and for some length of time, both our Lord's humility and meekness, by affections and actions sweetened with this spirit of meekness and humility, you will become, with the help of God, a really apostolic man.

66. Humility in High Places

ST. ROBERT BELLARMINE
To the Jesuit Provincial, June 16, 1599

It is very strange that you have received none of the five letters which I wrote to you with my own hand. I will try to make up for their loss by the length of this one. As for myself, I am doing my best to bear the burden of the purple which has been imposed on me with as little detriment to the welfare of my soul as possible. But I must own to you that I am very frightened and in much danger, for I now possess a rather grand and prosperous-looking suite, men are at my beck and call to do my least bidding with alacrity and care. Besides this, my position brings with it not a few creature comforts, and though I try not to give my heart to them, still, there they are. I am afraid, then, lest it be deservedly said to me, *Recepisti mercedem tuam.* So having no counsellor and not knowing what to do, I commend myself entirely to God's intimate friends that they may take me with them, who am unworthy of their company, to the "everlasting dwelling-places" which by my own efforts I could never reach. I have, indeed, a good will and firm purpose not to offend God, not to enrich nor aggrandize my relatives, not to aim at higher dignities but rather to fly from their approach with all my power, not to give scandal in anything, and to say Mass every day as I have always done. But I know well that this is not enough.

The thought of renouncing the purple is constantly in my mind, but how I am to do it I cannot see. I feel that my efforts would be unavailing and that men would say it was only another of my poses. Nor am I sure that the renunciation would be pleasing to God, seeing that it was by His will that I was forced to accept the dignity. To introduce novelties into my way of living by reducing the number of my suite or adopting a simple style in dress would give the impression that I was ambitious to initiate reforms which the most austere and upright cardinals have neither counselled nor adopted. St. Antoninus, for instance, teaches in his treatise *De Statu Cardinalium* that a certain degree of splendor is necessary, if the dignity of this sacred Order is to receive its due meed of respect from the world at large. I am trying as hard as ever I can to keep *my* splendor and dignity as modest as may be. Among those of my colleagues who are neither extravagant nor showy but follow a middle course that has, however, its own elegance and distinction, I hold the least elegant and distinguished place. Indeed within the limits of decorum and decency, I am just not shabby.

My reason for putting these matters before you, dear Father, is that you, as the guide and master of my soul, may admonish me if in anything I should do wrong, and that thus, by your means, I may be converted to wiser counsels. I will now give you some exact details. There are ten gentlemen in my suite, to perform various higher duties. Most of the ten have two servants each, but some have only one. Besides these, I have fourteen servants for ordinary house and stable work, so the sum total of the domestics does not exceed thirty. I told each of them privately when I engaged them that, according to the law of my house, swearing, impurity, or any other serious sin entailed instant dismissal. Each week I call them together and exhort them as earnestly as I can to lead good lives and to perform their religious duties. I continue to say Office at the canonical times as of old, and have not given up the practice of fasting on Wednesdays and Fridays which I adopted in the past.

I try never to send away a poor man disconsolate or empty-handed, but, as I am poor myself, I can only give little sums at a time. If ever I become rich, then I shall be lavish with my alms, according to the counsel of Tobias. Goodness knows, it is not the desire to hoard which prevents me from giving much to each petitioner, for I never had the slightest love for money or property. As for austerities, I am afraid I am not given to hair-shirts, sleeping on the ground, a bread and water diet, etc., for as I am now hastening towards my sixtieth year and my health is all but broken, I doubt whether I could support such hardships for long. Still, if ever a spiritual and prudent man should recommend them, I think, unless my self-love is playing me a trick, I would be quite ready to take them up. At first I decided to have only one carriage, but I soon discovered that a second was necessary for the convenience of my suite, without whom it is not permitted to attend the Papal services and consistories. I could, of course, get a lift from my friends on the way to these functions, but the return journey was the trouble. My friends' coaches were not available then, so if I had not a second carriage of my own the gentlemen-in-waiting would have been obliged to go home on foot, and that would not have been correct. The furniture of my house is as simple and plain as possible, and I did not allow my arms to be embroidered on the tapestries or couches in the vestibule, though it is the usual custom to have them put on. All the chairs except four are plain leather-covered ones. The four are in velvet, but are only produced when we have visits from cardinals, royal ambassadors, and other great people. The rest of the furniture is very ordinary stuff indeed, which nobody could call valuable. I wear no silk at all, and have nothing grander than plain, cheap wool in my wardrobe.

I am writing thus to you that you may relieve my doubts with your wise counsel, and tell me plainly what I ought to do. You are my intimate friend and that is why I open my heart to you, but I would not like others to be told what I have said. The pope wanted me to accept the bishopric of my native place, Montepulciano, but only on condition that I should not leave Rome. I did not accept his terms as I know how dangerous it is to be an absentee bishop. If, however, he would permit me to reside in the diocese I would not be so reluctant, because it seems to me that the episcopal office is more spiritual, more religious, more fruitful of good, and more secure, than that of the cardinalate alone, which though sacred has still much that is secular about it. I am not forgetting the difficulties and dangers involved in the care of souls, but when God calls, it is not for us to cry safety first. Obedience is, without doubt, the safest state, for, as St. Francis says, in obedience there is profit and in prelacy peril. But our choice should fall rather on that way of life which is most pleasing to God and at the same time least dangerous for our souls. Forgive the length of my letter and pray for me, Father. I shall be anxiously awaiting your good advice, and I beg you with all my heart to pull me with you to heaven, somehow, even though I be reluctant. Good-bye.

67. An Ecumenical Council

ST. IGNATIUS LOYOLA
To two Jesuit theologians, A.D. 1546

I should be slow to speak and should do so only after reflection and in a friendly spirit, particularly when a decision is to be given about matters before the Council or afterwards to be discussed by it. Rather should I profit by listening quietly in order to learn the frame of mind, the feelings and the intentions of the speakers, so that I might be the better able to answer in my turn, or to keep silent. When speaking about matters of controversy, it is advisable to enumerate the reasons on both sides that you may not appear prejudiced, nor must you allow yourself to give anybody cause for complaint. I should not mention the names of authors in my discourse, especially if they be men of consequence, unless I had first considered the matter thoroughly, and should keep on friendly terms with all, without favoritism. If the matters under discussion are so obviously right and just that one neither could nor should remain silent, I should then give my opinion with the greatest possible composure and humility, and conclude with *salvo meliori judicio*. Finally, should I wish to speak in a discussion on such a subject as acquired or infused qualities, it would be a great help not to consider my own leisure, nor to hurry for lack of time, that is to say, not to think of my personal convenience at all but rather to adapt myself to the convenience and condition of the person with whom I seek to deal so that I may influence him, to the greater glory of God.

Our Fathers going to Trent will best promote the glory of God among souls by preaching, hearing confessions, lecturing, teaching children, setting a good example, visiting the poor in the hospitals, and exhorting the neighbor. In such works each should strive according to his particular talent to encourage as much as possible the spirit of prayer and devotion, in order that all may beg God our Lord mercifully to pour forth His Divine Spirit on those who are engaged with the business of the Council. In preaching, I should not touch upon matters that are in controversy between the Protestants and the Catholics, but simply exhort the people to lead a good life and practice the devotions of the Church. I should move them to acquire a knowledge of their own hearts and a greater knowledge and love of their Creator and Lord, appealing to the intellect. While hearing confessions I should address my penitents in such words as might afterwards be repeated publicly by them, and impose as their penance some prayers for the Council. In giving the *Spiritual Exercises* here also prayers for the Council ought to be recommended. The teaching of children should be undertaken when opportunity offers, bearing in mind the preparedness and dispositions of both master and pupil. It will be well to start at the beginning and develop subjects in a greater or less degree according to the ability of the scholars, and at the end of the lesson or exhortation there should be prayers for the Council. The hospitals should be visited at such times of the day as are best for health, and you should hear the confessions of the poor people, comfort them, and also bring them little presents whenever you can, not forgetting prayers for the Council.

68. Papal Conclave

ST. ROBERT BELLARMINE
To the Jesuit Provincial, April 29, 1605

Quis novit sensum Domini, aut quis consiliarius ejus fuit? A pope was elected who, as you have heard, was a very good man, a friend of our Society, and full of intentions so excellent that if he could only have carried them into effect he would have proved himself a model shepherd of souls. I know this for certain because, on Palm Sunday, he chose to unveil his heart to me in a general confession, as he expressed it, not of sins but of good resolutions. On April 27 he died. Who can unriddle these judgments of God?

Here we are, then, once more preparing to enter the conclave, and we need prayers more than ever because I do not see in the whole Sacred College one who possesses the qualities which you describe in your letter. What is worse, the electors make no effort to find such a person. It seems to me a very serious thing that, when the Vicar of God is to be chosen, they should cast their votes, not for one who knows the will of God, one versed in the Sacred Scriptures, but rather for one who knows the will of Justinian, and is versed in the authorities of the law. They look out for a good temporal ruler, not for a holy bishop who would really occupy himself with the salvation of souls. I, for my part, will do my best to give my vote to the worthiest man. The rest is in the hand of Providence for, after all, the care of the Church is more the business of God than ours.

And now, Father, I earnestly commend myself to your prayers in this new peril. My daily prayer in the last conclave was our Lord's *Transfer calicem hunc a me,* and it shall be the same this time, for I find myself very far from possessing those qualities which you rightly demand in a Vicar of Christ. Help me then lest I enter into this temptation.

69. The Pope's Burden

ST. GREGORY THE GREAT
c. A.D. 590

Gregory to John, Bishop of Constantinople, Eulogius of Alexandria, Gregory of Antioch, John of Jerusalem, and Anastasius, ex-Patriarch of Antioch:

Unequal as I am to a task from which my whole soul recoils, I have been forced to take upon my shoulders the burden of the pastoral office. When I think of it, grief rushes upon me and my heart in sad foreboding can see nothing ahead but dark shadows that blot out everything else. Why does our Lord choose a bishop, I ask, if not to intercede for the offenses of the people? Now, how can I appear with any confidence to plead for others' sins before One in whose sight I feel no security about my own? Supposing someone tried to make me intervene on his behalf with one who was a stranger to me, a man of position whom he had angered. I should immediately reply: "I simply cannot. We are not intimate friends; I do not even know him." If then, merely as man to man, I might well feel diffident about pleading with one upon whom I had no claim, how dare I hold the office of intercessor for the people before God, when the deserts due to my past life give me little assurance of His friendship? Moreover, in the circumstances, an even graver fear oppresses me, for as we all know well, should the chosen mediator be in disfavour himself, he will merely fan the flame of the other's wrath. I am terrified that, whereas our Lord has hitherto patiently borne with their offenses, the body of the faithful committed to my charge may now perish through the addition of my guilt to their own.

But even if I somehow manage to control my fears, and turn to study my episcopal work in a more cheerful frame of mind, I lose heart again when I consider its magnitude. For I am acutely aware of the watchfulness demanded of a prelate: He must be pure in thought, exemplary in conduct, discreet in holding his tongue, edifying in speech, in compassion a friend to all, in contemplation exalted above all, a lowly companion of the welldoer, a tower of zeal for justice against the vices of the evildoer. As I have said elsewhere, one who governs must take the greatest care to keep his own thoughts pure; no defilement should pollute the man who has undertaken the specific task of cleansing the stains of sin from the hearts of others as well as his own. It is necessary that the hand whose work is to wash filth away should itself be spotless; otherwise its touch will contaminate everything it handles with the dirt clinging to its own surface, and so leave it worse than before. *Be ye clean,* the Scriptures tell us, *you that carry the vessels of the Lord* (Is 52:11). Those who carry the vessels of the Lord are the men who undertake by the example of their own mode of life to attract their neighbors' souls to the holiness of the inner sanctuary. Deep self-examination then should lead the pastor to realize the need for his own cleansing if, in the bosom of his own personal conduct, he is to carry living vessels to the eternal temple.

However, the burden of the pastoral office has been laid upon me, and the more I ruminate over these and many things besides, the more impossible I find it to be what I ought. This is especially so in these days, for in spite of bearing the title of Pastor, a man's time is so eaten up in external administration that it may be questioned whether he holds the office of Pastor or of worldly magnate. As pastor, he must strive his utmost to avoid being weighed down excessively by the external cares from which no one who wields authority over his fellow men can be entirely free; but in my position so many problems have to be dealt with every day that they both overwhelm the mind and sap the strength of the body. I grow weary beneath the heavy load of pastoral care. Therefore, venerable brother, I conjure you by the Judge whom we shall one day face, by the mighty throng of angels, by the Church of the first-born whose names are written in heaven, help me by your prayerful intercession, for otherwise the burden may prove to be beyond my strength. Bearing in mind the Scriptural injunction, *Pray for one another that you may be saved,* I likewise give to you what I ask of you. And in giving, I shall recover the gift, for when we are linked by the power of prayer, we as it were hold each other's hand as we walk side by side along a slippery path; and thus by the bounteous disposition of charity, it comes about that the harder each one leans on the other, the more firmly are we riveted together in brotherly love.

70. Five Hundred Years Later

ST. GREGORY VII
A.D. 1075

Gregory the bishop, servant of the servants of God, to Hugh, abbot of Cluny, health and apostolic benediction.

Were it possible, I wish you could know all the trouble that besets me, all the labor that mounts up day by day to weary me out and deeply distress me. Then your brotherly sympathy would incline you towards me in proportion to the tribulations of my heart, and your own heart would pour forth a flood of tears before our Lord to beg Him, by whom all things are made and who rules all things, to stretch forth His hand to me in my misery, and with His wonted lovingkindness set this wretched being free. Often indeed have I implored Him that even as He Himself has imposed the burden, so He would either take me from this life, or use me for the profit of our holy mother the Church. So far, however, neither has He rescued me from great afflictions, nor has my life proved useful, as I hoped it would, for the service of the Church with whose chains He has bound me.

Hence it comes about that between the grief which on the one hand assails me daily anew, and on the other the hope too long deferred, tossed at every turn by a thousand tempests, I endure a life which is a continual death. And still I wait for Him who has bound me with His fetters, brought me back to Rome against my will, and once there has encompassed me with difficulties beyond number. Again and again I implore of Him: Make haste, do not delay; come speedily, do not linger, and deliver me, for the love of Blessed Mary and St. Peter. But because praise has no value, nor hallowed prayer any speedy efficacy in the mouth of a sinner, I pray, beg, and beseech you with all assiduity to request those whose merit of life gains them a hearing, to plead to God for me with the same love and charity with which they ought to love the mother of us all.

71. *Sic transit gloria mundi*

ST. ROBERT SOUTHWELL
To his fellow-Catholics in prison, A.D. 1584

Our life is like the print of a cloud in the air, like a mist dissolved in the sun, like a passing shadow, like a flower that soon fadeth, like a dry leaf carried with every wind, like a vapor that soon vanishes out of sight. St. Chrysostom calleth it a heavy sleep, fed with false and imaginary dreams; again he calls it a comedy, or rather, in our days, a tragedy, full of transitory shows and disguised passions. St. Gregory Nazianzen calleth it a child's game, who buildeth houses of sand on the shore, which the returning wave washeth away; yea, as Pindar saith, it is no more than the shadow of a shade. It passeth away like the wind; it rideth past like a ship in the sea that leaveth no print of passage; like a bird on the air, of whose way there remaineth no remembrance; like an arrow that flieth to the mark, whose track the air suddenly closeth up. Whatsoever we do, sit we, stand we, sleep we, or wake we, our ship, saith St. Basil, is always sailing towards our last home. Every day we die, and hourly lose some part of our life; and even while we grow we decrease. We have lost our infancy, our childhood, our youth and all, till this present day; and this very day death by minutes is secretly purloining from us. This St. Gregory well expresseth, saying, "our living is a passing through life, for our life, with her increase, diminisheth. Future things are always beginning, present things always ending, and things past quite dead and done. No armor resisteth, no threatening prevaileth, no entreaty profiteth against the assault of death." If all other perils and chances spare our life, yet time and age will, in the end, consume it. Better it is, since death is nature's necessary wreck, to follow St. Chrysostom's counsel, "let us make that voluntary, which must needs be of necessity; and let us offer to God as a present, what, of due and debt, we are bound to render. What marvel if, when the wind bloweth, the leaf fall; if, when the day appeareth, the night end?"—"Our life," saith the same saint, "was a shadow, and it passed; it was a smoke, and it vanished; it was a bubble, and it was dissolved; it was a spider's web, and it was shaken asunder."

The Christian
in Life

72. Perfection for the Plain Man

ST. TERESA OF AVILA
To her brother, Toledo, January 2, 1577

Jesus be with you. I don't want to write at length, but when I begin to write to you I never know how to stop. It is the devil who is responsible for your regret at having bought La Serna: he wants you to cease thanking God for the great favor He showed you in that matter. Do understand once and for all that it was by far the best thing to do and it has given your sons more than property—it has given them prestige. Praise God for what you did, and don't imagine that, if you had a great deal of time, you would spend more of it in prayer. Get rid of that idea; it is no hindrance to prayer to spend your time well, as you are doing when you are looking after the property which you will hand on to your sons. Again and again God gives more in a moment than in a long period of time, for His actions are not measured by time at all.

So, when the Christmas holidays are over, try to get hold of someone and go through the deeds with him and put them into proper shape. Jacob did not cease to be a saint because he had to attend to his flocks, nor did Abraham, nor St. Joachim. Everything seems a trouble to us when we want to get out of doing some task; at least it is to me, which is why it is God's will that I should know no peace. It is a great favor from God that what other people would consider a pleasure is wearisome to you. But that must not make you give it up, for we have to serve God in His way, not in ours.

You can tell Teresa that there is no fear I shall love anyone else as much as I love her. I was very touched to read what you wrote to Seville about her, for they sent me the letters here, and our nuns were not a little delighted to hear them—I read them to them in recreation and enjoyed doing so too. No one will ever stop my brother from being a ladies' man—it would be the death of him if anyone did—but, as the ladies in this case are saints, he thinks it all quite safe.

It is well with us both just now. What great things our Lord is doing! He seems to be pleased to show forth His greatness in raising up wretched creatures and doing us all these favors—and I know of none more wretched than you and I. I must tell you that, for over a week, I have been in such a condition that, if it were to go on, I should hardly be able to attend to all my business. Since before I wrote to you I have had raptures again, and they have been most distressing. It is useless to resist them and they are impossible to conceal. I get so dreadfully ashamed that I feel I want to hide away somewhere. I pray God earnestly not to let them happen to me in public; latterly I have been going about almost as if I were drunk. Previously, for nearly a week, I had been in such a state that I could hardly think a single good thought, so severely was I suffering from aridity. In one way I was really very glad that this was so, as for some time before that I had been as I am now, and it is a great satisfaction to realize so clearly how little we can do of ourselves. Blessed be He who can do everything. Amen. I have said quite enough. Anything further is not suitable for a letter—it should not even be talked about.

As to your own experience, it is certainly a greater thing than you realize, and may be the beginning of much blessing if you do not lose this through your own fault. I have already experienced that kind of prayer: as a rule, after it is over, the soul remains in a state of peace, and then it sometimes engages in certain forms of penance. In particular, if the impulse has been very strong, the soul feels it cannot bear not to be doing something for God; for this is a touch of love which He bestows on the soul, and if it grows stronger you will understand that part of the verse which you now say you cannot; for it is deep grief and pain, which one experiences without knowing whence it comes, nor even if it comes from a wound at all, or what it is: we only feel a delectable pain, which makes us cry out and say:

> Thou woundest not, yet pain'st indeed,
> And painlessly the soul is freed
> From love of creatures....

• For when the soul really experiences a touch of this love for God, it withdraws from all creature-love without feeling the least pain, in such a way as to show that the soul is not shackled by any love for them, which could not be so if it had not this love for God. When God takes possession of the soul, He gives it more and more dominion over created things, and even if His presence is withdrawn and the satisfaction which the soul was enjoying disappears, He does not withdraw Himself from the soul, nor does it fail to grow very rich in graces, and, as time goes on, that becomes evident in the affections.

I think I answered your question about feeling as though nothing had happened after the experience was over. I cannot recall if it is St. Augustine who says: "The Spirit of God passes without leaving a trace, just as the arrow leaves no trace in the air." There are other occasions when the condition of the soul is such that for a long time it cannot return to itself: it is like the sun, whose rays give out heat even when it cannot itself be seen. The soul seems to belong to some other place, and to animate the body without being in the body, because one of the faculties is suspended.

Pay no attention to those evil feelings which come to you afterwards. I think the explanation of them must be that the soul's joy is so keen that it makes itself felt in the body. With God's help it will calm down if you take no notice of it. I am quite clear that they are of no account, so the best thing is to make no account of them. I was once told by a very learned person that a man had come to him in great trouble, because whenever he communicated a very evil thought came to him—much worse than the things you tell me about—and so he had been ordered not to receive Communion, except once a year when it is of obligation. Although not a man of much spiritual experience, this learned man saw the weakness of this, and told him to take no notice of his thoughts, but to communicate every week. He did so, and lost his fear of the thoughts, whereupon they left him. So take no notice of yours either.

You are doing very well, glory be to God, as regards the kind of meditation you are making—I mean when you are not experiencing a state of quiet. I do not know if I have answered all your questions, for, though I always reread your letters, I have not had time today. You must not give yourself the trouble of rereading the letters you write me. I never reread mine. If a word here or there should have a letter missing, just put it in, and I will do the same for you, for your meaning is quite clear, and rereading your letters would be a waste of time for you and all to no purpose.

I send you this hairshirt to use when you find it difficult to recollect yourself at times of prayer, or when you are anxious to do something for the Lord. It is good for awakening love, but you are on no account to put it on after you are dressed, or to sleep in it. It can be worn on any part of the body, and put on in any way so long as it feels uncomfortable. Even a mere nothing like this makes one so happy when it is done for God out of a love for Him. With the love you are feeling now, I don't want us to omit giving it a trial. Write and tell me how you get on with this trifle. For I assure you, the more faithfully we deal with ourselves, remembering our Lord's sufferings, the more of a trifle it seems to us. It makes me laugh to think how you send me sweets and presents and money, and I send you hairshirts. You must use the discipline only for short periods, too, for in that way you feel it all the more, and at the same time it will do you less harm. Do not punish yourself with it too severely, for it is of no great importance, though you will think it very imperfect of you not to. And remember, if it affects the kidneys, you must neither wear the hairshirt nor take the discipline, or it will do you great harm. God prefers your health and your obedience to your penances. Remember what He said to Saul. Be very careful not to go without your sleep and also to take enough collation, for when a person wants to do something for God he is apt not to realize he is doing himself harm until the harm is done. I can assure you that I have learned this from my own experience. Do not think that this blessing of sound sleep which God gives you is an unimportant one. I assure you, it is very precious. And I tell you once more, you must not try to do with less sleep: this is no time for you to do so. Remember that we middle-aged people need to treat our bodies well so as not to wreck the spirit, which is a terrible trial. So do as you are ordered: that is the way to do your duty to God.

My confessor, Dr. Velazquez, was here today. I discussed with him what you said about wanting to give up using the carpets and silver, as I should not like you to cease making progress in God's service because I was not helping you, but there are things in which I do not trust my own opinion. In this, however, he agreed with me. He says it is of no importance one way or the other; what matters is that you try to see how unimportant such things are and not become attached to them. It is right that you should have a suitably appointed house, as you will have to marry your sons one day. So just be patient for now: God always gives us opportunities to carry out our good desires, and He will give you a chance to carry out yours. May God watch over you for me and make you very holy. Amen.

73. Perfection for the Pretty Woman

ST. FRANCIS DE SALES
To a married woman, Annecy, May 3, 1604

It is impossible to supply you on the spot with all I have promised you, for I have not sufficient free time to put all the material together on the subject you have asked me to explain. I shall treat of it over several letters, and besides making things easier for me, that will give you breathing-space to digest my instructions.

You are filled with a great longing for Christian perfection; that is the noblest longing you could possibly have. Cherish it, increase it day by day. The means of achieving perfection differ according to diversity of vocation, for nuns, widows, and those in the married state are all bound to seek after perfection but not by the same road. Your way, Madam, since you are married, is to live in close union with God and your neighbor and whatever relates to them.

The principal means of union with God must be found in the reception of the sacraments and in prayer. As to the use of the sacraments, you should never allow a month to pass without receiving Holy Communion, and communicate oftener according to the progress you are making in God's service, and the advice of your spiritual directors. Concerning Confession, however, I should strongly advise you to go much more frequently, especially if you have fallen into some fault which troubles your conscience, as so often happens to the beginner in the spiritual life. Nevertheless, if you lack the necessary opportunity to make your confession, contrition and penance will suffice.

In the matter of prayer, you should make it assiduously, especially meditation to which you are rather well-adapted, I imagine. Every morning then, devote somewhat less than an hour to it either before the daily round, or else before you sup in the evening, but take care never to make it after dinner or supper, because to do so will injure your health. To make it well, you will find it a help to know beforehand the exact subject upon which you are going to meditate, so that from the very beginning of your prayer, you have the matter prepared.

Over and above that, make frequent ejaculatory prayers to our Lord, and do it at all times and wherever you are, keeping your eyes always on God in your heart and your heart in God. Take pleasure in reading Luis of Granada's studies on prayer and meditation; no one can instruct you better than he, nor with such animation. I should like you to allow no day to go by without spending from between half an hour to an hour in reading some spiritual book; that will compensate for a sermon. There you have the chief means of uniting yourself to God.

And now to the ways and means that aid us to establish right relations with our neighbor: they are very many, but I shall mention only a few. We must see our neighbor in God who would have us show him love and consideration. Such is St. Paul's advice (see Eph 6) when he instructs servants to obey God in their masters and their masters in God. We must put this love into practice by showing our neighbor outward marks of kindness; and although at first it may seem to go against the grain, we ought not to give up for all that, because our goodwill and the habit formed by constant repetition will finally conquer the repugnance of our lower nature. We must occupy our prayer and meditation with the problem, since we must first pray for the love of God, and then always petition for that of our neighbor, especially of those to whom we are not humanly attracted.

I advise you to go to the trouble of making an occasional visit to the hospitals. Comfort the sick, compassionate their ailments, make it clear that the sight of their sufferings affects you, and pray for them in addition to giving them practical help. But in all you do, take scrupulous care never in any way to irritate your husband, your household, or your parents by overmuch church-going, exaggerated seclusion, or neglect of your family duties. Or again, as sometimes happens, don't let it make you censorious of others' conduct, or turn up your nose at conversations which fail to conform to your own lofty standards, for in all such matters charity must rule and enlighten us, so that we comply graciously with our neighbor's wishes in anything that is not contrary to God's law.

You must not only be prayerful and lead a spiritual life, but you must make it congenial to each and every one around you. Now they will admire it, if you make it serviceable and pleasant. The sick will esteem your devotion if it brings them loving consolation; your family, if they realize it makes you more mindful of their well-being, more approachable in a crisis, more gentle in reproof, and so forth; your husband, if he sees that as your spiritual life advances, the more do you smile upon him and prove your love for him by your sweet bearing; your parents and friends, if they note in you a greater generosity, loyalty, and courteous yielding to their wishes so long as the latter do not transgress God's will. In a word, as far as you possibly can, make your piety attractive.

I have written a short pamphlet on perfection in the Christian life, of which I enclose a copy. Take it in good part along with this letter: they both issue from a heart entirely devoted to your spiritual welfare; it desires nothing so ardently as to see God's work perfected in your soul.

I beg you to give me a share in your prayers and Communions, and assure you in return of a lifelong remembrance in mine.

74. The Christian

BLESSED JOHN OF AVILA
To a spiritual disciple, c. A.D. 1563

I have received your letter, and to tell you the truth, if my many occupations did not often prevent me from answering you, I should ask you to write very frequently, as it is always a great pleasure to receive news of yourself and your family. But as I owe you so much already, let me add this debt to the score, and our Lord will repay you all.

You ask me to tell you how to become a good Christian, and I am most glad to hear your question, for to wish to be a good Christian is to have already started well on the road. But take care not to resemble the many, whose knowledge of God's Will, as it does not make them follow it, only condemns them to more severe punishment; for, as Christ tells us: *That servant who knew the will of his lord, and did not according to his will, shall be beaten with many stripes* (Lk 12:47). Therefore, to ask to be shown the way of God is to lay oneself under no small obligation, but as I believe you wish to learn it with the full intention of practicing all that it involves, it is my duty to direct you in it.

Good works are of two kinds. Some are exterior, such as prayer, fasting, and almsgiving; abstaining from swearing, falsehood, and murmuring; avoiding injuring or annoying people and other things of a similar kind. Some also are purely spiritual or interior, such as fervent love for God and our neighbor, an intense realization of our own unworthiness, deep gratitude for the divine mercies, and such a profound reverence for the Almighty that we realize our own nothingness in the sight of His greatness. There are also many other religious sentiments which cannot be enumerated. Corporal good works are the easiest to perform, and a man is much to blame if he omits these, for can any one be careful in greater matters who neglects lesser ones? If we cannot restrain our tongue, or control our bodies and employ them in good works, can we complain that God does not call us to higher things?

The Temple of God in Jerusalem had one gate for the people and further on another through which none but the priests might pass. So, to hear Mass, to honor one's elders, to abstain from speaking or acting wrongly, and other duties of the same kind, are common to all Christians, whether they be the friends of God or not; but a heart full of faith and charity is the special gift of His friends, and is the distinguishing mark between the sons of perdition and of salvation. As the Jews had to walk through the first portal to reach the second, so Christians pass by good actions to purity of heart. Not that these works in themselves make the heart holy, which can only be effected by the gift of God's grace: but this, by His great mercy, He bestows on those who do their best to serve Him as far as their weakness will allow them. What we need, above all other things, is a new heart, but this is the last thing we should think ourselves capable of obtaining by our own power. No man has faith who does not believe that he has received his being from God; neither has he faith, who thinks that any other than the Almighty can give him strength to become good, for holiness is a higher gift than mere existence. Those who imagine they can attain to holiness by any wisdom or strength of their own will find themselves after many labors, and struggles, and weary efforts, only the farther from possessing it, and this in proportion to their certainty that they of themselves have gained it.

Humility and self-contempt will obtain our wish far sooner than will stubborn pride. Though God is so exalted, His eyes regard the lowly, both in heaven and on earth, and we shall strive in vain to please Him in any other way than by abasing ourselves. The Son of God came down from heaven and taught us by His life and words the way to heaven, and that way is humility, as He said: *He that humbleth himself shall be exalted* (Lk 18:14). Therefore, if you wish God to give you a new heart, you must first of all amend your deeds, and then lament your faults and accuse yourself of your sins. Do not extenuate your defects, but judge yourself justly; let not your self-love blind you, but when conscience accuses you of wrong, do not forget it, but keep it before your eyes and manifest it to Jesus Christ, your savior and physician. Weep for it before Him, and He will comfort you without fail. No force can prevail with a Father like the tears of his child, nor is there anything which so moves God to grant us, not justice, but mercy, as our sorrow and self-accusation. Call upon the Almighty, for He will not be deaf to your cries; show Him your wounded soul, for you have not to deal with one who is blind; speak to Him of all your miseries, for He is merciful and will heal them. Go to confession and Holy Communion, and when you are united to your Savior, your soul will melt with devotion, and you will say: *How great is the multitude of thy sweetness, O Lord, which thou hast hidden for them that fear thee* (Ps 30:20).

Be sure, too, to show to your neighbor the same love which God has shown towards you. If you are harsh to others, you will find God harsh to you, for you know His fixed decree: *With what measure you mete, it shall be measured to you again.* Do not be niggardly, then, to other people, for fear that God may treat you in the same way. He will pardon you many crimes for the one offense you forgive your neighbor; He will be long-suffering with you in return for a little patience shown towards others; He will reward you with abundant riches for the small alms you bestow. Strive earnestly, therefore, to keep the law of charity, for in that is your life.

In these few words you see the rule by which you must live; watch carefully over your words and actions. Practice prayer, and beg Christ to grant you a newness and singleness of heart; do nothing to injure others, but rather do them all the good you can by word and deed, and thus you will fulfill your duty both to God, your neighbor, and yourself. *This do and thou shalt live.* Know, however, that if you are to be a friend of God, you must prepare yourself for trials, for without them all your virtue is like an unwalled city, which falls at the first onslaught. Patience is the guardian of all the other virtues, and, if it fail, we may lose in one moment the labor of many days. Our Master and Redeemer tells us: *In your patience you shall possess your souls* (Lk 21:19); without it, we lose control over ourselves, because anger, like wine, robs us of our reason. Brace up your heart to suffer afflictions, for without the battle there is no victory, and the crown is only for the conqueror. Do not think that your burden is heavy; it is very light, compared with what you deserve to have to bear and with what Jesus Christ our Lord bore for your sake; it is slight indeed in comparison to the reward it will bring you. Remember that we shall soon quit this world, and then all the past will seem to us like a short dream, and we shall see that it is better to have labored than to have rested here. Learn how to profit by your sorrows, for they bring great riches to the soul. They cleanse it from past sin; what fire is to gold, that tribulation is to the just man, whose heart it purifies. Trials only injure the wicked, for instead of being grateful to God they murmur against Him. Their punishment does them no good, because they turn their sufferings into sins, and so lose where they might have gained, earning hell by painful labor. Do not imitate them, but let your courage increase with your trials. God proves His sons by sorrow, and no one will be crowned but he that has been through the combat. St. James says: *Blessed is the man who endureth tempta- tion, for when he hath been proved, he shall receive the crown of life* (Jas 1:4), which God promises to those who love Him. If only we realized the value of this crown, how gladly should we now suffer affliction! Would that we understood how blessed, both now and hereafter, are the tears we shed in this life. We should abase ourselves to the dust here, so that we might stand high in heaven, and should despise all earthly pleasures, were they given us, in comparison with the heavenly joys for which we hope. Soon the vanity of this world will be unmasked, and the kingdom of God will be revealed. Live here as a stranger, your body on earth, but your heart above, so that when our Lord calls you, He may not find you sleeping, but ready to go with Him, and to hear the sweet words: *Well done, thou good and faithful servant, enter thou into the joy of thy Lord* (Mt 25:21).

75. A Good Confession

St. Alphonsus Liguori
To his Redemptoristine nuns, c. A.D. 1773

Everyone knows that for a good confession three things are necessary: an examination of conscience, sorrow, and a determination to avoid sin. Spiritual souls who go frequently to confession and guard against deliberate venial sins have no need to spend a long time in the examination of conscience and had they committed any mortal sins they would know it without any examination. They would be conscious too of venial sins if fully deliberate, by the consequent remorse. Besides, there is no obligation to confess all our venial transgressions; therefore we are not obliged to make a strict search after them, and much less after the number, the circumstance, the manner, or the causes of them. It is sufficient to confess the most grievous, and to mention the rest in general terms. St. Francis de Sales is so consoling on this point. "Do not feel worried if you do not remember all your little peccadilloes in confession," he says, "for as you often fall imperceptibly, so you are often raised up imperceptibly," that is, by acts of love or the other good deeds virtuous souls are accustomed to perform.

In the second place, sorrow is essential; this is the principal condition necessary for obtaining pardon. The most sorrowful, not the lengthiest confessions, are the best. The proof of a confession is found, says St. Gregory, not in the multitude of the penitent's words, but in his compunction of heart. Some people are troubled because they do not feel sorrow; they wish to shed tears and to feel a tender contrition every time they receive the sacrament; and because in spite of all their efforts they are unable to excite this sorrow, they always feel uneasy about their confessions. But you must realize that true sorrow consists not in feeling it, but in wanting it. All the merit of virtue lies in the will. Thus, in discussing faith, Gerson has declared that sometimes a man who wishes to believe has more merit than another who does believe. And St. Thomas says that the essential sorrow necessary for the sacrament of Penance is a displeasure at having committed sin, and this is found, not in the sensitive part of the soul, but in the will. Take care not to make forced efforts to arouse sorrow. Remember that the best interior acts are those performed with the least violence and with the greatest sweetness, for the Holy Ghost orders all things sweetly and peacefully. That is why Ezechias described his sorrow in the words: *Behold in peace is my bitterness most bitter.*

In the third place, a purpose to sin no more is essential; and this purpose must be firm, universal, and efficacious. Some people say: I wish never more to commit this sin, I wish never more to offend God. Alas for the word *wish!* A firm purpose of amendment says with a resolute will: I will never more commit this sin, I will never more offend God deliberately.

Secondly, it must be universal. The penitent must resolve to avoid all sins without exception—all mortal sins, that is to say.

Spiritual souls should determine to avoid all deliberate venial sins, but as for indeliberate ones, it is sufficient to guard against them as far as one is able; it is quite impossible to avoid all indeliberate sins.

Thirdly, it must be efficacious. It is not enough for penitents to make up their minds to renounce sin, it is necessary also to remove the occasions of it; otherwise all their confessions, though they should receive a thousand absolutions, will be invalid. Not to remove the proximate occasion of mortal sin is in itself a mortal sin. And, as I have already shown in my *Moral Theology*, he that receives absolution without a firm purpose of removing the proximate occasion of mortal sin, commits a new mortal sin and is guilty of sacrilege.

But one may perhaps be tempted to conceal a sin in confession. Some Christians, through human respect and through fear of losing the esteem of others, easily continue for months and years to make sacrilegious confessions and Communions. But how can a Christian that has been so daring as to sin grievously against the divine majesty, find an excuse before God for concealing a sin in confession in order to avoid the transient and trifling confusion that would arise from confessing it to a priest? It is but just that the man who has despised God should humble and confound himself. However, the devil will endeavor to fill the mind of such sinners with many delusions and vain fears. One will say: My confessor will rebuke me sternly if I reveal this sin. Why should he rebuke you? Tell me, were you a confessor, would you speak harshly to a poor penitent, who had come to manifest his miseries to you in the hope of being raised up from his fallen state? Another will argue: But the confessor will, at least, be scandalized at my sin, and will dislike me for it. All nonsense! Far from being scandalized, he will be edified when he sees with what good dispositions and sincerity the sinner makes his confession, in spite of the shame that covers him. Has the priest not heard similar or possibly even far more grievous sins from others? Would to God you were the only sinner in the world! As for the dislike, on the contrary the confessor will esteem the penitent the more when he realizes the confidence placed in him, and will try all the more zealously to help him.

Have courage, then, and conquer by your generosity the shame that the devil magnifies so much in your mind. It will be enough to begin to reveal the sin you have committed: all your ridiculous apprehensions will vanish on the spot. And believe me when I tell you that afterwards you will feel more happy at having confessed your sins than if you had been made monarch of the whole earth. Recommend yourself to the Blessed Virgin Mary, and she will obtain for you strength to overcome all repugnance. And if you lack the courage to disclose your sins at once to the confessor, say to him: "Father, I need your help. I have committed a certain sin which I cannot bring myself to confess." The confessor will then adopt an easy means of dragging from its den the wild beast that would devour you. All you will have to do is to answer Yes or No to his interrogations. And behold, both the temporal and the eternal hell have disappeared, the grace of God is recovered, and peace of conscience reigns supreme.

76. Let Be!

ST. JOHN CHRYSOSTOM
To Olympias, A.D. *404*

To grieve to excess over the failings for which we must render an account is neither safe nor necessary. It is more likely to be damaging or even destructive. Still worse is it then and perfectly useless to wear oneself out grieving over others' misdeeds. Above all, it is playing into the hands of the devil, and harmful to the soul.

To illustrate my point, I shall tell you an old story. A certain man of Corinth had received the benefit of the holy waters, was purified through the initiation of baptism, had been a partaker at the tremendous rites of the holy table, and in a word, was a sharer of all the mysteries which are ours. Many say that he held the position of teacher. After this holy initiation and all the inestimable benefits to which he had been admitted, and in spite of holding an important position in the Church, he fell into most grievous sin. Looking upon his father's wife with lustful eyes, he did not stop at desire but translated his unbridled will into deed. This brazen act passed beyond fornication and even adultery; it was much worse.

Blessed Paul heard about it, and being at a loss for a suitable and sufficiently grave term for this sin, made the magnitude of the crime clear by another means. *In a word,* he says, *it is heard that there is fornication among you, and such fornication as is not mentioned even among the heathen.* In an effort to emphasize the enormity of such a crime, he does not say, "such as is not perpetrated," but *such as is not mentioned.*

Accordingly, he hands him over to the devil, cuts him off from the whole Church, and allows nobody to partake with him at the common table. It is not right, he declares, even to eat together with such a person, and peremptorily orders that the severest penalty be inflicted upon him; he makes use of Satan as the instrument of vengeance to punish the man's flesh.

And yet he who cuts the offender off from the Church, and refuses to let anyone eat at the same table with him, who orders all to grieve on his account, he who drives him away from all directions as though he were a real plague spot, who has shut him out from every house, handed him over to Satan, and demanded so heavy a penalty for him, this very Paul, when he sees that the man is contrite and repentant for the sins he has committed, and that his deeds prove that he truly has turned over a new leaf, completely reverses his policy. He now orders the same people to whom he had issued these instructions, to adopt the very opposite line of conduct. He who had said: "Cut him off, turn him away, grieve over him, and let the devil seize him," now says—what? *Confirm your charity towards him, lest such a one be swallowed up with overmuch sorrow, and we should be over-reached by Satan. For we are not ignorant of his devices.*

Cannot you see that the tendency to grieve beyond measure comes from the devil and is the work of his cunning? Through urging to excess, he converts the healing medicine into a noxious poison, and whenever he falls into excess, a man hands himself over to the devil. That explains why Paul says, *lest we be over-reached by Satan.* His words amount to this: "This sheep was covered with a terrible disease; he was set apart from the flock and cut off from the Church, but he has corrected the evil and has become the good sheep that he was before. Such is the power of repentance. Let us welcome him wholeheartedly, let us receive him with outstretched hands, let us embrace him and clasp him to our breasts, let us make him one of us. For if we will not, we give the devil the advantage. Through our carelessness he seizes upon, not what is his own but him who had become ours; he submerges him in an excess of grief, and makes him his own for the future." Therefore St. Paul goes on to say: *For we are not ignorant of his designs;* we know well enough how often, when plans for helping someone go awry, he makes use of them to trip up the unwary.

Well now, Paul does not allow a man who has himself fallen into sin—and such a sin!—to indulge in too great a grief, but rather encourages him, urges him on, and busies himself in doing all he can to remove the weight of his despondency. He points out that immoderation is inspired by Satan, and marks a gain for the devil—is in fact a proof of his villainy and the fruit of his wicked designs. How then can it be anything but the greatest folly and madness where other people's sins and their final reckoning are in question, so to grieve and afflict the soul as to involve oneself in a cloud of melancholy culminating in turmoil, confusion, and unbearable agony of mind?

77. Scrupulosity

ST. JOHN OF THE CROSS
To a Carmelite nun, A.D. 1589–1591

Jesus, Mary. In these days be employed inwardly in desiring the coming of the Holy Spirit, and both during the festival and afterwards continue in His presence, and let your care and esteem for this be such that nothing else attracts you, neither consider aught else, whether it be trouble or any other disturbing memories; and during the whole of this period, even though there be omissions in the house, pass them over for the love of the Holy Spirit, and for the sake of what is necessary to the peace and quiet of the soul wherein He loves to dwell.

If you can put an end to your scruples, I think it would be better for your quietness if you were not to confess during these days. When you do confess, let it be after this manner: with regard to advertences and thoughts, whether they have respect to judgments or whether to unruly representations of objects or any other movements that come to you without the desire and collaboration of your soul, and without your desiring to pay attention to them, do not confess these or take any notice of them or be anxious about them, for it is better to forget them, although they trouble your soul the more; at most you might describe in general terms the omission or remissness that you may perchance have noted with respect to the purity and perfection which you should have in the interior faculties—memory, understanding, and will. With respect to words, confess any excess and imprudence that you may have committed as regards speaking truly and uprightly, and out of necessity and with purity of intention. With regard to actions, confess the way in which you may have diverged from the path to your true and only goal, which you should follow without respect of persons—namely, God alone.

And, if you confess in this way, you may rest content, without confessing any of these other things in particular, however much interior conflict it may bring you. You will communicate during this festival, as well as at your usual times.

When anything disagreeable and displeasing happens to you, remember Christ crucified and be silent.

Live in faith and hope, though it be in darkness, for in this darkness God protects the soul. Cast your care upon God for you are His and He will not forget you. Do not think that He is leaving you alone, for that would be to wrong Him.

Read, pray, rejoice in God, your Good and your Health, and may He give you His good things and preserve you wholly, even to the day of eternity. Amen. Amen.

78. Obey!

ST. ALPHONSUS LIGUORI
To a penitent, A.D. 1766

What joy you give me when you tell me that you continue to go to Holy Communion. But I do not feel happy about the rest of your letter where you speak of the silly fears which you are allowing to grip you once again. All your apprehensions spring from the devil and they will lead you, I am afraid, to give up your Communions. You tremble for your past? I tremble for your future. Are you going to return to your old habit of wailing: "I can't. It's impossible"? Can't you see that the devil's deception has convinced you in the past that all your confessions and Communions were sacrilegious? I assure you, in the name of God, that you are in a state of grace. Were you to make your confession to me, I should formally forbid you under pain of grievous sin to make any reference to your past life, no matter how scrupulous you felt about it.

You will reply: But what am I to do when I am in the throes of such fears? What are you to do? Believe what I and so many others have told you, namely, that when doubts and scruples of conscience assail you, you yourself are ignorant, unbalanced, and incapable of forming a judgment. Believe that. And therefore believe the truth when it is told you. On my part, I repeat to you, in the name of God: Do not discontinue your Holy Communions, however violent or persistent your doubts. I take the responsibility for this advice, I am answerable for it to God. As long as you have not committed any quite recent and fresh sin which is undoubtedly mortal, a sin to which you have given your full consent, a sin which was fully deliberate, always receive Communion without going to confession. I say *a quite recent sin,* for if it belongs to the past you must say absolutely nothing about it again in the confessional. Possibly you will have to put up with the fears that torment you until you die. There is only one course of action—go ahead in blind obedience.

I ask you to keep this letter and do not mention the word sacrilege to me again. When you feel troubled, read my letter and be of good heart. Before God, I see plainly that by so doing you will follow the right road and become a saint; act otherwise, and you will risk the loss of your soul, as others have lost theirs because they would not submit their judgment to that of another. Blind obedience is praised by all theologians, by all the holy Fathers, by the whole Church. Practice it and you will be safe.

79. Am I in a State of Grace?

ST. GREGORY THE GREAT
To Gregoria, Lady-in-Waiting to Augusta, A.D. 593

Your Ladyship's long-awaited letter has reached me. With scrupulous and minute care, you accuse yourself therein of manifold sins; yet Almighty God is merciful, and knowing as I do your deep love for Him, I am confident that the Voice of Truth is pronouncing upon you that same verdict which He delivered in favor of a holy woman I need not name: *Her sins, many as they are, shall be forgiven her, because she has loved much* (Lk 7:47). Now what is surest proof of her forgiveness? Why, that she then followed our Lord, sat at His feet and listened to His word (Lk 10:39). She transcended the active life which still occupied her sister Martha, and undoubtedly was then exalted to the life of contemplation. Think of the earnestness with which she searched for her buried Lord after she had stooped and failed to find His Body. There she remained in tears before the door of the sepulcher even though His disciples had departed. That was why she was found worthy to behold Him alive whose dead body she had been seeking, and she it was who announced to the disciples His resurrection. So through the wonderful providence of God's goodness, a woman's lips brought the news of life because in Paradise a woman's lips had dealt death. On a second occasion also, in company with the other Mary, she saw our Lord after He had risen, drew near to Him, and clung to His feet. Pause, I beg you, and consider precisely whose feet they were, and what the hands that clasped them. The woman we are talking about, the city's most notorious sinner, touched with her polluted hands the feet of him who sits at the right hand of the Father, high above the angels. Let us try to penetrate if we can, to probe the inmost depths of this heavenly love, on whose wings grace bears aloft a woman whom sin had plunged into the depths of the abyss. Here, beloved daughter, here you see the fulfillment of the promise given us by the prophet, when his voice proclaimed this era of Holy Church: *In that day there shall be a fountain open to the house of David for the washing of the sinner and of the unclean woman* (Zec 13:1). Truly has the house of David become to us an open fountain for the cleansing of sinners, for in it we are washed from the filth of sin in the open stream of His mercy by the Son of David, our Savior.

But when your Ladyship threatens in your letters to give me no peace until I assure you that the forgiveness of your sins has been revealed to me, you make a request that is difficult and to no purpose: difficult, in the first place, because I am unworthy of revelations; pointless, I tell you, because you are not meant to be unconcerned about your sins, except possibly on the last day of your life when you can no longer muster strength to grieve over them. But until then, your offenses should always arouse compunction, and ever in fear and trembling you should daily wash them away in your tears. Paul the apostle, as we know, was caught up to the third heaven and led into Paradise, where he heard secret words unlawful for man to utter; yet for all that, he was kept in suspense. *I chastise my body,* he declared, *and bring it into subjection, lest perhaps after preaching to others I myself should be rejected* (1 Cor 9:27). He had been carried up even into heaven, yet he still experienced disquiet, and has one who dwells very much on earth any right to freedom from fear? Weigh my words well, most beloved daughter: very often security is the mother of negligence. Therefore in this world you are not meant to feel safe; that would give birth to carelessness. *Blessed is the man that is always fearful* (Prv 28:14), says holy Writ; and again: *Serve ye the Lord with fear, and rejoice unto him with trembling* (Ps 2:11). Your soul then must needs be filled with uncertainty during the brief sojourn of this life, if it is afterwards to rejoice in the happiness of safety for evermore. May Almighty God fill your soul with the grace of His Holy Spirit, and when the tears you have shed in prayer are wiped away, may He bring you to joy everlasting.

80. On Daily Holy Communion

St. Gregory VII
A.D. *1074*

Bishop Gregory, servant of the servants of God, to his beloved daughter in Christ, Matilda, health and benediction in the Lord.

He alone who searches the secrets of the heart knows the extent of my tender care and unceasing solicitude for you and your well-being. He understands it far better than I. You have not failed, I take it, to give the matter thought? You realize that just as I have kept your interests in mind with unwearied charity, so ought you to show equal consideration for me. You should not brush it all aside in order to concentrate solely on your own soul's salvation. For I have told you before, and shall tell you again in obedience to the heavenly proclamation: *Charity seeketh not her own* (1 Cor 13).

Now, by God's help, I have furnished you with weapons to use against the prince of this world, and among others I have indicated the most powerful of all, namely, the frequent reception of the Body of our Lord. Secondly, I have bidden you entrust yourself wholeheartedly to the sure fidelity of our Lord's mother. This led me during the course of our letters to quote St. Ambrose's opinion with regard to receiving our Lord's Body. "If we proclaim the death of the Lord," he tells us in his 4th Book *On the Sacraments,* "we proclaim the remission of sins. If as often as the Lord's Blood is shed, it is poured forth for the remission of sins, I ought to receive it always, so that my sins may always be forgiven. I who am always committing sin ought always to have a remedy." And the same saint goes on to ask: "If it is daily bread, why do you receive it only at the end of the year, after the Greek custom in the East?" Receive daily what will benefit you every day. Live in such a way that you may be worthy to receive it every day. He who does not deserve to receive daily, does not deserve to receive at the end of the year. Remember that holy Job offered sacrifice for his sons every day, for fear they had committed sin either in heart or in speech. As often as the sacrifice is offered, the Lord's death, the Lord's resurrection is shown forth together with the remission of sins. You appreciate the fact, and yet you do not eat this daily bread of life? A man suffering from a wound needs a remedy. The wound is our being slaves to sin; and the remedy? The heavenly and adorable sacrament.

Pope Gregory repeats the same thought in the fourth Book of his Dialogues: "We must despise this present world with our whole heart," he says, "since we have already seen how it passes away, and we must immolate to God the daily offering of our tears and the daily sacrifices of His Body and Blood. For this victim, through a divine mystery, renews for us the death of the Only-begotten, and it alone saves our soul from eternal death. It is true that rising from the dead He dies no more, death shall no more have dominion over Him; but it is true also that whilst living in Himself with an immortal and incorruptible life, He is yet immolated for us once more in the mystery of the holy oblation. In that oblation, His Body is received, His Flesh sacrificed for the people's salvation, His Blood is poured forth, not now upon the hands of unbelievers but into the mouths of the faithful. Let us consider then the benefits we derive from this sacrifice, which continues to reenact the Passion of the only-begotten Son for our forgiveness. Can any believer doubt that, at the voice of the priest in the hour of immolation, the heavens are opened; in that mystery of Jesus Christ, the choirs of angels are present; things above are united to things below, earthly joined to heavenly, the visible and invisible made one?"

The ancient father, John Chrysostom, addresses his neophytes in much the same strain. "Lo! Christ has taken His Bride to Himself!" he cries. "See with what sustaining food He nourishes you. He Himself forms the substance of the meal and all its nutriment. As a woman, compelled by natural affection, hastens to feed her babe from her overflowing breast, so also Christ ever nourishes with His Blood those whom He regenerates." And to the monk Theodore, John adds: "Mortal nature is a slippery kind of thing: it is, to be sure, quick to give way but not too slow to put right, and as it easily falls, so it quickly rises."

Daughter, it is our duty to have recourse to this unique sacrament, to seize upon this unique remedy. I have taken the trouble to write to you at some length, most beloved daughter of Blessed Peter, in order to make your faith and fidelity in receiving our Lord's Body increase more and more. This is the treasure, these the gifts—not gold or precious stones—that your soul asks of me for love of your heavenly homeland, for love, that is to say, of the Prince of heaven. And you ask them of me, even though you might deservedly receive far better from other priests.

As for our Lord's mother, to whom especially I have entrusted and do entrust you, and shall never fail to entrust you until we see her as we long to do—what am I to say of her whom heaven and earth cease not to praise though they can never do so as she deserves? But this you must hold as certain: as she is higher, holier, more perfect than every other mother, so much the more is she kind and gentle towards her erring but repentant sons and daughters. So make a firm resolution never to commit another sin, prostrate yourself before her, and pour forth your tears from a contrite and humbled heart. You will find her, I can assure you beyond all doubt, more accessible, more tender in the love she bears you, than any natural mother could be on earth.

81. Walk Humbly

ST. JOHN OF THE CROSS
To one living in the world, Segovia, October 12, 1589

May Jesus be in your soul. I have done anything but forget you; just think, how could I forget one who is in my soul, as you are? While you are walking in that darkness and in those empty places of spiritual poverty, you think that everyone and everything are failing you; but that is not surprising, for at these times it seems to you that God is failing you too. But nothing is failing you, nor have you any need to consult me about anything, nor have you any reason to do so, nor do you know one, nor will you find one: all that is merely suspicion without cause. He that seeks naught but God walks not in darkness, in whatever darkness and poverty he may find himself; and he that harbors no presumptuousness and desires not his own satisfaction, either as to God or as to the creatures, and works not his own will in any way whatsoever has no need to stumble or to worry about anything. You are progressing well; remain in quietness and rejoice. Who are you to be anxious about yourself? A fine state you would get into if you did that!

You have never been in a better state than now, for you have never been humbler or more submissive, nor have you ever counted yourself and everything in the world as of such little worth; nor have you ever known yourself to be so evil, nor God to be so good, nor have you ever served God so purely and disinterestedly as now, nor do you any longer go, as you may have been apt to do, after the imperfections of your will and your own resolution. What do you desire? What kind of life do you imagine yourself as living in this world? How do you imagine yourself behaving? What do you think is meant by serving God, but abstaining from evil, keeping His commandments and walking in

His ways as best we can? If this be done, what need is there of other apprehensions, or of any other illumination or sweetness whether from one source or from another? In these things as a rule the soul is never free from stumbling blocks and perils, and is deceived and fascinated by the objects of its understanding and desire, and its very faculties cause it to stray. And thus God is granting the soul a great favor when He darkens the faculties and impoverishes the soul so that it may not be led astray by them; and how can it walk aright and not stray, save by following the straight road of the law of God and of the Church, and living only in true and dark faith and certain hope and perfect charity, and awaiting its blessings in the life to come, living here below as pilgrims, exiles, and orphans, poor and desolate, with no road to follow and with no possessions, expecting to receive everything in Heaven?

Rejoice and put your trust in God, for He has given you signs that you can quite well do so, and indeed that you ought to do so; should you do otherwise, it will not be surprising if He is wroth at seeing you so foolish, when He is leading you by the road that is best for you and has set you in so sure a place. Desire no way of progress but this, and tranquilize your soul, for all is well with it, and communicate as is your wont. Confess, when you have something definite to say; there is no need to talk. When you have anything to say you will write about it to me, and write to me quickly and more frequently.

I have been somewhat indisposed, but now am well again, though Fray Juan Evangelista is ailing. Commend him to God, and me likewise, my daughter in the Lord.

82. Spiritual Nakedness

ST. AMMONAS THE HERMIT
To his disciples, A.D. 340[?]

1. To my dearly beloved in the Lord. If anyone has been stripped of the heavenly garment of the new life, which is the Spirit of Truth and the power which comes from Him, he must go on pleading tearfully with the Lord until He clothes his soul in the power which comes from above in place of the shame and confusion with which it is now covered. For just as bodily nakedness is a source of confusion and dishonor for men, so, too, do God and His saints turn their faces away from those who are not clothed in the Holy Spirit. If Adam felt shame when he saw that he was naked, how much more shame is going to be felt by the soul which is stripped of its Lord! So anyone who has been stripped of the clothing of the Spirit must be ashamed of himself; let him realize his own disgrace and blush for his nakedness; let his spirit cry out loudly to God, and let him carry on the struggle within his heart until the heavenly glory, appearing visibly above him, comes to clothe him. Glory be to the immeasurable mercy! When the woman suffering from a flow of blood truly believed and touched the hem of the Lord's clothing, her flow of blood dried up. In the same way, every soul which is wounded by sin and punished by a flood of evil thoughts, will be saved if it draws near to the Lord in faith, and the stream of its evil thoughts will be dried up through the power of Jesus Christ, the Lord of the world.

2. For, although the soul may have been wounded by the enemy in the struggle and blinded by the darkness brought by its sins, yet even such a soul as this, provided that its good will holds firm and that it thirsts for the God-Jesus and calls to Him to come and save it, will still be healed through the mercy of the

Lord. And once the soul has seen the true light, it will never again be blind; once it has been healed of its wounds, it will never again have to suffer from its evil passions.

3. That is why, my dearly beloved, you must ask day and night for this divine power to be granted to you. It will remove the veil from the eyes of the interior man, and take away all his bitter thoughts and evil plans. It will cleanse and purify the eyes of your heart, enabling them to contemplate God in all purity. And it is this power, too, which will purge your soul of all worldly cares. That is why, my dearly beloved, you must this instant implore God to send the Paraclete down to you from above, for the Lord has Himself promised to send the Holy Spirit to all who ask it of Him, to let Himself be found by all who look for Him, and to open to all who knock at His door. And His promise is true.

4. It is, indeed, essential for a man to take up the struggle against his thoughts, if the veils woven from his thoughts and covering up his intellect are going to be removed, thus enabling him to turn his gaze without difficulty towards God and to avoid following the will of his wandering thoughts. When they do begin to wander, however, he must recollect them and distinguish the good intention in the soul from the thoughts which come from the Evil One. Indeed, those who watch continually over their innermost thoughts have to keep up an unceasing struggle. But the man who clings with all his heart to the will of God follows neither his own will nor that of Satan but solely God's will, as it is written: *My son, do not follow after the desires of your soul, but turn it aside from its own concupiscence* (Eccl 5:2). For concupiscence always gives birth to sin (see Jas 1:15), and the man who follows his own will is like one who follows the will of his enemy (see Eccl 18:31).

5. When souls wishing to please God first enlist as disciples, it is the Spirit of penance who comes down on them. Then, when He has purified and cleansed them of all the foulness of their sins,

He leads them in purity and joy to the Holy Spirit, and from that moment keeps pouring out on them a fragrant perfume all the days of their life. Henceforward, they find their delight in God Himself, in the love which He bears them. Glory be to His immeasurable mercy throughout all ages. Amen.

83. Pilgrim, Not Vagabond

ST. ROBERT SOUTHWELL
To a priest, A.D. *1589*

I am much grieved to hear of your unsettled way of life, visiting many people, at home with none. We are all, I acknowledge, pilgrims, but not vagrants; our life is uncertain, but not our road. The curse made Cain a vagabond and wanderer upon the earth. Conscience wounded by sin renders life also uneasy. Inconstancy is a disease of the mind, always changing to new places, never able to find a holy thought wherein it can rest. Variety of company is the mother of idleness and instability, and is more apt to corrupt than to perfect the disposition, however good. Who is more sun-burnt than he who is always travelling? A change of objects maybe feeds the eyes, but they suffer heavier damage from the wind and dust. Virtue is seldom found in the highway, and rare is the company from which you come forth more innocent. Experience is dear, if bought with danger to a good life. It is better to be ignorant of other men's manners, than to be a stranger at home. It is difficult to adapt one canvas to so many different models. Diversity begets confusion, but perfects not art. It is difficult to imitate even one thing correctly. Graft your thoughts into some good stock, suck the sap from a fruitful root. Change of juices does not ripen, but rots the fruit. He who is familiar with all is friend to none. You will never be your own, if always with everybody. Among many strangers you will have but few friends.

Transplant not your mind into such varieties; suffer it to take root in some one soil. Plants frequently transplanted sooner wither than blossom. It is an unwholesome appetite that tastes of everything and relishes nothing. He who sips of all and sticks to none is unsteady of heart. Recall, then, your senses. Restrain your wandering mind. Think upon a new course. Count yourself worthy of something to which you may in future adhere. Be at home somewhere, and there live by rule; then go forth to other places, like a guest looking towards home. Imitate the bees which suck the honey from the flowers, and immediately return to the hive, and there go about domestic duties, which begin with prudence and end with profit. I wish you to place a measure to your social disposition, not as I would cage a bird, or condemn an owl to the dark. There is a medium between mute solitude or silent obscurity, and a continual change of company; both these extremes are equally bad; the mean between them is best when we converse, whenever there is a call to do so, and collect at stated times. Set before your eyes nature herself; the seasons, day and night, are lessons of this kind of life. Some circumstances call us abroad, others invite us to retirement. Learn while at home how to behave in company, and instruct your mind how to nourish in secret holy thoughts, which in the exercise of every virtue will prove to you sweeter than all possible delights; wherewith may you live both a long and a holy life (which from my heart I wish you). Farewell.

84. Watch Your Step

ST. ANSELM
C. 1095

To his dearly beloved sisters and daughters Archbishop Anselm wishes health, and together with God's blessing, imparts his own for what it is worth.

I rejoice and thank God to learn of the high purpose and the holy relationship you share in the love of God and in sanctity of life. Your affection for me, beloved daughters, which in truth I hold dear, makes you beg me to send you some advice which will instruct and inspire you to live a meritorious life. Since then I ought to comply with your earnest petition if I can, I will try to set down a few points helpful to your purpose.

My dear daughters, every praiseworthy or blameworthy act derives its good or bad qualities solely from the will. For from the will comes the root and source of those acts that lie within our power; and even if we cannot fulfill our aim, yet each one will be judged before God according to his intention. So do not look so much at what you accomplish as at what you aim at doing; not so much at your deeds as at your intention. Every act performed with a right, that is an upright, intention is good; and one performed with an evil intention is not good. In virtue of his righteous intention a man is designated just, precisely as in virtue of his evil intention he is designated unjust. If you wish to live a virtuous life, then keep unceasing watch over your will in matters both great and trifling. In things that are within your own power, and in things that are beyond you, let it not swerve a hairsbreadth from the straight path. If you want to test whether your intention is right—it is undoubtedly so if it is in accordance with God's will. Therefore, when you resolve upon or prepare to do anything of importance, you must ask yourselves: Does God approve my determination to do this, or does He not? If your conscience answers you: I am certain that God approves this desire of mine, that He is pleased with my intention, then whether you can or whether you cannot carry out your plan, yet you should hold fast to your intention. But if your conscience warns you that God does not wish you to persevere in your project, then you must abandon it with all your might; and if you really and truly want to be rid of it, you must as far as possible shut out from your heart all thought and remembrance of it.

Now if you want to drive away a wicked thought or desire, just grasp this little piece of advice I am going to give you, and stick to it. Do not argue with perverse thoughts or evil desires, but when they attack you, occupy your mind vigorously with some profitable meditation or plan until they vanish away. No thought or intention is ever expelled from the heart except by some other thought or intention incompatible with it. You must maintain your position in regard to bad thoughts and intentions in such a way that while you strain every nerve to recover good ones, your mind will scorn even to remember or notice the others. Now if when you wish to pray or to busy yourself with some good train of thought, you are beset by ideas such as you ought not to admit, you must never consent to give up the good work you had begun because of their importunity, otherwise the devil who has instigated them will rejoice at having caused you to forsake your good beginnings. Conquer them rather by despising them in the way I have suggested. Do not be grieved or worried at their attack, so long as you disregard and give no consent to them, as I have pointed out. If you are upset, they may take advantage of your dejection to return to your memory and renew their annoyances. It is a fact that the human mind has a habit of remembering whatever pleases or displeases it far more frequently than anything it feels or considers to be beneath its notice.

In much the same way a person ought to be very careful in keeping to her holy resolution in regard to any unbecoming impulse in body or soul, such as a temptation to impurity, anger, envy, or vainglory. These temptations will most easily be eradicated when we refuse to let ourselves notice them or advert to them, or do anything under their influence. Nor must you be afraid that impulses or thoughts of this kind will be imputed to you as sin, so long as your will in no way entangles itself with them, because there is no condemnation for those who are in

Christ Jesu, who walk not according to the flesh. To walk according to the flesh means to give deliberate consent to the flesh. The flesh is the Apostle's name for every vicious impulse of soul or body, which he expresses in the words: *The flesh lusts against the spirit, and the spirit against the flesh*. Suggestions of this kind are in practice easily suppressed if we trample on them as soon as they appear, in the way I have recommended; but it becomes difficult when once we have let them worm their way into our minds.

May the almighty and merciful Lord grant you absolution and remission of all your sins, and make you progress always with humility to an ever-higher life and never fall away. Amen.

85. God Alone

ST. JOHN OF THE CROSS
To a religious, his penitent, April 14, 1589

The peace of Jesus Christ, son, be ever in your soul. I received Your Reverence's letter, in which you tell me of the great desires that our Lord gives you to occupy your will with Him alone, and to love Him above all things, and in which you ask me to give you a few directions as to how you may achieve this.

I rejoice that God has given you such holy desires and I shall rejoice much more at your putting them into execution. To this end you should notice that all pleasures, joys, and affections are ever caused in the soul by the will and desire for things which appear to you good, fitting, and delectable, since the soul considers these to be pleasing and precious; and in this way the desires of the will are drawn to them, and it hopes for them, and rejoices in them when it has them, and fears to lose them; and thus, through its affections for things and rejoicing in them, the soul becomes perturbed and unquiet.

So, in order to annihilate and mortify these affections for

pleasures with respect to all that is not God, your Reverence must note that all that wherein the will can have a distinct joy is that which is sweet and delectable, since this appears pleasant to it, and no sweet and delectable thing wherein it can rejoice and delight is God, for, as God cannot come within the apprehensions of the other faculties, so neither can He come within the desires and pleasures of the will; for in this life, even as the soul cannot taste of God essentially, so none of the sweetness and delight that it tastes, howsoever sublime it be, can be God; for, further, all that the will can have pleasure in and desire as a distinct thing, it desires in so far as it knows it to be such or such an object. Then, since the will has never tasted God as He is, neither has known Him beneath any apprehension of the desire, and consequently knows not what God is like, it cannot know what it is like to taste Him, nor can its being and desire and experience attain to the knowledge of the desire for God, since He is above all its capacity.

And thus it is clear that no distinct object from among all objects that the will can enjoy is God. Wherefore, in order to become united with Him, a man must empty and strip himself of every inordinate affection of desire and pleasure for all that can be distinctly enjoyed, whether it be high or low, temporal or spiritual, to the end that the soul may be purged and clean from all inordinate desires, joys, and pleasures whatsoever and may thus be wholly occupied, with all its affections, in loving God. For, if in any wise the will can comprehend God and become united with Him, it is by no apprehensible means of the desire, but by love; and, as neither delight nor sweetness nor any pleasure that can pertain to the will is love, it follows that none of these delectable feelings can be a proportionate means whereby the will may unite itself with God, but only the operation of the will, for the operation of the will is very different from its feeling; it is through the operation that it becomes united with God, and has its end in Him, who is love, and not through the feeling and apprehension of its desire, which makes its home in the soul as its end and object. The feelings can only serve as motives for love if the will desires to pass beyond them, and not otherwise; and thus delectable feelings do not of themselves lead the soul to God, but cause it to rest in themselves; but in the operation of the will, which is to love God, the soul sets on Him alone its affection, joy, pleasure, contentment, and love, leaving all things behind and loving Him above them all.

Wherefore, if any man be moved to love God otherwise than by the sweetness which he feels, he is already leaving this sweetness behind him and setting his love on God, whom he feels not; for, if he set it upon the sweetness and pleasure that he feels, dwelling upon this and resting in it, this would be to set it upon creatures or things pertaining thereto and to turn the motive into the object and the end; and consequently the act of the will would become harmful; for, as God is incomprehensible and inaccessible, the will, in order to direct its act of love towards God, has not to set it upon that which it can touch and apprehend with the desire, but upon that which it cannot comprehend or attain thereby. And in this way the will remains loving that which is certain, in very truth, by the light of faith, being empty and in darkness, with respect to its feelings, and transcending above all that it can feel with the understanding, and with its own intelligence, believing and loving beyond all that it can understand.

And thus he would be very ignorant who should think that, because spiritual delight and sweetness are failing him, God is failing him, and should rejoice and be glad if he should have them and think that for this reason he has been having God. And still more ignorant would he be if he went after God in search of this sweetness, and rejoiced and rested in it; for in this case he would not be seeking God with his will grounded in the emptiness of faith and charity, but spiritual sweetness and pleasure, which is of creature, following his taste and desire; and thus he would not then love God purely, above all things (which means to set the whole strength of the will upon Him), for, if he seizes hold upon that creature and clings to it with the desire, his will rises not above it to God, who is inaccessible; for it is impossible that the will can rise to the sweetness and delight of divine union, or embrace God or experience His sweet and loving embraces, save in detachment and emptying of the desire with respect to every particular pleasure whether from above or from below; for it is this that David meant when he said: *Dilata os tuum, et implebo illud* (Ps 80:11).

It must be known, then, that the desire is the mouth of the will, which opens wide when it is not impeded or filled with any morsel—that is, with any pleasure; for, when the desire is set upon anything, it becomes constrained, and apart from God everything is constraint. And therefore, in order for the soul to succeed in reaching God and to become united with Him, it must have the mouth of its will opened to God alone, and freed from any morsel of desire, to the end that God may satisfy it and fill it with His love and sweetness, and it may still have that hunger and thirst for God alone and refuse to be satisfied with aught else, since here on earth it cannot taste God as He is; and furthermore, that which it can taste, if it so desire, as I say, impedes it. This was taught by Isaiah when he said: *All you that thirst, come to the waters,* etc. (Is 55:1). Here he invites those that thirst for God alone to the fullness of the divine waters of union with God, though they have no money—that is, no desire.

Very meet is it, then, if your Reverence would enjoy great peace in your soul and achieve perfection, that you should surrender your whole will to God, so that it may thus be united with Him, and that you should not employ it in the vile and base things of earth.

May His Majesty make you as spiritual and holy as I desire.

86. Prayer

St. Augustine
To a noble lady, A.D. 411

You asked me, I remember, to write you something on prayer, and I promised to do so as soon as He to whom we pray should give me time and opportunity. So I now feel it my bounden duty to discharge my debt and in the love of Christ meet your devout request. How much your desire gladdened me as showing your high sense of a high duty, words cannot express.

In the darkness of this world where pilgrim-wise we journey far from the Lord, as long as we walk by faith and not by sight (see 2 Cor 5:6-7), the Christian soul ought to account itself desolate and never cease to pray, learning to fix the eye of faith on the divine word of the holy Scriptures as *on a light shining in a dark place until the day dawn and the day-star arise in our hearts* (2 Pt 1:19). For the ineffable source from which this lamp borrows its light is the Light that shines in darkness but the darkness does not comprehend it. To see it, our hearts must be purified by faith: *Blessed are the clean of heart for they shall see God* (Mt 5:8); and *We know that when he shall appear we shall be like to him, because we shall see him as he is* (1 Jn 3:2)—after death, true life; after desolation, true consolation; a life which delivers our souls from death and a consolation which restrains our eyes from tears.

Why do we scatter our desires and why fear that we shall not pray as we ought and why ask therefore what to pray for? Why not rather say with the Psalmist: *One thing I have asked of the Lord, this will I seek after; that I may dwell in the house of the Lord all the days of my life; that I may see the delight of the Lord and may visit his temple.* For there *all the days* are not differentiated by their coming and going: the beginning of one is not the end of another: they are all unending, constituting as they do a life which is itself without end. In order to obtain this life of bliss, true blissful Life Himself has taught us to pray, not in long rigmaroles as though the more wordy we were, the surer we were heard, because we are addressing One who, as our Lord tells us, knows what is needful for us before we ask Him (Mt 6:7, 8). It may seem surprising, however, that after forbidding us to speak much, He who knows what we need before we ask should say to us: *Men ought always to pray and faint not.* He proceeds to give us the example of the widow who desired revenge against an enemy. By her constant entreaties she forced an unjust judge to give way not from motives of justice or mercy but overcome through sheer weariness of her importunity. So are we taught how our merciful and just Lord God will of a certainty give ear to persevering prayer, when this widow by dint of continual begging prevailed over the indifference of an unjust and wicked judge. Moreover, she obtained her desire which was nothing less than vengeance, and so what will be the readiness and lovingkindness with which God will fulfill the holy desires of those who He knows have forgiven others their trespasses? Our Lord gives us a similar lesson in the story of the man visited by a friend on a journey. The man had not the wherewithal to set a meal before him and wanted to borrow three loaves from another friend of his—in which, perhaps, there is a figure of the Trinity of Persons in one substance. Finding him and all his servants asleep he knocked in a way so persistent and so annoying that the friend was completely roused from his slumbers and gave him as many as he wanted, not because he felt at all kindly disposed towards him but simply to avoid further disturbance. Therefore if a man is forced to give away even against his will because someone in need would give him no rest until he did, with how much more merciful kindness will He give who never sleeps but rather rouses us from sleep to make us ask from Him?

It is to impress this lesson upon us that He adds: *Ask, and it shall be given you; seek, and you shall find, knock, and it shall be opened to you. For everyone that asketh receiveth; and he that seeketh findeth; and to him that knocketh it shall be opened. And which of you, if he ask his father for bread, will he give him a stone? Or a fish, will he for a fish give him a serpent? Or if he shall ask an egg, will he reach him a scorpion? If you then, being evil, know how to give good gifts to your children, how much more will your Father from heaven give the good Spirit to them that ask him?* (Lk 11:9-13). We have here those three things commended by the Apostle: by the fish is signified faith, either because of the water of Baptism, or because it remains unharmed amid the tempestuous waves of this world; in contrast with which is the serpent that with his poisonous guile persuaded men to disbelieve God. By the egg is signified hope, because the life of the young bird is not yet evident but is to be—it is not seen but hoped for, because *hope which is seen is not hope* (Rom 8:24); in contrast with which is the scorpion, for the man who hopes for eternal life forgets the things that are behind and stretches forth to those that lie before, since it is dangerous to look back; but the scorpion is to be feared because of what lies in its tail—its sharp and poisonous sting. Bread signifies charity, for *the greatest of these is charity* (1 Cor 13:13) and bread surpasses all other food in worth; in contrast to which is the stone, for hearts that are hardened refuse to exercise charity.

Thus when we practice faith, hope, and charity with continual desire, we pray always. But at the same time we also set aside stated hours and times devoted to explicit prayer to God according to the Apostle's instruction: *Let your petitions be made known to God* (Phil 4:6), not indeed as though we are giving God information, because He knows them before we say a word, but rather that in the presence of God we ourselves should realize all we need and wait patiently upon Him. It is, therefore, neither wrong nor unprofitable to spend a long time in prayer (although, as I have said, in desire we ought always to be in an attitude of prayer), provided that we do not neglect other good and necessary works. To spend a long time in prayer is not, as some think, the same as praying "with much speaking." Multiplied words are one thing, long-continued warmth of desire is another. It is written of our Lord Himself that He spent the whole night in prayer and that being in an agony He prayed the longer.

We are told how the monks of Egypt prayed very frequently but very briefly. Their prayer was sudden and ejaculatory so that the intense application so necessary in prayer should not vanish or lose its keenness by a slow performance. By this practice they show clearly enough that just as, on the one hand, this close attention must not be exhausted if it cannot last long, on the other if it can be sustained it must not be abruptly snapped. Far be it from us to spend our prayer in much speaking, or to refuse to pray much so long as the soul is rapt in fervent intensity. To speak much is to employ a superfluity of words to ask for the one thing necessary, but to pray much is to have a heart throbbing with a glowing abiding love for Him to whom we pray. Usually prayer is a question of groaning rather than speaking, tears rather than words. For He sets our tears in His sight and our groaning is not hidden from Him who made all things by His Word and does not ask for words of man.

For us human beings, however, words are a necessity, not because they acquaint God with what we want or change His designs but because they help us to see into ourselves and face our needs. When therefore we say: *Hallowed be thy name,* we stir up in ourselves the desire that God's name, essentially holy in itself, may also be esteemed holy by men and not despised; it brings no profit to God but to men. And when we say: *Thy kingdom come,* although it is bound to come whether we wish it or not, we arouse a longing in our own souls for that kingdom, that it may come within ourselves, that we may be found worthy to reign therein. When we say: *Thy will be done on earth as it is in heaven,* we beg of God the grace of obedience so that we may do His will as the angels do in the heavens. When we say: *Give us this day our daily bread,* we use the word "today" to signify this present life and ask for a sufficiency of temporal blessings; and because bread exceeds all the rest in value it is used to express the whole of our needs: or else we refer to the Sacrament of faith which we are bound to receive in this present life, not indeed for this present life but to obtain the happiness of eternal life. When we say: *Forgive us our trespasses as we forgive them that trespass against us,* we remind ourselves that what we are asking for, the same have we to do; we must merit the boon of forgiveness. When we say: *Lead us not into temptation,* we call to mind how we are to beg God not to withdraw His help for fear we be deceived and in our weakness yield to some temptation or be overcome by its strength. When we say: *Deliver us from evil,* we reflect upon the fact that we are not yet in possession of that bliss where no ill is to be suffered. And this last petition of the Lord's prayer is so comprehensive that in whatever trouble he finds himself, a Christian may well use it to give utterance to his tears and vent his groans, he may begin his prayer with this petition, employ it throughout, and conclude with it.

For whatever other words we use, if we pray rightly and fittingly, we say nothing more than is already to be found in the Lord's prayer. Whosoever asks for anything that cannot find its place in that prayer from the Gospel is making, if not exactly unlawful, at least unspiritual prayer. If you run through the petitions of all holy prayers, I believe that you will find nothing that is not summed up and contained in the Lord's prayer. In praying, therefore, we are quite free to use any words that please us, but we must ask for the same things. We are left no choice in the matter. It is faith, hope, and charity that lead to God the soul that prays, i.e. the soul that believes, hopes, desires, and seeks for guidance as to what to ask God by a study of the Lord's prayer.

And whoever begs from God that "one thing" and seeks after it, does so in perfect confidence, because that one thing is the only true, the only happy life in which, with bodies and souls immortal and incorruptible, we shall contemplate the joy of the Lord for evermore. All other things we desire and quite rightly demand with a view to this one end. In it is the fountain of life for which we now thirst in prayer as long as we live in hope, not yet seeing the things we hope for, trusting under the covert of His wings before whom is all our desire, that we may be inebriated with the plenty of His house and made to drink of the torrent of His pleasure. For with Him is the fountain of life and in His light we shall see light (Ps 35:8-10).

87. *Ne Quid Nimis*

ST. FRANCIS DE SALES
To a lady of high rank, Anneçy, April 26, 1617

[Probably in deference to his correspondent, who may have feared the letter should go astray, St. Francis refers to her throughout in the third person as Barbe-Marie.]

Dearly beloved daughter, here is my reply to your letter of the 14th.

1. Tell that endearing Barbe-Marie who loves me very much and whom I love even more, to talk as freely as she likes about God wherever she feels it may do good, and cheerfully ignore what her listeners may say or think about her. To put it briefly, I've already made her duty plain: never do or say anything to win praise, never leave anything undone or unsaid for fear of being praised. And it is not hypocritical if one's deeds fail to match one's words. Good gracious! Where should we be if it were? I

should have to hold my tongue to avoid playing the hypocrite, since it would follow that were I to speak of perfection I should assume I was perfect. Certainly not, my very dear child. I no more believe I am perfect because I talk about perfection than I should believe myself Italian because I speak Italian. However, I do believe that I am acquainted with the language of perfection; I have learned it in conversation with those who spoke it.

2. Tell her to powder her hair since she does it with a right intention; going into detail over a thing like that isn't worth the trouble. There is no need to get your mind entangled in such cobwebs. The hair of my daughter's mind is even finer than the hair of her head, and that is why it causes her trouble. She must not split hairs as she does, or fritter away time on objections which simply do not matter to our Lord. So give her instructions to go ahead in all confidence, and to steer a middle course by the attractive virtues of simplicity and humility, instead of carrying things to extremes by subtle distinctions and argument. Let her boldly powder her hair then. After all, don't pheasants, those pretty creatures, give their feathers a good dust-bath so as not to breed lice?

3. Let her never lose an opportunity of a sermon or good work for want of saying: Look sharp! But say it sweetly and calmly. If when at table she realizes that the Blessed Sacrament is being carried by, let her accompany it only in desire if anybody else is present; if she is alone, she may go and accompany it provided that she can arrive in time without making a fuss, and afterwards let her return peacefully and resume her meal, for our Lord would not allow even Martha to serve Him with indiscriminate zeal.

4. I have told her that she may use firm and resolute language when it is called for, in order to make a certain person fulfill his duty, but her words will carry the more weight in proportion as they are spoken in a low tone, are ruled by

reason, and are completely free from passion.

5. Let her advance in prayer either by using points of meditation, as I have said, or in the way she has been accustomed to pray—it matters little. I seem to remember that I simply told her to prepare the points, and at least when she begins, to try to linger over them. If she finds it to her liking, it is a sign that God wishes her to follow this method at least for the present. However, should His sweet presence afterwards steal over her, let her yield to it and also to the conversation she makes in the name of God Himself; this method is quite good, to judge from the account she gives in your letter; but all the same, it is sometimes necessary to speak to this mighty All, and be ready for our nothing to face an encounter with something. Now since you read my books I shall say no more, except to tell you to go forward with simplicity, candor, freedom, and the guilelessness of a babe, now carried in your heavenly Father's arms, now led by His hand.

I am very pleased that my books have gained admittance into that mind of yours which was so foolhardy as to think it was self-sufficient. But the books are the product of a father's heart, and you happen to be that father's dear daughter, since such is God's good pleasure. To Him be glory and honor for ever.

88. Recipe Against Melancholy

St. Teresa of Avila
To a layman, Segovia, July 3, 1574

May the grace of the Holy Spirit be with your Lordship. I tell you, here and now, that if you ever address a letter to me in that way again, I shall not answer it. I don't know why you want to displease me, as you do every time you write, though I had not properly realized how displeased it could make me until today. Will your Lordship please find out from the Father Rector how he addresses me: nothing more should be put than that, and the form of address you use is altogether at variance with the spirit of my Order. I was glad to hear that the Father Rector is well, as I have been anxious about him. I beg your Lordship to give him my remembrances.

This seems to me extremely unsuitable weather for you to undergo your cure in. May the Lord grant it will turn out as I shall beseech Him it may. May His Majesty also bring your servants back safe and well. That is my prayer to Him, but I wish you would not worry about it so much. What a bad effect all that worry must have on your health! Oh, if we realized these truths, how few earthly things would trouble us!

Take no notice of that feeling you get of wanting to leave off in the middle of your prayer, but praise the Lord for the desire you have to pray: that, you may be sure, comes from your will, which loves to be with God. It is just melancholy that oppresses you and gives you the feeling of constraint. Try occasionally, when you find yourself oppressed in that way, to go to some place where you can see the sky, and walk up and down a little: doing that will not interfere with your prayer, and we must treat this human frailty of ours in such a way that our nature is not subjected to undue constraint. We are seeking God all the time, and it is because of this that we go about in search of means to that end, and it is essential that the soul should be led gently. But in this matter, and in all others, my Father Rector will understand what is best for you better than I.

89. Friend to Friend

St. Bernard
A.D. *1149*

To the reverend father and lord Peter, by the grace of God Abbot of Cluny, the humble devotion of Bernard, styled Abbot of Clairvaux.

O you good man, what have you done? You have praised a sinner, you have numbered a good-for-nothing amongst the blessed! You must now pray that I shall not be led into error if, in my delight at such great praises, I were to forget the sort of person I am. This almost did happen when I read the letter in which you made me out to be blessed. If words could do that, how happy I would be. Even now I would call myself happy, but by your favor not by my own deserts. Happy to be loved by you and happy in loving you. Would that I could enjoy your company, I do not say always, nor even often, but just once or twice in a year. For a long time now we have been united in the closest friendship, and an equal affection has rendered us equals. What could a person of my lowly attainments have in common with a man like you, if you were not so tolerant of my limitations? Thus it has come about that both my lowliness and your magnanimity have been so blended that I could not be lowly without you nor you magnanimous without me. I say this because my son Nicholas has greatly disturbed me by telling me that he noticed that one of my letters to you concluded with bitter words. Believe me who love you that nothing could have come from my heart or left my lips which would have offended your ears. My many occupations are to blame, because when my secretaries have not fully grasped my meaning they are apt to write too sharply, and I have not time to read through what they have written. Forgive me this time, for whatever I may do with other letters, I shall in future look through my letters to you and trust no one's ears or eyes but my own. Greet for me all your holy brethren, and pray them to pray for me.

90. A Letter at Last!

ST. ANSELM
C. *1090*

To Dom Gondulph, my revered master, dearest brother, most loyal friend, Brother Anselm sends greeting.

Whenever I make up my mind to write to you, soul most beloved of my soul, whenever I make up my mind to write, I feel puzzled to know how best to begin. My feeling towards you is indeed sweetness and song to my heart, and I wish you the greatest blessings my mind can devise. From the moment I laid eyes on you, you know how deeply I loved you; I hear reports of you that make me long after you, God alone knows to what extent; and so wherever you wander my affection follows you, and wherever I remain, my desire encircles you. But when you beg me by your messengers, urge me by your letters, importune me by your gifts to keep you in remembrance, then *let my tongue stick fast to the roof of my mouth if I remember thee not* (Ps 136:6), if I find in anyone but Gondulph the very perfection of friendship. How should I ever forget you? How could he perish from memory who is impressed upon my heart as a seal on wax?

Now tell me: why do you complain with such a mournful face that you never receive a line from me? Why do you ask with such affection that I should write frequently, when you have me always with you in thought? When you keep silence, I realize that *you love me;* and when I make no sign, *surely thou knowest that I love thee* (Jn 21:16)? You are constantly present in my mind because I never for a moment doubt you, and I hereby swear to you that you can feel equally certain of me. Since then we are aware that each is present to the other's consciousness, we have only to send each other a word to allow us to share our joys together and likewise our anxieties. You will learn more fully from the bearer than from the writer of this letter how things are going with me, to make you rejoice or grieve accordingly. Give my greetings to your Dom Osbern in place of my own dear dead Osbern. Farewell, farewell, beloved, and in order to pay you back for your pertinacity, I pray and pray and pray, remember me, and do not forget the soul of my dear Osbern. If prayer for both of us should seem too much of a burden, then drop me—but do remember him.

91. The Parting of Friends

ST. PETER CANISIUS
To the German Jesuit Novices in Rome, May 1548

My Brothers in Christ, dear and desired, I have so much to tell you, so many things glad and sad to say, that I scarcely know how to begin my letter. It is a very sweet experience when a man folds his friend to his heart and looks upon his face again, especially when that friend has come from far away bringing with him the expectation and ardent desires of many a month. So, too, men cannot help feeling a certain corresponding sadness when they have reason to believe that the long-sought means and opportunities to improve their friendships may be removed from them, not for a time only but for good. In this way I think it is possible that both you and I may find some small trouble taking possession of our souls, you at seeing your old friend Canisius, the one man you knew in Rome, spirited suddenly far away from you just as you arrived in the City, and I, because deprived of the chance to welcome my eagerly awaited brothers, among the first of our

Society's sons from Germany, after their long and arduous journey. That journey, however, had a happy end, for it placed you in the center of all that is mighty and magnificent in the world and gave you, as you now know, the best of fathers and the truest of brothers to delight your hearts.

As for the solid development of our friendship, we must not measure that by our nearness to one another in the flesh, which is a mean and vulgar standard, for it consists rather in likeness of soul and harmony of will. Since, then, our endeavors to serve Christ are of one pattern and our ways of life very similar, how can we, with the breath of the Holy Spirit upon us, be anything but united wherever we are? How can the miles between us sunder our souls, or ever silence the converse of heart with heart?

So, since our souls have come from God and are soon to be gathered to Him again in heaven, let us despise, dearest brothers, the perishable globe of this earth, this dark prison that keeps from us the glorious eternal light and involves us, beaten and troubled, in the tangles of a thousand errors, snares, vanities, and concupiscences. One refuge and solace alone remains, which is that we who are bound to one another by charity's beautiful engagements should graft and establish our souls in Christ, serve Him with a freeman's service, drink of His spirit, win Him in our sufferings and our dying, and possess Him in everlasting beatitude.

92. The Gift of Sleep

St. Teresa of Avila
To a Carmelite friar, Avila, December 1577 [?]

... I praise our Lord, who gives your Paternity that tranquillity and the desire to please Him in everything. It is wonderful mercy on His part that He should occasionally grant you illumination in the shape of such great favors. After all, His Majesty will give you help proportionate to your trials; and so, as you are suffering great trials, you will enjoy great favors too. Blessed be His name for ever and ever.

I assure you, my Father, it will be a good thing if your Paternity can sleep. You see, you have a lot of work to do and, until your head gets into a hopeless state, you do not realize how you are overtaxing your strength. And you know how important it is that you should be well. So, for the love of God, look at the thing from another point of view, and stop devoting the hours in which you ought to be asleep either to making plans—however necessary they may be—or to prayer. Please do this out of kindness to me, for often, when the devil sees that someone is very fervent in spirit, he keeps drawing his attention to things which seem of great importance for the service of God, so that if he cannot prevent good being done in one way, he will do so in another.

93. Use Your Common Sense!

ST. CATHERINE DEI RICCI
To a layman, Prato, January 6, 1561

You tell me you do not feel well, and I quite believe it although I do not see what can be done. Religious who are separated from the world and have neither business nor family obligations are bound to lead a much more mortified and rigorous life than others. But you as the head of a great house with all the cares of a family upon your shoulders ought to be very prudent about preserving your life and health, not for the sake of enjoying this world's pleasures but in order to support your family as you should, and to give your children a true Christian training. I would remind you that we shall have to give an account at the judgment of our indiscretion as well as of our self-indulgence.

Now that you are at Florence, I am afraid no one will think of giving you broth and biscuits for supper, and therefore I am sending you a basket of chestnuts with the injunction to eat at least four every evening. We have to aim at life not death, at doing good in order to honor and glorify God in ourselves. I wish you would not do things beyond your strength: you will injure yourself irreparably. For instance, you ought not to have gone from here. You were told so often enough, but you only answered, "Whether it snow, or whether it hail, go I will." It is useless to argue with a man who has made up his mind, and you were determined to go, come what might, although I was very sorry to hear it and had I been able, would have kept a single drop from falling on your dear head. But you would not obey me who am so full of concern for you. Then came your accident and your difficulty in getting home.

Here we are at nine o'clock on Tuesday evening, and I assume that you have ended your day and retired to bed. I feel sure that this weather is really injurious to your health, so I do beg you to take care of yourself in all simplicity at least until mid-April. Do it for the love of our Lord, and in order to gain time to work for God—for that should be our true aim.

The wine arrived, and I was given some of it at collation last night after I had read your letter, for my throat had swollen very much on hearing of your troubles. But your news was so bitter that the sweetness of the wine was lost on me. This morning, however, I found the taste sweet, and thank you for the gift. Last night and this morning I remembered you and offered to our Lord your body, soul, and heart, your memory, understanding, and will. They are like the six water-pots and I implored Him to change their water into wine. I prayed that, as wine purifies and preserves, so your mind may be purified from all that disturbs it, and your good will preserved by means of meritorious works. I beg you likewise to be mindful of me, and look forward to the day when we shall see each other, not at St. Peter's, nor at Florence nor Prato, but in Paradise, in the fruition of Jesus and His blessed Mother and the whole court of heaven.

94. The Rhythm of Life

ST. ROBERT SOUTHWELL
To his friend, Thomas Howard, September 30, 1591

There is in this world a continual interchange of pleasing and afflicting accidents, still keeping their succession of times, and overtaking each other in their several courses. No picture can be all drawn of the brightest colors, nor a harmony consorted only of trebles; shadows are needful in expressing of proportions, and the bass is a principal part in perfect music: the condition of our exile here alloweth no unmingled joy; our whole life is tempered between sweet and sour, and we must all look for a mixture of both. The wise so wist, prepared both for the better and the worse; accepting the one, if it come, with liking, and bearing the other without impatience, being so much masters of every turn of fortune, that none shall work them to excess. The dwarf groweth not on the highest hill, nor doth the tall man lose his height in the lowest valley. And as a base mind, though most at ease, will be dejected, so a resolute virtue is most impregnable in the deepest distress.

They evermore most perfectly enjoy their comforts, who least fear their contraries; for a desire to enjoy carrieth with it a fear to lose, and both desire and fear are enemies to quiet possession, making men less owners of God's benefits, than tenants at His will. The cause of our troubles is, that our misfortunes happen, either to unwitting or unwilling minds. Foresight preventeth the one, necessity the other: for he taketh away the smart of the present evils that attendeth their coming, and is not dismayed by any cross, that is armed against all.

Where necessity worketh without our consent, the effect should never greatly afflict us; grief being bootless where it cannot help; needless where there was no fault. God casteth the dice, and giveth us our chance; the most that we can do is to take the point that the cast will afford us, not grudging so much that it is no better, as comforting ourselves that it is no worse. If men were to lay all their evils together, to be afterwards divided by equal portions amongst them, most men would rather take what they brought than stand to the division; yet such is the partial judgment of self-love, that every man judgeth his self-misery too great, fearing he shall find some circumstance to increase it and make it intolerable: thus by thought he aggravates the evil.

When Moses threw his rod from him it became a serpent, ready to sting, and affrighted him so much as to make him fly; but being quietly taken up, it was a rod again, serviceable for his use and no way hurtful. The cross of Christ and the rod of every tribulation, seemeth to threaten stinging and terror to those who shun and eschew it, but they that mildly take it up and embrace it with patience may say with David, *thy rod and thy staff have been my comfort.* In this, affliction resembleth the crocodile: fly, it pursueth and frighteth; follow, it flieth and feareth; a shame to the constant, a tyrant to the timorous.

Hold not your eyes always upon your hardest haps; there are fairer parts in your body than scars. Let God strip you to the skin, yea to the soul, so He stay with you Himself: let His reproach be your honor, His poverty your riches, and He in lieu of all other friends. Think Him enough for this world that must be your possession for a whole eternity.

95. Neighborly Justice

ST. THOMAS MORE
To his wife, Woodstock, September 3, 1529

Mistress Alice, in my most hearty wise I recommend me to you.

And whereas I am informed by my son Heron of the loss of our barns and our neighbors' also with all the corn that was therein, albeit (saving God's pleasure) it were great pity of so much good corn lost, yet sith it hath liked Him to send us such a chance, we must and are bounden not only to be content but also to be glad of His visitation. He sent us all that we have lost and sith He hath by such a chance taken it away again His pleasure be fulfilled; let us never grudge thereat but take in good worth and heartily thank Him as well for adversity as for prosperity and peradventure we have more cause to thank Him for our loss than for our winning, for His wisdom better seeth what is good for us than we do ourselves. Therefore I pray you be of good cheer and take all the household with you to church and there thank God both for that He hath given us and for that He hath taken from us and for that He hath left us, which if it please Him He can increase when He will and if it please Him to leave us yet less, at His pleasure be it.

I pray you to make some good ensearch what my poor neighbors have lost and bid them take no thought therefor, for and I should not leave myself a spoon there shall no poor neighbor of mine bear no loss by any chance happened in my house. I pray you be with my children and your household merry in God and devise somewhat with your friends what way were the best to take for provision to be made for corn for our household and for seed this year coming, if ye think it good that we keep the ground still in our hands, and whether ye think it good that we so shall do or not, yet I think it were not best suddenly thus to leave it all up and to put away our folk off our farm, till we have some-what advised us thereon; howbeit if we have more now than ye shall need and which can get them other masters, ye may then discharge us of them, but I would not that any man were sud-denly sent away he wot nere whither. I shall, I think, because of this chance get leave this next week to come home and see you, and then shall we further devise together upon all things what order shall be best to take.

96. The Refugee Problem

St. Francis Xavier
To a fellow-Jesuit, Manapad, June 1544

I arrived back on Sunday evening having heard very bad news about the Cape Comorin Christians. The Badagas, I learned, were carrying them off as slaves, and the Christians, to save themselves, had taken refuge on some rocks out in the sea, where they are now dying of hunger and thirst. The winds were so contrary when I set out with twenty *tônis* to the succour of the fugitives, that neither by rowing nor by towing the boats with ropes from the shore could we reach the Cape. When the winds subside we shall have another try, and I shall do all in my power to help the poor souls whom it is the most pitiful thing in the world to see in such dire straits. Many of them arrive daily in Manapad, despoiled of everything and without food or clothing.

I have been along the land route to the Cape to meet the stricken Christians. They made the most lamentable sight you could imagine, here a group perishing for lack of food, there some old men vainly endeavoring to keep pace with the others. And the dead were all about, and husbands in mourning, and wives bringing babes into the world by the roadside, and many other sights to move one to tears. If you had seen what I have seen you would be as much heartbroken. I directed all the poor souls to Manapad and now the place is full of them. Oh, beg the Lord God to move the hearts of the rich so that they may have pity on those hapless ones. I have written to the headmen asking them to send alms for the unhappy Christians, but have told them that they are not to exact any contributions from poor people. Our hope is in God, so do not let them bring pressure to bear on anybody, whether rich or poor.

I have sent instructions to Father Coelho to get the boats launched and in readiness to embark all the villagers of your area, in case of emergency, for I am sure the Badagas will attempt to surprise you and capture the Christians. Make the people keep a vigilant watch on the mainland, as those Badagas who are mounted, pounce at night and capture the folk before they have time to get into their boats. Keep a close eye on your Christians, for they have so little sense that to save two *fanams* they would abandon their sentry duties. Make them launch all their boats at once and put their belongings into them, and get the women and children to pray, now as never before, for we have none to help us but God. Above all, see to it that a most vigilant watch is maintained at night and that spies are posted on the mainland. I greatly fear that with the moon now at the full they may come to the Coast by night on a foray, so mind that your people are on the alert during the night hours. May our Lord be your protector.

97. In Sickness

BLESSED JOHN OF AVILA
To a layman, A.D. 1560

You may well be content to serve our Lord in illness, for when He calls people to suffer instead of working for Him, He is calling them to a higher state. During our earthly exile, it is most fitting that we should carry the cross with Christ, who loved it so dearly that He chose to die on it. We can do this better in sickness than in health, for illness is repugnant to flesh and blood and can never cause vainglory. Great were the works of Christ in His mortal life, but greater far were His sufferings, which exceeded those of the whole world. This idea explains St. James's words: *My brethren, count it all joy, when you shall fall into divers temptations,* and again: *Patience hath a perfect work* (Jas 1:2, 4). Accept your illness then willingly, and be grateful to our Lord who sent it. If you bear this cross and burden well, He will send you interior and more painful trials, which He keeps for His dearest friends, to conform them to Himself. For though Christ's visible cross was great, it was not to be compared to that which, unknown to men, He bore in His soul.

Though you may think that God has taken you away from other work because you performed it badly, yet thank Him none the less for doing so. To be corrected by the hand of so loving a Father needs rather humility to restrain our excessive joy than patience to bear our punishment well. However, I fear that you may not profit by this sickness as you should, for sometimes beginners become lax in their religious duties when suffering from an illness which is not dangerous to life. How foolish it is to change physic into poison, and injure our souls with the thing God sends us for a remedy. Call on Him for aid with all your heart, that as He has weakened your body by His touch, your soul may run to Him the more swiftly. This infirmity is sent that your flesh may expiate its sins by suffering pain; so do not turn this chance of discharging your past debts into a time for incurring fresh ones.

Watch carefully over your conduct: do not think your body must have everything it wants, but by the aid of the Holy Ghost, offer it to Christ crucified, and He who let Himself be hung between two thieves will not drive you away. Although you cannot now keep up your customary reading and meditation as you would wish, still, do all you can without serious injury to your health. Our Lord is so good and so powerful that He gives strength to those He sees to be doing their best. Sometimes He bestows more favors on people who lie ill in bed and are unable to pray, than on others who spend hours in prayer. Perhaps He will show you this mercy, which depends solely on His good pleasure.

In conclusion, I beg you, for the love of God, not *to be carried about by every wind of doctrine* (Eph 4:14), but to preserve your high esteem for those persons through whose hands you have received divine mercy. Imitate the man in the Gospel who was born blind: he considered his cure a proof of his Master's goodness who had worked it, and would let no one persuade him to the contrary. He said: *If he be a sinner, I know not: one thing I know, that whereas I was blind, now I see* (Jn 9:25). Though this man said: *If he be a sinner,* yet he was evidently convinced of our Lord's justice, as is shown by his persistently maintaining it in his answers to the Jews, and also by Christ's making Himself known to him in the temple as the reward of his faith.

I beg our Blessed Lord who died for you to remain with you.

98. Astringent Advice

BLESSED SEBASTIAN VALFRÈ
To an invalid, A.D. 1690

Everything, whether you are well or sick, reduces itself to conforming yourself to God's sweet will; and one who can make good use of sickness will not be less perfect than one who makes good use of health and prosperity. We are too apt to judge of results by our own desire as to what they should be, and not according to what will conduce to our growth in holiness. Fever may hinder your prayers, but it cannot prevent you from being humble. Die when it pleases God you should, and if only His will be done in all things, all will be well. We have a father in our Congregation who has been dying, you might say, for twenty years and who cannot observe the Rule. Yet he is the joy and edification of the whole house on account of his patience, gentleness, and charity.

Try to understand these four great truths:

1. Every illness and every trial is permitted by God as the means whereby we can best ensure our salvation and as the material most fitted for our sanctification. Take your illness as a penance given you by God, who knows the extent of your debts to Him as well as the best way in which you can discharge them. He demands this payment and wants to be given it in coin of His own choosing. You should be content to do as He wishes, for He is satisfied with far less than you owe Him.

2. Read into everything God's explicit will. Love it and adore it, and trust in Him without seeking anything beyond His will, without even wanting to find out how long your trial is to continue. Suffer for our Lord, offering all to His most sacred Heart. Suffer with our Lord, uniting your sufferings to His. Receive them from His hand. Do not look for them, but do not refuse them, and value them as precious marks of favor which He

bestows on you. Do not desire to exchange them for others, but do not torment yourself by adding to them. Try to increase your knowledge of God by their means; be of good heart and be patient. Do not fix your eyes on the lash that scourges you, but at the loving hand and heart wielding it; kiss and adore. Do not even make known how much you suffer except, as far as it is fitting, to the physician of your body and the father of your soul.

3. God is not content to see you merely suffering with patience. He wants you to be grateful, and to approve of what He does. You are not the only one in the world! So many of the elect are suffering on earth; and so many of the blessed envy you from heaven and would change places with you if they could.

4. Feel a more lively gratitude towards those who brace you up and invigorate you in your pain than towards those who merely commiserate you. An unpitied pain wins greater merit before God. Never say to God: "Enough," simply say: "I am ready!" When it is all over, you will not regret having suffered; rather you will regret having suffered so little and suffered that little so badly. Finally, do not give trouble to those who wait on you, and do not be exacting with your nurses.

99. Inordinate Fear of Death

St. Francis de Sales
To a penitent, Annecy, April 7, 1617

I am seizing the earliest opportunity to write and fulfill my promise by laying before you a few thoughts which, if you reflect on them, may lessen that fear of death which terrifies you so much when you are ill or with child. Although the fear is in no way sinful, yet it is a pity, because your heart cannot be united to God in love so closely as it might be were it not so deeply agitated.

First of all, I assure you that if you persevere in a life of God's service, as I see you are doing, you will find that the apprehension will gradually calm down. Moreover, as your soul steers clear of harmful emotions and becomes ever more firmly fixed in God, you will notice yourself setting less value on this mortal existence and the stupid pleasure one takes in it. So go on steadily in the life of prayer you have begun, and advance daily from one step to the next along your present path. You will find that in a short time the terrors will diminish and no longer play such havoc with your feelings.

Secondly, often fill your mind with thoughts of the great gentleness and mercy with which God our Savior welcomes souls at death, if they have spent their lives in trusting Him, and striven to serve and love Him, each according to his calling. O how good you are, Lord, to the upright of heart! (see Ps 72:1).

Thirdly, frequently lift up your heart towards our Redeemer in holy confidence mingled with profound humility, as if to say: I am wretched, Lord, but You will take my wretchedness and lay it in the bosom of Your mercy, and lead me by Your fatherly hand into the joy of Your inheritance. Weak, abject, and poor as I am, in that moment You will look on me with love, for I have hoped in You and desired to be all Yours.

Fourthly, do your utmost to arouse in yourself a love of heaven and the life of the blessed. Make it a subject of continual meditation. You will find a fair number of considerations set out in the *Introduction à la Vie dévote*, in the meditation on the glory of heaven and the choice of Paradise (Part 1, Ch. 16, 17); in proportion as you value and long for eternal happiness, so you will weaken your dread of parting from this mortal and fleeting life.

Fifthly, never read books or even passages in books which deal with death, judgment, and hell because, thanks be to God, you have made a firm resolution to live a Christian life, and need no such incentives of fear and terror to goad you on.

Sixthly, often make acts of love of our Lady, the saints, and the holy angels. Make friends with them. Talk to them frequently, using words of praise and tenderness. When you have gained familiar access to the citizens of the heavenly Jerusalem above, you will grieve far less at bidding farewell to those of the mean city here below.

Seventhly, repeatedly adore, praise, and bless the most holy death of our crucified Lord, and place your confidence whole-heartedly in that merit of his which will win you a happy death—say over and over again: "O divine death of my sweet Jesus, you will bless mine and it shall be blessed. I bless you and you will bless me, O death more desirable than life." So it was that during his mortal illness St. Charles had a picture of our Lord's burial hung where he could see it, together with the prayer on the Mount of Olives. In that critical moment St. Charles wanted to strengthen himself by his Redeemer's Passion and Death.

Eighthly, occasionally recall that you are a daughter of the Catholic Church and rejoice in that fact, for the children of such a Mother will always die a happy death so long as they intend to live according to her laws. At the hour of death, so the blessed Mother Teresa says, it is the greatest consolation to die a "Daughter of Holy Church."

Ninthly, end all your prayers on a note of confidence. Say for instance: *O Lord, Thou art my refuge* (Ps 141:6); *my soul trusteth in Thee* (Ps 56:2). *O God, who has ever trusted in Thee and been put to shame?* (Eccl 2:11). *In Thee, O Lord, have I hoped, and I shall never be confounded* (Ps 30:1). When you make ejaculations during the day and when you receive the Blessed Sacrament, always speak words of love and trust in our Lord, such as: You, O Lord, are my Father. O God, You are the lover of my soul, the King of my heart, the Beloved of my being. O sweet Jesus, You are my dear master, my help, my refuge.

Tenthly, always look upon those you love most dearly and from whom it would be bitter grief to part as the very ones who will keep you company for all eternity in heaven—your husband, your tiny John, your father. "O darling little son, by God's help, he will enter one blessed day into life everlasting. There he will rejoice in my happiness and make merry, and I shall likewise rejoice in his and make merry, and nothing shall ever separate us more." Say the same of your husband, father, and so forth, and it will come the more readily to your lips, since your dear ones serve and fear God. You are inclined to depression, and therefore go to the *Introduction à la Vie dévote* and see what I have to say about sadness and how to remedy it.

Here, my dear Madam, is all I can say for the moment on this subject. I have said it with a heart filled with tenderness towards you, and I beg you to give me a place in yours, and offer me up frequently before the divine mercy. In return, I shall never cease to petition that God may bestow on you His blessing.

Live happily and joyfully in God's love.

100. Ripeness Is All

ST. ANSELM
c. 1076

To his sometime companion and brother-monk, once loved as friend and equal, and now in the same love become his Lord and Father, to Ernest, Bishop of Rochester, Brother Anselm wishes in this life health and wholeness, and perfect felicity in the life to come.

When I learn that your body is worn out by sharp and incessant pain that brings you pretty well to the point of death, the news saddens me and humanly speaking fills me with grief. However, the thought that this is precisely the way your soul is being made ripe for eternity refreshes me and I watch your growth in holiness with spiritual gladness. Your Reverence is surely well aware that afflictions and the cauterization of the flesh burn away the rust of sin and perfect the life of the just. Holy Scripture assures us that God scourges every son whom He receives (Heb 12:6); it tells us further that tribulation works endurance, endurance tried virtue, tried virtue hope, and hope does not disappoint (Rom 5:3), and adds that patience does its work perfectly (Jas 1:4). This teaches us beyond all doubt that we shall find joy in suffering in proportion as we have striven in hope, and have labored for the perfection of the work, namely, our inheritance as sons. For if God is well-pleased so long as we do not deny His ordinances, what supreme pleasure we must afford Him when we accept His will with cheerfulness in sufferings that touch our own person! And although He is sovereign justice yet is He sovereign Mercy too, and never would He compel us to expiate anew in the next world the sins for which He has seen us hasten to make ready atonement in this life.

So we may confidently expect that at the Judgment the severity of the Judge will give place to clemency so long as we endure His severity here and now. By dwelling on these and like considerations, my Reverend Lord, your holy Paternity knows perfectly well that as the flesh fails, the soul advances; out of the body's infirmity springs the soul's health; where vengeance is due, pardon is meted out; the very suffering gives birth to consolation, the very grief to joy.

May the almighty and all-merciful God bring you into harmony with His will in all things during your life on earth that He may order all things in harmony unto your everlasting bliss hereafter. Sweetest Father and my reverend Lord, I beg your Paternity never to forget your loyal servant, absent in body albeit present in spirit. May you flourish evermore in the Lord, in body as well as in soul.

The Christian
in Death

101. Death No Stranger

ST. ROBERT SOUTHWELL
To his friend, Thomas Howard, September 30, 1591

Death is too ordinary a thing to seem any novelty, being a familiar guest in every house. Since his coming is expected and his errand not unknown, neither should his presence be feared nor his effects lamented. What wonder is it to see the fuel burned, the spice pounded, or the snow melted? and as little fear it is to see those dead, that were born upon condition once to die. Night and sleep are perpetual mirrors, figuring in their darkness, their silence, and the shutting up of the senses, the final end of our mortal bodies; and for this some have intituled sleep the eldest brother of death: but with no less convenience it might be called one of death's tenants, near unto him in affinity of condition, yet far inferior in right, being but the tenant for a time of that, of which death is the inheritor: for, by virtue of the conveyance made unto him in Paradise, that dust we are, and to dust we must return, he hath hitherto shown his seigniority over all, exacting of us not only the yearly, but hourly reverence of time, which ever by minutes we defray unto him: so that our very life is not only a memory, but a part of our death, since the longer we have lived, the less we have to live. What is the daily lessening of our life, but a continual dying? Not the quantity but the quality commendeth our life; the ordinary gain of long livers being only a greater burthen of sin.

Our life is but lent; a good whereof to make, during the loan, our best commodity. It is a debt due to a more certain owner than ourselves, and therefore so long as we have it, we receive a benefit; when we are deprived of it, we suffer no wrong. We are tenants at will of this clayey farm, not for any term of years; when we are warned out, we must be ready to remove, having no other title but the owner's pleasure. It is but an inn, not a home; we came but to bait, not to dwell; and the condition of our entrance was finally to depart. If this departure be grievous, it is also common—this today to me, tomorrow for thee; and the case equally affecting all, leaves none any cause to complain of injurious usage. Some are taken in their first step into this life, receiving at once their welcome and farewell, as though they had been born only to be buried. Some live till they be weary of life, to give proof of their good hap that had a kindlier passage; yet tho' the date be divers, the debt is all one, equally to be answered of all, as their time expireth: for who is the man that shall live and not see death, since we all die, and like water slide into the earth?

In paradise we received the sentence of death; and here as prisoners we are kept immured, tarrying but our time till the jailer call us to our execution. Whom hath any virtue eternized, or desert commended to posterity, that hath not mourned in life and been mourned after death? Even the Blessed Virgin, the mother of God, was thrown down as deep in temporal miseries, as she was advanced high in spiritual honors; none amongst all mortal creatures finding in life more proof than she of her mortality. For tho' she had the noblest son that ever woman was mother of, not only above the condition of men, but above the glory of angels; being her son only, without temporal father, and thereby doubling the love of both parents in her breast; yea, tho' he was God, and she the nearest creature to God's perfections, no prerogative either acquitted her from mourning, or him from dying; and tho' they surmounted the highest angels in all preeminences, yet were they equal with the meanest men in the sentence of death.

Seeing therefore that Death spareth none, let us spare our tears for better uses, it being an idol-sacrifice to this deaf and implacable executioner. And for this, Nature did promise us a weeping life, exacting tears for custom at our first entrance, and suiting our whole course to this doleful beginning; therefore they must be used with measure that must be used so often, and since we cannot end our tears, let us at the least reserve them. Learn to give sorrow no long dominion over you. Some are so obstinate in their own will, that even time, the natural remedy of the most violent agonies, cannot by any delays assuage their grief. They entertain their sorrow with solitary musings, and feed their sighs and tears; they pine their bodies, nursing their heaviness with a melancholy humor, as though they had vowed themselves to sadness; unwilling it should end till it had ended them, that being true which Solomon observed, *that as a moth the garment, and a worm the wood, so doth sadness pervade the heart.* But this impotent softness fitteth not sober minds. It is for the most part the fault, not of all, but of the silliest women who, next to the funeral of their friends, deem it a second widowhood to force their tears, and make it their happiness to seem most unhappy; as tho' they had only been left alive, to be a perpetual map of dead folks' misfortunes. Much sorrow for the dead is either the child of self-love or rash judgment. If we shed our tears for the death of others as a mean to our contentment, we show but our wound—perfect lovers of ourselves: if we lament their decease as their hard destiny, we attach them of evil deserving with too peremptory a censure, as though their life had been a rise, and their death a leap into final perdition: for otherwise, a good departure craveth small condoling, being but a harbor from storms, and an entrance into felicity.

It could not displease you to see your friend removed out of a ruinous house, and the house destroyed and pulled down, if you knew it were to be built in a statelier form, and to transfer the inhabitant with more joy into a fairer lodging. Let then your sister's soul depart without grief; let her body also be altered into dust; withdraw your eyes from the ruin of this cottage, and cast them upon the majesty of the second building, which St. Paul saith shall be incorruptible, glorious, strange, spiritual, and immortal. Think it no injury that she is now taken from you, but a favor that she was lent you so long; and show no unwillingness to restore God his own, since hitherto you have paid no usury for it. Consider not how much longer you might have enjoyed her, but how much sooner you might have lost her, and take our Sovereign's right for a sufficient reason for her death. Let him, with good leave, gather the grape of his own vine, and pluck the fruit of his own planting, and think such curious works ever safest in the artificer's hand, who is likeliest to love them, and best able to preserve them. Since God was well pleased to call her, she not displeased to go, and you the third twist to make a triple cord, saying, our Lord gave, and our Lord took away, as it hath pleased our Lord, so hath it fallen out: the name of the Lord be blessed.

102. On Preparation for Death

BLESSED JOHN OF AVILA
To a friend, A.D. 1565

You ask me to give you some advice about saving your soul: a most reasonable demand and well worth meeting if only my ability were equal to my good will.

When a man first comes to the use of reason, he should begin so to regulate his life that at death his days may all have been spent in preparation for worthily receiving the crown of glory. When he reaches maturer age, the forerunner of death, he must repent and make amends for any past negligence. This is the time to renew our courage and to exert ourselves to remedy the weaknesses of our youth and to devote ourselves with fervor to making ready for death.

This preparation consists not only in setting ourselves free from both debts and mortal sin, but in doing penance for our past faults, so that when our good and evil deeds are put into the balance of justice, with the divine mercy added to the right side of the scale, our attachment to God's service may weigh as much as our former attachment to the world. We ought to give alms, to be charitable, devout, patient, and humble, in order to compensate for our former defects in these virtues. Busy like a honey-making bee, with a holy fervor, we should try to get nearer and nearer to God; for at our time of life the hour approaches when we must appear before Him. How shall we answer our Sovereign judge, if we have thrown away those later years He has most mercifully given us, in which to amend the past and prepare ourselves for heaven?

Therefore, care less for temporal things and attend instead to those which are more important.

Withdraw your heart from the world before God takes your body from it: keep your mind in perfect peace however much it is occupied in business. A man who is travelling post-haste concerning a matter which is of life and death to him, does not turn his head to look at anything as he passes. You must cultivate the same indifference to mundane matters. Say in your heart, "I am being led captive to death and what is this world to me? I am going to God; I will not entangle myself in earthly things." If in spite of all our efforts, we often find our attention distracted from religious matters, what would it be if we took no pains to be recollected? Consider that you are only beginning to serve God: remember your former good resolutions and beg God to assist you in carrying them out, for you have more experience as to the best means of keeping them now than you had before.

Your life consists in drawing nearer to God: to do this you must endeavor to detach yourself from visible things and remember that in a short time they will all be taken from you. Practice spiritual reading and prayer; go to confession and Holy Communion; and let the one object of your life be to serve God and to bear with things contrary to your will. Be most tender in your love for God and your neighbor; act in as charitable a way as possible to others, and be firm as a rock in bearing the trials sent you by Divine Providence. Good works are of no use unless we bear the cross as well, nor do sufferings profit us unless we lead a Christian life. If this seem hard to us, let us contemplate our Lord and Master, and realize His many labors and pains. What He was, that He wishes His followers to be, each in his own measure, for He asked and obtained from His Father that where He was there might His servants also be. Therefore we must not fear to follow Him in His pains here below and yet wish to share with Him in His present bliss. Although it is the more painful part to partake of His sorrows, yet it is the better, for we shall enjoy our Lord's presence more fully for having toiled for Him here. *If we suffer with Him, we shall also reign with Him.* Do not let us be incredulous about this promised reward nor slow in trying to gain it, for after a brief time of toil we shall enjoy eternal happiness.

Kindly consider this letter as written to your wife as well as to yourself. You must help each other and walk together in the right path so as to be companions in heaven mutually enjoying the sight of God, for He has joined you together on earth.

103. *De profundis*

BLESSED SEBASTIAN VALFRÈ
To his own soul, A.D. 1709

The sorrows of death compass me, and the pains of death take hold upon me, when I consider the uncertainty of that last passage, not knowing whether my hereafter will be terrible or blessed; for no man knoweth whether he be worthy of love or hatred. My heart is filled with terror by the import of those awful words: *Oportet nos presentari ante tribunal Christi, ut referet unusquisque quae gessit, sive bonum, sive malum.* That is, we must present ourselves before the judgment-seat of Christ, where each must bear the burden of what he has done, whether it be good or evil. I fear that last day, that day of tribulation and anguish, of calamity and misery, of mist and darkness, that day in which, if the just have reason to fear, how much more should I, an impious, wretched, and ungrateful sinner! I am terrified by the thought of the cruel teeth of the infernal monster which lurks ready to devour me, unless I prepare myself to escape from its fangs. I will therefore enter within myself at once and make my choice now, preferring to die to this life rather than perish eternally. Grant, O Lord, that Thy Sacred Body may be my last refection, and Thy sweet Name, Jesus, the last word on my lips. Unite my will with Thine. Hide me in Thy riven side. Be Thou my light, that I may not remain in darkness. Come, O Jesus, and do not tarry. Take me from my misery. Draw me to Thee, and receive me into glory, O Thou my beginning and last end. Thou art the sun of my soul, and my only solace, my satisfaction and the sole repose of my spirit; Thou art my Creator, my Redeemer, and my God.

104. Reassurance

ST. BERNARD
A.D. *1151*

To his dear and intimate friend Suger, by the grace of God Abbot of St. Denis, Brother Bernard sends glory from within and grace from on high.

Fear not, man of God, to put off the earthy man which is holding you down to the earth, and which would bring you down even to the regions under the earth. It is this which troubles, burdens, and aggrieves you. But why trouble about your clothing of flesh, when you are about to put on the garb of immortality in heaven? It is ready for you, but it will not be given to you already clothed; it will clothe you, but not while you are still clothed in the flesh. Wait patiently, and be glad to be found naked and unclothed. God Himself wishes man to be clothed, but not while he is still clothed in the flesh. The man of God will not return to God, until what he has of the earth has gone back to the earth. These two, the man of God and the earthy man, are at variance one with the other, and there will be no peace for you until they are separated; and if there should be peace, it would not be the peace of God, nor would it be peace with God. You are not one of those who say: "Peace, when there is no peace." The peace which passes all understanding is awaiting you, and the righteous are waiting for this peace to be given you, and the joy of the Lord awaits you.

And I, dear friend, am torn by the desire to see you, that I may receive a dying man's blessing. But no man can arrange his life just as he wishes, and so I cannot dare to promise what I am not sure of being able to perform; yet I will try to do my best to do what I am not yet able to see my way to doing. Perhaps I shall come, perhaps I shall not. But whatever happens I, who have loved you from the first, shall love you without end. I say with all confidence that I can never lose one whom I have loved unto the end: one to whom my soul cleaves so firmly that it can never be separated, does not go away but only goes before. Be mindful of me when you come to where I shall follow you, so that I may be permitted soon to come after you and come to you. In the meantime be sure that I shall never lose the dear memory of you, although to my sorrow I lose your dear presence. Yet God can keep you with us in answer to our prayers, He can still preserve you for those who need you, of this there can be no doubt.

105. A Plea for Forgiveness

ST. PHILIP HOWARD
To his wife, A.D. *1595*

Mine own good Wife, I must now in this world take my last farewell of you, and as I know no person living whom I have so much offended as yourself, so do I account this opportunity of asking you forgiveness, as a singular benefit of *Almighty God,* and I most humbly and heartily beseech you even for His sake, and of your charity to forgive me in all whereinsoever I have offended you, and the assurance thereof is a great contentment to my soul at this present, and will be a greater I doubt not when it is ready to depart out of my body; and I call God to witness it is no small grief unto me that I cannot make you recompense in this world for the wrongs I have done you; for if it had pleased God to have granted me longer life, I doubt not but you should have found me as good a Husband to my poor ability by His grace, as you have found me bad heretofore. He that knows all things, knows that which is past is a nail in my conscience, and burden the greatest I feel there: my will is to make satisfaction, if my ability were able: but tho' I should live never so long, I could never do it further than by a good desire to do it, which while I have any spark of breath shall never be wanting.

I beseech you for the love of God to comfort yourself whatever shall happen, and to be best pleased with that, which shall please God best and be His will to send. For mine own part I find by more arguments than those I understand from you, that there is some intent (as they think who work it) to do me no good, but indeed to do me the most good of all: but I am, I thank God, and doubt not but I shall be by His grace, ready to endure the worst which flesh and blood can do against me.

106. One Word More

St. William Howard
To his wife, December 29, 1680

I have, I give God humble thanks, slept this night some hours very quietly. I would not dress me until I had by this given you thanks for all your great love and kindness to me. I am very sorry that I have not deserved it from you. God reward you! Were I to live numbers of years, I assure you I would never omit any occasion to let you know the love I bear you. I cannot say what I would, nor how well and many ways you have deserved.

God of His infinite Mercy send us a happy meeting in heaven! My last request unto you is that you will bear my death as well as you can, for my sake. I have now no more to do but as well as I can (though not so well as I would) to recommend my sinful soul unto the mercy of the Holy Trinity, who, through the Passion, Blood, and merits of our Savior, I hope will mercifully grant me a place (though the lowest) in heaven. God grant it, and bless you and ours!

107. Tomorrow May Be Too Late

St. Robert Southwell
To his father, October 22, 1589

I am not of so unnatural a kind, of so wild an education, or so unchristian a spirit, as not to remember the root out of which I branched, or to forget my secondary maker and author of my being. It is not the carelessness of a cold affection, nor the want of a due and reverent respect that has made me such a stranger to my native home, and so backward in defraying the debt of a thankful mind, but only the iniquity of these days, that maketh my presence perilous, and the discharge of my duties an occasion of danger. Nature by grace is not abolished, nor destroyed, but perfected. And if its affections be so forcible, that even in hell, where rancor and despite and all feelings of goodness are overwhelmed by malice, they moved the rich glutton by experience of his own misery, to have compassion of his kindred, how much more in the Church of God, where grace quickeneth, charity inflameth, and nature's good inclinations are abetted by supernatural gifts, ought the like piety prevail? If the most frozen and fierce mind cannot but thaw and melt with pity even when it knows a person to suffer his deserved torments, how much less can the heart of a child consider those that bred him into this world, to be in the fall to far more bitter extremities, and not bleed with grief at their uncomfortable case? Where can the child owe so great service as to him to whom he is indebted for his very life and being? With young Tobias I have travelled far, and brought home a freight of spiritual substance to enrich you, and medicinable receipts against your ghostly maladies. I have in this general famine of all true and Christian food, with Joseph, prepared abundance of the bread of angels for the repast of your soul. And now my desire is that my drugs may cure you, and my provision feed you, by whom I have been cured and fed myself. Despise not, good sire, the youth of your son, neither deem your God measureth his endowments by number of years. Hoary senses are often couched under youthful locks, and some are riper in the spring than others in the autumn of their age.

For these many years I have studied and practiced spiritual medicine, acquainting myself with the beating and temper of every pulse, and travailing in the cure of maladies incident to souls. If therefore I proffer you the fruit of my long studies, and make you a present of my profession, I hope you will construe it rather as a dutiful part than as any point of presumption. He may be a father to the soul that is a son to the body, and requite the benefit of his temporal life by reviving his parent from a spiritual death.

Now to come to the principal drift of my discourse; most humbly and earnestly I am to beseech you that, both in respect of the honor of God, your duty to His Church, the comfort of your children, and the redress of your own soul, you would seriously consider the terms you stand in, and weigh yourself in a Christian balance, taking for your counterpoise the judgments of God. Take heed in time that the word "Thecel," written of old against Baltassar and interpreted by young Daniel, be not verified in you; remember the exposition, "you have been weighed in the balance and found wanting." Remember that you are in the balance, that the date of your pilgrimage is well nigh expired, and that it now behoveth you to look forward to your country. Your strength languisheth, your senses become impaired, and your body droopeth, and on every side the ruinous cottage of your faith and feeble flesh threateneth a fall. Having so many harbingers of death to preadmonish you of your end, how can you but prepare for so dreadful a stranger? The young may die quickly, but the old cannot live long. The prerogative of infancy is innocence; of childhood reverence; of manhood maturity, and of age wisdom; and seeing that the chief property of wisdom is to be mindful of things past, careful of things present, and provident of things to come, use now the privilege of nature's talent to the benefit of your soul. To serve the world you are now unable and, though you were able, you have little wish to do so, seeing that it never gave you but an unhappy welcome, a hurtful entertainment, and now doth abandon you with an unfortunate farewell. You have long sowed in a field of flint, which could bring you nothing but a crop of cares and afflictions of spirit, rewarding your labors with remorse, and for your pains repaying you with eternal damages. It is now more than a seasonable time to alter your course of so unthriving a husbandry, and to enter into the fields of God's Church; in which, sowing the seed of repentant sorrow and watering it with the tears of humble contrition, you may reap a more beneficial harvest and gather the fruit of everlasting consolation. Remember, I pray you, that your spring is spent and your summer overpast; you are now arrived at the fall of the leaf, yea, the winter colors have already stained your hoary head.

Be not careless, saith St. Augustine, though our loving Lord bear long with offenders; for the longer He stayeth without finding amendment, the sorer will He punish when He cometh to judgment. What is the body without the soul but a mass of corruption? and what the soul without God but a sepulcher of sin? If God be the way, the truth, and the life, he that goeth without Him strayeth, he that liveth without Him dieth, and he that is not taught by Him erreth. Well saith St. Augustine, that God is our true and chief life, from whom to revolt is to fall, and to return is to rise. Be not you, therefore, of the number of those who begin not to live until they be ready to die, and then after a foe's dessert, come to crave of God a friend's entertainment. Some think to share heaven in a moment, which the best scarce attain in the godliness of many years; and when they have glutted themselves with worldly delights, they would fain pass at once from the diet of Dives to the crown of Lazarus, and from the servitude of Satan to the freedom of the Saints. True it is that a thief may be saved upon the cross and find mercy at the last gasp, but well saith St. Augustine that though it be possible, yet is it scarcely credible, that his death should find favor whose whole life hath deserved wrath, and that his repentance should be accepted, which more through fear of hell and love of himself than of God or hatred of sin, crieth for mercy? Wherefore, good sire, make no longer delay, but being so near the breaking up of your mortal house, take time, before straitened by extremity, to satisfy God's justice. Though you suffered the bud to be blasted and the flower to fade; though you permitted the fruit to perish and the leaves to wither away; yea, though you let the boughs decay and the very trunk corrupt, yet alas! keep life in the root for fear the whole trunk become fuel for the fire. Death is in itself very fearful, but much more terrible in regard to the judgment that it summoneth us unto. Your soul will then experience the most terrible fears, if you do not recover yourself into the fold and family of God's Church.

O dear sire, remember that the Scripture terms it a fearful thing to fall into the hands of the living God, who is able to crush the proud spirit of the obstinate, and to make His enemies the footstool of His feet. Wrestle no longer against the struggles of your own conscience and the forcible admonitions that God doth send you. Embrace His mercy before the time of rigor and return to His Church, lest He debar you His kingdom. He cannot have God for his Father that refuseth to possess the Catholic Church for his mother. You have been, alas! too long an alien in the tabernacles of sinners. Turn now the bias of your heart towards the sanctuary of salvation and the city of refuge and hasten with jealous progress to Christian perfection.

Howsoever therefore the soft gales of your morning pleasures lulled you in slumbers; howsoever the violent heat of noon might awake affections, yet now in the cool and calm of the evening retire to a Christian rest, and close up the day of your life with a clear sunset; that leaving all darkness behind you, and carrying in your conscience the light of grace, you may escape the horror of eternal night, and pass from the day of mortality to the Sabbath of everlasting rest; and humbly desiring that my sincere affection may find excuse of my boldness, I here conclude.

108. Farewell

St. Aloysius Gonzaga
To his mother, Rome, June 10, 1591

The Peace of Christ.

May the grace and consolation of the Holy Spirit be always with Your Most Illustrious Ladyship. Your Ladyship's letter found me still living in this world of death but I am very soon going to praise God for ever in the land of the living. I thought by now to have made already that last passage, but the violence of the fever abated in its main course and fierceness, and has brought me quietly to the glorious feast of the Ascension. Since then, because of a great concentration of catarrh in my chest, it has increased, so that quite gradually I am on my way to the dear and sweet embrace of the Heavenly Father, on whose breast I hope to be able to rest, in security, and for ever. Now if charity, as St. Paul says, makes us weep with those who weep, and rejoice with those who are joyful, great must be the joy of your Ladyship, Lady Mother, for the grace that God does you in my person. I confess that I am bewildered and lose myself at the thought of the divine goodness, a sea without shore and fathomless, of God who calls me to an eternal rest after such short and tiny labors—summons and calls me to heaven, to that supreme Good that I sought so negligently, and promises me the fruit of those tears that I sowed so sparingly. Take care, take care, dear Mother, to do no injury to that infinite Goodness, as it would be, without doubt, to grieve for as dead, one who must now live before God to help you by his prayers far more than he could do on earth.

Not long will last that separation: there we shall see one another again and be happy without ever growing tired, united together with our Redeemer, praising Him with all our strength, and singing for ever His mercies. I do not at all doubt that, leaving aside all that the reasoning of human nature says, we shall easily open the door to faith and to that simple and pure obedience to which we are held by God, offering Him freely and promptly that which is His, and all the more willingly the dearer to you is the thing that He takes from you, believing firmly that what God does is all of it well done, taking away what He first had given us, and for no other reason than to put it in a safe and sure place, and to give to it what we all desire for ourselves. I have said all this for no other reason than to satisfy the desire I have that Your Most Illustrious Ladyship and all my family may receive this my departure as a dear gift, and that you may accompany me and help me with your Mother's blessing to pass this gulf and reach the shore of all my hopes. I have done it with all the better will because I have nothing else left with which to give you some little proof of the love and filial reverence that I owe you. I end by asking once more very humbly for your blessing.

109. On the Further Shore

ST. PETER DAMIAN
To a friend at the point of death, c. 1065

I entrust you to God almighty, dearest brother, and commit you to Him who created you, that when death overtakes you and you pay the debt of mortal nature, you may return to your Maker who formed you out of the earth. As your soul departs from your body, may the shining cohorts of angels hasten to greet you, the tribunal of apostles acquit you, the triumphant ranks of white-robed martyrs accompany you, the lily-bearing bands of glorious confessors surround you, the choir of virgins bring up your train with rejoicing, and in blest tranquillity may the patriarchs receive you into their loving embrace. May our Lord Jesus appear before you gentle and eager of countenance and assign you a place amid those who stand in His presence for evermore.

May you never know terror of darkness, hissing of flame, torment, or torture. May the foul fiend and all his minions reel back at your approach; as you advance encircled by angels, may he tremble and flee into the monstrous chaos of eternal night. *Let God arise and let his enemies be scattered, and they that hate him flee before his face. As smoke is driven away, so let them vanish, as wax melts before the fire, so let sinners perish before God* (Ps 67). Let the legions of hell then be filled with confusion and shame, and let not Satan's satellites presume to bar your course.

May Christ who suffered for you rescue you from punishment; may Christ who was crucified for you deliver you from your cross; may Christ who deigned to die for you redeem you from death. May Christ the Son of the living God set you in His verdant paradise of everlasting delight, and may the true Shepherd recognize you as a sheep of His own flock. May He absolve you from all your sins and haply appoint you to sit at His right hand in the company of His elect. May you see your Redeemer face to face, and standing evermore in His presence, gaze upon Eternal Truth revealed in all its beauty to the eyes of the saints. Finally, may you take your place among the ranks of the blessed, and enter into the sweetness of the Beatific Vision for ever and ever. Amen.

110. From the Arena

St. Théophane Vénard
*From his cage in Tonkin,
To his family, January 20, 1861*

I write to you at the beginning of this year which will be my last on earth. I hope you got the little note announcing my capture on the feast of St. Andrew, when God permitted me to be betrayed by a traitor, but I bear him no grudge. I sent you a few lines of farewell from that village, before I had the criminal's chain fastened round my feet and neck. I have kissed that chain, a true link which binds me to Jesus and Mary, and which I would not exchange for its weight in gold. The mandarin treated me with every possible consideration. His brother came at least ten times to try to persuade me to trample the cross under foot rather than see me die so young!

At the end of a couple of days I arrived at Kecho, the ancient capital of the Tonkin kings. Can you picture me sitting quietly in the middle of my wooden cage borne by eight soldiers, besieged on all sides by a huge crowd who almost barred the passage of the troops? "What a pretty little fellow that European is!" I heard some of them saying. "He is gay and cheerful as if he were going to a feast. He doesn't look a bit afraid!" My catechist Khang, shouldering his terrible wooden yoke, walked behind my cage. I prayed God's Holy Spirit to strengthen us both, and I begged the Queen of Martyrs to help her faithful child.

To begin with, the judge gave me a cup of tea which I drank without ceremony in my cage. Then after the usual interrogatory:

"Trample the cross under foot, and you will not be put to death."

"What! I have preached the religion of the Cross all my life until this very hour, and you expect me to abjure it now? I do not set so high a price upon this world's pleasures as to want to purchase them by apostasy."

The mandarins then proceeded to question my catechist, and inflicted ten strokes of the knot which he bore without flinching. God never failed to supply him with the strength to make a glorious confession of the Faith.

Since then I have been placed in my cage at the door of the

prefect's house, guarded by a company of Cochin-Chinese soldiers. Now I await in patience the day when God will allow me to offer Him the sacrifice of my blood. I do not regret this world; my soul thirsts for the waters of eternal life. My exile is over. I am approaching the soil of my true country; earth vanishes, heaven opens, I go to God. Adieu, dearest father, sister, brothers, do not mourn, do not shed tears over me, live the years that lie ahead in unity and love. One day we shall meet one another again in heaven. It is three long weary years since I have had news of you, and I do not know who is taken, who left. The prisoner of Jesus Christ salutes you. In a very short time now the sacrifice will be consummated. God have you always in His holy keeping. Amen.

Melanie, my darling sister and friend, I want to send you a special word of love and farewell. Our hearts have been one from childhood. You have never had a secret from me, nor I from you. When as a schoolboy I had to leave home for College, it was you who used to pack my trunk and soften with tender words the pain of parting. It was you who entered into all the joys and trials of College life, and strengthened my vocation for the Foreign Missions. It was with you I passed that solemn night of February 26, 1851, which was our last meeting on earth, when we exchanged our inmost thoughts and entered into each other's hopes of sanctity in a way that reminded me of St. Benedict and St. Scholastica. And when I crossed the ocean and came to water this Ammonite country with my sweat and blood, your letters brought me strength, joy, and comfort. So it is only fair that you should be in mind in this last hour, and that I should send you a few words of love and undying remembrance. It is midnight. Round my wooden cage I can see nothing but banners and swords. In the corner of the hall where my cage stands, a group of soldiers are playing at cards; another group at draughts. From time to time the sentries strike the hour of the night on their tom-toms. About two feet from my cage, a feeble oil-lamp throws a wavering glimmer on this sheet of Chinese paper and enables me to trace these few lines. From day to day I expect my sentence—perhaps tomorrow? Probably I shall be beheaded. At the news, my darling, you will shed tears—they must be tears of joy! Think of your brother wreathed by the halo of martyrdom, bearing in his hand the palm of victory. Within a few short hours my soul will quit this earth, exile over, and battle won. I shall mount upwards and enter into our true home. There among God's elect I shall gaze upon what eye of man cannot imagine, hear undreamt-of harmonies, enjoy a happiness the heart cannot remotely comprehend. But first of all the grain of wheat must be ground, the bunch of grapes trodden in the wine-press. May I become pure bread and wine perfectly fit to serve the Master! I trust it may be so through the mercies of my Savior and Redeemer and through the protection of His Immaculate Mother. That is why even as I stand in the arena in the thick of the fight I dare to intone the hymn of triumph as if assured of victory. And I leave you, my dearest sister, to till the field of virtue and good works. Reap an abundant harvest for the everlasting life which awaits us both. Gather up faith, hope, charity, patience, gentleness, sweetness, perseverance, and a holy death, and so we shall go hand in hand now and for evermore. Goodbye, Melanie. Goodbye, beloved sister of mine. Adieu!

111. Death of a Husband

BLESSED JOHN OF AVILA
To a widow, A.D. 1568

I have delayed writing to you, for I thought that my words could do little to mitigate the great sorrow which they tell me you are suffering. It seemed to me that I could help you better by interceding on your behalf with the God of all consolation, than by anything I could say. However, I am strongly urged to send you a letter, and as it is so much desired and our Lord is able to fulfill His purposes even by such means as this, I must not fail to comply with the request. God grant that my words may bring to your heart the comfort I wish it.

It is our Lord's will that you should taste of the sorrows of this vale of tears, and not of the milder but of the most bitter kind. May His Name be ever blessed, His judgments adored and His will fulfilled, for the creature owes its Creator reverence and subjection in all things, be they pleasant or painful. To test our obedience, and to teach us what great things we are bound to do and to suffer for so great a Master, God is accustomed to deprive us of what is as dear to us as the light of our eyes.

Abraham had a strong affection for his son Isaac, and that was the point on which the Almighty tried him. Job fondly loved his seven sons, and God took them from him in one day. In this manner He treats all those who are dear to Him, while He bestows great graces on them by this means.

I know that human nature cannot understand this. It thinks only of the grief and the loss, and cares for nothing else. But if God dwells in us, we must restrain our feelings, and make them subservient to reason and to His will. Whatever our suffering may be, we must not let it overwhelm us. Remember our Lord's anguish, which wrung from Him a sweat of blood, and made Him cry out: *Father, not my will but thine be done.* If we would be known as His disciples we must say the same, for as His servants on earth, and His companions in heaven, He will have none but those who take up their cross and follow Him, as sheep do their shepherd, even though the path lead to death.

Tell me, what right have we to complain of our trials, for they enable us to rid ourselves of our sins and make us like to the Son of God? It would be monstrous for slaves to refuse to obey a law their master kept, or for an adopted son to rebel against what the true son bore. Who was ever more beloved by the Eternal Father than His only-begotten Son? Yet who was ever afflicted with so many sufferings as He? He was the *Man of sorrows, and acquainted with grief.* Count the drops of water in the ocean, and then you may number His afflictions. As the Son of God endured such anguish, being sorrowful even unto death, ought we to pass our lives without tasting one drop of the vinegar and gall with Him? How ashamed should we feel at seeking to share His joys, but leaving Him alone in His agony! Let none deceive themselves, but let them feel assured that, as the King of heaven entered His kingdom through tribulations, we must reach it by the same path. There is but one way—Christ, and Christ crucified. If we seek a different road, we shall not find it. We should lose ourselves by any other path, and find that, however hard the sufferings of this world may be, those in the next world are far worse. Oh! the blindness of the sons of Adam, who think nothing of the future as long as they can enjoy the present; who do not care for what profits them, but only for what pleases them, and subordinate their reason to their passions. They weep when they ought to be glad, and rejoice when they have cause to mourn. Earthly happiness, like smoke, gradually fades away until it is no more seen. The years we pass here are but as a brief dream, from which we awake to find that it has all been an illusion. When sorrow comes to us, however light it may be, we forget our past joys, and the remembrance of them is only grief to us.

If this world is so treacherous a delusion, why not seek the other? Day by day we see our life slipping from us; let us strive for that which will bring us eternal happiness. If, in the past, prosperity has often made us think that we could find happiness here, may our eyes be anointed with the gall of suffering, so as to give us light to see the misery of this world, which is not our own country, but a land of wretched exile. Let us raise our hearts, that our conversation may be in heaven. Our Lord has sent you this trial to make you cling closer to Him, since you have less on earth to care about. Do not fancy that He takes pleasure in your pain: for He is merciful, and feels a tender pity for your tears. He has embittered your cup with this drop of wormwood so that, as all human consolation is taken from you, your heart may rest on Him alone. God has deprived you of one happiness only to give you another in its place, as is His wont: He has taken your husband from you, that He Himself may fill his place, for He is called the "Father of the forsaken." Your widowhood will bring with it many trials, and you will often miss your husband's care: many of your friends will show you but little kindness or fidelity, and some will even prove ungrateful. When this is so, God wishes you to have recourse to Him, and to make Him the confidant of all your trouble. Open your soul to Him as your true Father. If you call on Him with all your heart and trust yourself in His hands, you will find Him a sure refuge in all your difficulties, and a guide on your way. Without knowing how, you will often find that your affairs have succeeded beyond your highest expectations. Experience will show you how true a friend the Almighty is to those in tribulation; how He dwells with them and provides for them. If, sometimes, He does not grant all you desire, it will be to give you something that is better for you; this is how the heavenly Physician treats the sick who go to Him wishing to be cured, rather than to taste pleasant medicines. Do not withdraw yourself from His hands, however painful His remedies may be. Ask Him not to do your will in what He does, but to do His own.

Let prayers and tears be your weapons, and these, not useless tears for what our Lord has taken from you, but life-giving tears, which may gain pardon for your husband's soul and salvation for your own.

For what purpose, dear Lady, does the unmeasured grief serve to which they tell me you yield, except to add sin to sorrow? For, you know, that as we should not indulge in foolish mirth, neither must we indulge in excessive grief; but both in the one and the other we must be obedient to God's holy law. Why do you complain? Why, I ask, do you complain? Either you are a sinner, and this affliction is to cleanse your soul, or you are righteous, and must be tried, that you may win your crown. Whichever you be, it is right that you should render heartfelt thanks to your Creator, that you should be resolute in loving the end to be gained by your sufferings, nauseous as the medicine may be. This is what the Holy Scriptures mean when they relate how Esther kissed the top of King Assuerus' rod. Do not let the years pass in endless sorrow, but lift up your heart to our Lord, and prepare yourself for that passage from life which you have seen others take before. You have already yielded enough to nature: dry your eyes, and do not spend the time which was given you to gain eternal life in mourning over death. Remember how our Lord drove from the house those who were mourning the death of a young maiden, saying: *She is not dead, but sleepeth,* in peaceful rest, as does your husband, for he both lived and died a true servant of Christ. Why should you be so grieved because God has taken the man you loved from this unhappy world into the place of salvation? If it bring you trials, accept them willingly, that your husband may rest in peace. If his absence afflict you, take comfort from the thought that you will soon rejoin him, for the days of this life are brief, and it is but of little consequence which of us dies first. It is well to believe that our Lord took him because he was ready for death, and that you have been left here that you may prepare yourself for it. You served God earnestly during your married life; continue to do so now that you live in the state of widowhood; accept its special trials with patience, so that if you gained thirty-fold before, you may now earn sixty-fold. Thus although your life may not be a very happy one, it will greatly profit your soul, for by it you will purge away your sins, you will imitate Christ on the cross, and you will hold the certain hope of gaining His eternal kingdom. To this end, with tears and prayers you must beg our Lord for His grace: you must read books of devotion, and receive the heavenly bread of the most Blessed Sacrament. Raise up your dejected heart and take courage to go on your way; you have a long road to traverse before you reach heaven, and you will not arrive there without suffering more afflictions still. The gem you desire to win is of inestimable value, and no price can be too great to purchase it. God never costs too dear, however much we pay for Him. Rejoice in the hope of possessing Him, for He is one day to be yours. Do not murmur at your troubles, but say: "I look for so great a good to come, that I do not feel my present misery." I pray and hope that our Lord Jesus Christ may accomplish all this in your soul.

112. Death of a Brother

St. Teresa of Avila
To her nephew, Valladolid, December 28, 1580

IHS

May the grace of the Holy Spirit be with you, my son. You will imagine how terribly grieved I am to have to give you such bad news in this letter. But I realize you would only hear it from somewhere else, and other people would not point out to you what consolation you may derive from so great a trouble, so I would rather you had the news from me. If we think well upon the miseries of this life, we shall rejoice at the joy of those who are already with God.

Two days after the feast of St. John, His Majesty was pleased to take to Himself my good brother, Lorenzo de Cepeda. It happened very suddenly, as the result of a hemorrhage. He had made his confession and received Holy Communion on St. John's day, and for a person of his temperament I think it was a blessing he did not linger; for, as far as his soul was concerned, I am certain death would have found him prepared at any time. Just a week before, he had written telling me he had only a short time to live, though he did not know on exactly what day he would die.

He died like a saint, commending himself to God, so we may believe, according to our Faith, that he spent only a short time in purgatory, or perhaps no time at all. For although, as you know, he had always been a servant of God, he had latterly reached such a point that he would have liked to have nothing to do with earthly things at all; and, unless he was with people whose conversation was about His Majesty, he would find what they said so wearisome that it was all I could do to cheer him. So he had retired to La Serna, in order to have more time alone, and it was there that he died—or rather, began to live. If I could write you a few intimate details of his spiritual life, you would realize how indebted you are to God for having given you so good a father, and how you must live in such a way as to be like his son. But in a letter I cannot add to what I have just said except to tell you to take comfort and to believe that where he is now he can do you more good than while he was on earth. I myself miss him very much—more than anyone else does, except good little Teresita of Jesus, though God has made her so sensible that she has taken it like an angel—which indeed she is, and a splendid nun and very happy in her vocation. I hope in God she will be like her father. I had no lack of worry over Don Francisco before seeing him settled down as he is now. He has been so much sought after in marriage in Avila that I was afraid he might choose someone unsuitable for him. So far Don Francisco has lived a life of great virtue, for he is a very good Christian. Please God I may hear the same said of you. As you know, my son, everything comes to an end, but the good or the evil we do in this life is endless and eternal.

Pedro de Ahumada is well, and so are my sister and her children, though they are in the direst necessity, for my brother—God rest his soul!—used often to help them. Her son, Don Gonzalo, was here not long ago. He is very fond of you, as other people are whom you deluded into having a good opinion of you—though personally I should have been glad if you had been better. Please God you may be better now, and may His Majesty give you the virtue and sanctity that I beseech for you. Amen.

113. The Kingdom of Eternal Bliss

St. Aelred
To his sister, c. *1160*

Let the glorious procession go into the high Jerusalem, the everlasting city of heaven. Christ Himself will be at its head, and all the members of His Body that are gathered together in Him shall follow in His train. There the glorious King shall reign in them, and they in Him. And they shall receive the kingdom of eternal bliss as their inheritance that was prepared for them even before the world was created. We cannot know what that kingdom will be like, and so how can we write about it? But this I know for sure, and I make so bold as to say—that you will lack nothing that you desire, and you will not have anything that you would rather be without. There shall be no weeping nor wailing, no sorrow nor dread, no discord nor envy, no tribulation nor temptation. There will be no such thing as corruption, suspicion, or ambition; no such thing as the sickness of old age, death, or poverty; no trace of need or weariness or faintness. And where none of these things is to be found, what else may there be but perfect joy and mirth and peace; perfect security, and unmarred love and charity; perfect riches, beauty, and rest; health and strength and the perfect sight of God? And in that everlasting and perpetual life what more could you want? God our creator will be clearly seen, known, and loved. He will be seen in Himself as He reigns in perfect bliss. He will be seen in His creatures as He governs and rules all things without the least trouble or toil, as He keeps all things unwearyingly, and as He gives Himself to all things in the measure that they can receive Him, without any lessening of His Godhead. The face of God that the angels desire to gaze upon, shall be seen in all its sweetness, lovableness, and desirability. But who may speak of the clearness and brightness of that vision?

There shall we see the Father in the Son, the Son in the Father, and the Holy Ghost in them both. There God our creator will be seen, not as in a mirror or in darkness, but face to face, as the Gospel says. There God will be seen as He is, when the promise that He made in the Gospel is fulfilled: "Who loves me shall be loved by my Father, and I shall love him and show him my own self." And it is from this clear sight of Him that that blissful knowledge comes of which Christ speaks in the Gospel: "This is eternal life, that they may know Thee, the one true God, and Jesus Christ whom Thou didst send." From this knowledge there springs so great a fervor of blissful desire, so much fullness of love, so much sweetness of charity, that the completeness of bliss may not take away the joyful desire, nor may the desire stand in the way of completeness. And how can we say all this in a few words? Surely, sister, it is in this way: "Eye hath not seen, nor ear heard, what God has made ready for those who love Him."

114. Christianity a Glorious Profession

ST. ROBERT SOUTHWELL
To his fellow-Catholics in prison, A.D. 1584

What a glorious dignity is it, how great a felicity, to fight under God as a ruler, and to be crowned by Christ as the judge of the combat! The time is come for you to take repose, and enjoy the felicity of the land of promise. You have been on mount Sinai, when thunders began to be heard, lightnings to flash, and a thick cloud to cover the mount: now you are called unto mount Thabor where, enjoying his glory you may say with St. Peter, *It is good for us to be here!* Our country is heaven, our parents the patriarchs. There a great multitude of our friends expect us, a vast number desireth our coming—secure and certain of their own salvation, and only solicitous for ours. What unspeakable comfort is it, to come to the sight and embraces of them! How great is the contentment of their abode, without fear of dying, and with eternity of living! There is the glorious choir of apostles, the company of rejoicing prophets, the innumerable multitude of martyrs, there are the troops of fair virgins. In the sight of God we shall have the fullness of felicity, which neither eye hath seen, nor ear heard, nor man's heart conceived. No fear shall affright us, no presumption puff us up, no love disquiet us, no anger incense us, no envy gnaw us, no pusillanimity quail us; but courage, constancy, charity, peace, and security shall replenish and establish our hearts. And as for our bodies, they shall be of most comely and gracious features; beauteous and lovely; healthful, without any weakness; always in youth, and in the flower and prime of their force; personable of shape, as swift as our thought, subject to no penal impression, incapable of grief, as clear as crystal, as bright as the sun, and as able to find passage through heaven, earth, or any other material impediment, as in the liquid and yielding air. There, plenty cloyeth not; there, gaiety offendeth not; there, continuance annoyeth not; there, hunger is satisfied, yet not diminished; there, desire is accomplished, but not dulled. Neither is their joy contained in their persons alone; for each by loving others as himself, delighteth in the happiness of others as much as in his own, and what he hath not in himself, he possesses in the society he is in; so that he hath as many joys as he has fellows in felicity; and because all love God more than themselves, they take more pleasure in his bliss than of all their joys besides.

Finally, to conclude with the words of St. Bernard, "What now remaineth, my dearest, but that you be warned of perseverance, which alone ensures renown to man, and reward to his virtues? For without perseverance, neither does the champion obtain the conquest, nor the conqueror his crown. The accomplishing of virtue is the virtue of courage; she is the nurse to our merits, and the mediatrice to our need. She is the sister of patience, the daughter of constancy, and the lover of peace; she is the knot of friendship, the band of agreement, and the bulwark of godliness. Take away perseverance, and no service hath any value; no good turn any thanks; no prowess any praise. In fine, not *he who beginneth, but he who persevereth unto the end, shall be saved.*"

SOURCES

(PL = Patrologia Latina; PG = Patrologia Graeca)

Letter

1. *Works:* Mary Magdalen's Funeral Tears; The Triumphs over Death; and An Epistle of Comfort &c. by the Rev. Robert Southwell. Edited by W. Jos. Walter (London, Keating & Co., 1822), pp. 128, 140.

2. *Saint Peter Canisius S.J.: 1521-1597* by James Brodrick, S.J. (London, Sheed & Ward, 1935), p. 176.

3 PG, 52, Letter I, col. 549.

4. *The Life of St. Philip Neri* by A. Capecelatro (Burns Oates, 1894). A modified translation of the letter addressed to Francesco Vai given by Fr. Thomas Alder Pope, Vol. II, p. 475.

5. *Records of the English Province of the Society of Jesus,* by Henry Foley, S.J., Vol. IV, pp. 355-358.

6. *Edmund Campion* by Richard Simpson (John Hodges, 1896), pp. 174-76.

7. *The Travels of Mother Frances Xavier Cabrini,* Foundress of the Missionary Sisters of the Sacred Heart of Jesus, as related in several of her letters, published by Giovanni Serpentelli, Streatham Hall, Exeter, 1925, pp. 169-92.

8. *Sainte Louise de Marillac: Ses Écrits* (Paul Castelin, 1961), Letter 447, p. 559.

9. *Jesuit Relations,* 39, 175. Before this famous instruction to young Jesuits eager to join the Huron mission had reached France, five recruits were already on the way, among them, St. Isaac Jogues and St. Charles Garnier. Three years after he had written this appeal, St. John Brébeuf met his terrible martyrdom on March 16, 1649. He was baptized in boiling water, had red-hot hatchets hung back and front over his body, his feet were cut off, a jaw split asunder with an axe, and the Indians finally tore out his heart and gorged on his blood.

10. *Ibid.* The letters from the missionaries themselves, to be found in R.G. Thwaites, *Jesuit Relations* (73 vols., 1897-1901), are, of course, the primary source of information concerning the group of martyrs canonized in 1930. St. Isaac Jogues was finally rescued by the Dutch, and returned to France by way of England towards the end of 1643. He was grievously distressed because his mutilated

hands prevented him from saying Mass. The impediment was removed by Pope Urban VIII with the remark: "It would be unjust that a martyr of Christ should not drink the blood of Christ."

11. *Mother Philippine Duchesne: 1769-1852* by Marjory Erskine (Longmans, 1926). A combination of extracts from letters quoted on pp. 239-41 and pp. 277-79.

12. *The Travels of Mother Frances Xavier Cabrini*, pp. 252-56.

13. *Letters of St. Vincent de Paul*, translated and edited by Joseph Leonard, C.M. (Burns Oates, 1937), Letter I, p. 34. To Monsieur Comet, advocate of the Presidential Court of Dax.

14. *The Life and Work of Blessed Robert Francis Cardinal Bellarmine S.J., 1542-1621* by James Brodrick, S.J. 2 vols. (Burns Oates, 1928), Vol. 2, p. 323.

15. *Vie du Bienheureux Jean Gabriel Perboyre*, Prêtre de la Congrégation de la Mission (Paris, Gaume et Cie, 1890). A combination of letters to M. Lacarière of St. Eustache, Paris, p. 192, and to M. Pierre Martin, Lazarist at Paris, pp. 195, 303 and 205.

16. *Life of J. Théophane Vénard*, translated from the French by Lady Herbert (Burns Oates, 1888), Letter to Abbé Paziot, pp. 156-64. Wherever possible, the letters have been checked and modified by reference to *Bienheureux Théophane Vénard*, Lettres choisiés par le Père Jean Guennou (Editions du Soleil Levant, 1960).

17. *Vie du Vénérable François-Regis Clet*, Prêtre de la Congregation de la Mission, Martyrisé en Chine, le 18 Fevrier 1820, by M. Demimuid (Paris, Gaume et Cie, 1893), pp. 344-47. Letter to M. Richenet.

18. *Life*, pp. 103 *seq.*

19. *Les Bienheureux de la Société des Missions-Étrangères* by Adrien Launay (Paris, 1900), pp. 217 and 251. Blessed Simon did not desert Fr. Delamotte. He decided to take him to Annin, prepared a boat, and took off with the priest and a few faithful Christians, but the attempt had already been notified to the authorities. Guards from the river bank ordered him to draw in. As he did so, the priest leapt from the boat and took to flight, but was pursued and captured. His arrest was Simon's doom. He was at once imprisoned, tortured, and put to death.

20. Translated from the Greek text of Bishop Lightfoot (Macmillan, 1926).

21. *Life*, pp. 50 *seq.*

22. *The Spirit of St. Jane Frances de Chantal* as shown by her letters, translated by the Sisters of the Visitation (Longmans Green, 1933), Letter 243, p. 57. The translation has been modified.

23. Process of Beatification *Summarium Additionale* G. Alla Molt' Illustre Signore Nepote, la Signora Maria Bellarmini. In forwarding the transcript of the Italian original of this letter which he very kindly made, Fr. Joseph Crehan, S.J., added this instructive comment: "About the subjection of the wife, one has to remember that St. Thomas held that husbands had the right to beat their wives, and in the Roman civil law *patria potestas* made him the lord of the family in a much stronger sense than would have been the case even then in English law, in which the influence of Christianity had been able to make itself felt much more powerfully than it had in Roman law."

24. *Letters*, Letter 516, p. 81.

25. *Lettres de Sainte Thérèse de l'Enfant Jésus*. Letter to Madame Pottier, née Céline Maudelonde, daughter of Mme Guérin's eldest sister. Céline married Gaston Pottier, a Normandy lawyer, on June 19, 1894.

26. PL, 22, col. 562-64. The recipient of this letter was probably St. Amandus of Bordeaux, with whom St. Paulinus of Nola also corresponded.

27. PL, 54, col. 1136-137.

28. *Lettres de Saint François de Sales à des gens du monde*, by M. Eugène Veuillot (Paris, 1865), Letter XVII, p. 118; *Oraison*, p. 124.

29. PL. 33, Ep. XCVIII, col. 359. To regard the sacrament of Baptism as a magical formula is a contingency unlikely to occur among Western peoples at least in the crude form this letter suggests, but it is conceivably not infrequent in pagan—"mission"—countries, and in a small way among ignorant folk who readily have recourse to superstitious remedies.

30. *Œuvres de Saint François de Sales* (Annecy 1911), Tome XVII, Letter 1539, p. 7. To Madame de Payzien.

31. *The Letters of Saint Teresa of Jesus*, translated and edited by E. Allison Peers (Burns Oates, 1951), Vol. II, Letter 398, p. 904.

32. *Profilo Biografico del monaco D. Placido Riccardi, 1844-1915*, by I. Schuster (Rome 1922), pp. 110-13.

33. PL, 22, Ep. CVII. To Laeta.

34. *Lettres*, p. 9: Letter to Louise Magdelaine, 1860-1939. Sister M.

Aloysia was Pauline's class-mistress at the Visitation Convent of Le Mans.

35. *Life*, p. 16.

36. *The Life and Illustrious Martyrdom of Sir Thomas More*, by Thomas Stapleton, S.T.D., translated for the first time into English by Philip Hallett (London, Burns Oates, 1928), Letter 23, p. 106.

37. *Letters*, Vol. I, Memorandum, p. 260.

38. Pietro Braido, *Lettera da Roma del 10 maggio 1884.* Estratto da "Orientamenti Pedagogici," Anno VI, Numero 4, Società Editrice Internazionale.

39. *Life* (Stapleton), Letter 27, pp. 111 and 115.

40. *Sexdecim monita Sancti Thomae de Aquino* pro acquirendo scientiae thesauro (Art Catholique, Paris, 1921).

41. *Life* (Stapleton), Letter 30, p. 101.

42. PG, 31, col. 563.

43. *The Letters of Saint Bernard of Clairvaux*, translated and edited by Bruno Scott James (London, Burns Oates, 1953), Letter 365, p. 436.

44. *Works of St. Alphonsus de Liguori*, edited by Rev. Eugene Grimm, C.SS.R. (Benziger Bros., 1891), Vol. XVIII, Letter 38, p. 94. The translation has been slightly modified.

45. *The Vocation of Aloysius Gonzaga* by C.C. Martindale, S.J. (Sheed & Ward, 1927), pp. 190-93. Rodolfo had first abducted and then secretly married Elena Aliprandi. Aloysius insisted that the marriage be publicly announced in order to terminate the scandal.

46. *La Confidante de l'Immaculée par une Religieuse de la Maison-Mère* (Nevers, St. Gildard, 1925), p. 243.

47. *St. Catherine dei Ricci* by F.M. Capes (Burns Oates), pp. 94-95.

48. PL, 22, Ep. XVIII.

49. PG, 32, col. 409.

50. *Life*, p. 57.

51. Source untraced. Quoted in *Letters from the Saints* by Claude Williamson (Catholic Book Club 1958).

52. *Letters, op. cit.*, Letter 112, p. 169. To the parents of Geoffrey of Péronne.

53. Saint Ignatius Loyola, *Letters to Women*, edited by Hugo Rahner, S.J. (Herder-Nelson, 1960), p. 398.

54. *Letters, op. cit.*, Letter 357, p. 433.

55. *Vie*, p. 47.

56. *Letters, op. cit.* A combination of Letters 221 and 355 to St. Louise

de Marillac.

57. *The Letters of Saint Teresa,* translated by the Benedictines of Stanbrook (Thos. Baker, 1924), Vol. IV, Letter CCCI. St. Giles' was the College of the Society of Jesus at Avila.

58. *Lettres,* Letter 18, To Sister Agnes of Jesus.

59. PG, 47, col. 623. The treatise *On the Priesthood* from which this passage is an extract is cast in the form of a dialogue between the writer and his friend Basil. The work has always been regarded as one of the greatest classics of Christian literature.

60. *Letters, op. cit.,* Letter 781, p. 307. The probable recipient of this letter, Paul Carcireux, rejected St. Vincent's advice and left the Congregation in order to assist his father.

61. *Letters of Blessed John of Avila,* selected and translated by the Benedictines of Stanbrook (Burns Oates, 1904), Letter 4.

62. *The Life and Work, op. cit.,* vol. II, p. 108.

63. PG, 47; Book 6, ch. 2.

64. *Saint Francis Xavier* by James Brodrick, S.J. (Burns Oates, 1952), pp. 332-337. An occasional sentence has been added for sequence from the same letter in Fr. Coleridge's *Life and Letters of St. Francis Xavier* in the Quarterly Series (Burns Oates, 1872).

65. *Letters, op. cit.* St. Vincent had not mistaken his man. In spite of real holiness, Fr. Escart's intemperate zeal led him to strike a friend dead in a fit of insanity. He died in Rome whither he had gone to obtain absolution for his crime.

66. *Life, op. cit.,* Vol. I, pp. 422-25: Letter to the Jesuit Provincial, Fr. J.B. Carminata, S.J.

67. Quoted in Fr. Brodrick's *Saint Peter Canisius,* p. 89. Letter from St. Ignatius to FF. Laynez and Salmeron.

68. *Life, op. cit.,* Vol. II, p. 115: Letter to Fr. J.B. Carminata, S.J.

69. PL, 77, col. 468.

70. PL, 148, col. 400.

71. *Works, op. cit., An Epistle of Comfort,* pp. 167-69.

72. *Letters* (E. Allison Peers): A combination of Letters 158, 163 and 168.

73. *Œuvres,* Annecy ed., Vol. XII, Letter 217, p. 267. To Madame la Présidente Brulart.

74. *Letters, op. cit.,* Letter 19.

75. *Works,* ed. Grimm, Vols. X and XI, pp. 527 *seq.*

76. PG, 52; Letter 2, To St. Olympias.

77. *The Complete Works of St. John of the Cross,* translated and edited by

E. Allison Peers, Vol. III (Burns Oates, revised edn. 1953), Letter 20, p. 268.

78. *Works,* ed. Grimm, Vol. 19, Letter 528, p. 189.
79. PL, 77, col. 878.
80. PL, 148, col. 326.
81. *The Complete Works,* Vol. III, Letter 18, p. 265: To Juana de Pedraza.
82. *A Letter of St. Ammonas the Hermit* (Extrait de 'Collectanea Ord. Cist. Ref.,' avril-juin 1962).
83. *Records of the English Province S.J.,* Vol. I, p. 338.
84. PL, 159, col. 167.
85. *The Complete Works,* Vol. III, Letter 11, p. 255.
86. PL 33, Ep. CXXX, To Proba.
87. *Œuvres,* Anneçy ed., Vol. XVII, Letter 1031, p. 386. To Madame la Présidente Blanc de Mions.
88. *Letters* (E. Allison Peers), Letter 59, Vol. I, p. 147. To Don Teutonio de Braganza.
89. *Letters* (B. Scott James); a combination of Letters 306 and 308, pp. 377-78.
90. PL, 158, Ep. IV, col. 1068.
91. *Life, op. cit.,* p. 121.
92. *Letters* (E.A. Peers), Letter 203, p. 495.
93. *Life, op. cit.;* a combination of three letters to Filippo Salviati, pp. 184-87.
94. *Works, op. cit., Triumphs over Death,* p. 111.
95. *Life* (Stapleton), Letter 33, p. 92.
96. *Saint Francis Xavier* (J. Brodrick, S.J.); a combination of four letters to Father Francis Mansilhas, pp. 174-79.
97. *Letters, op. cit.,* Letter 7.
98. *The Life of the Blessed Sebastian Valfrè* by Lady Amabel Kerr (London Catholic Truth Society, 1896), pp. 141-43.
99. *Œuvres,* Anneçy ed., Vol. XVII, Letter 1295, p. 371. To Madame de Veyssilien.
100. PL, 158, Ep. 44, col. 1115.
101. *Works, op. cit.,* p. 109. Southwell's *Triumphs over Death* was originally written to Thomas Howard, Earl of Suffolk on the death of his sister, Lady Margaret Sackville.
102. *Letters, op. cit.,* Letter 8.
103. *Life,* p. 440. This address to his own soul is drawn from Bl. Sebastian's *Spiritual Testament,* written as death approached.

104. *Letters,* Letter 411, p. 480.

105. *Catholic Record Society,* Vol. 21, pp. 315-17.

106. Quoted in *Sir William Howard,* Viscount Stafford, 1612-1680, by S.N.D. (London, Sands & Co., 1929), p. 208.

107. Foley *Records,* Series I, pp. 339 *seq.*

108. *The Vocation of Aloysius Gonzaga,* p. 225.

109. PL, 144, col. 497. The Church has incorporated this letter into her Rite for a departing soul.

110. *Life, op. cit.,* pp. 170 and 183.

111. *Letters, op. cit.,* Letter 5.

112. *Letters* (E.A. Peers), Letter 342. Lorenzo had forebodings of his end. "I cannot think how you can know you are going to die soon or why you have these ridiculous ideas or are oppressed by what will not happen," his sister assured him on June 19, 1580. Exactly a week later he died. Even great saints are not infallible.

113. *A Letter to his sister* by St. Aelred of Rievaulx, from the Latin and Middle English versions edited by Geoffrey Webb and Adrian Walker (London, A.R. Mowbray & Co. Ltd., 1957), p. 60.

114. *Works, op. cit.,* p. 106.

BIOGRAPHICAL NOTES
AND INDEX

(References to the letter(s) written by each saint will be found at the end of the notes.)

Aelred, St., was born at Hexham in 1110, and after a good education became master of the household to St. David, King of Scotland. Bidding farewell to the Court and the world, Aelred became in 1134 a monk at the recently founded Cistercian abbey of Rievaulx, whose austere observance he practiced with great fervor and devotion. In 1147 he became Abbot of his monastery, where he presided over three hundred monks. Besides minor writings, his books on *Spiritual Friendship* and *The Mirror of Charity* reveal a very attractive personality, filled with a tender devotion towards God and an unusually sympathetic affection for his fellowmen. He was himself "one whom I might fitly call friendship's child; for his whole occupation is to love and be loved." He died at Rievaulx on January 12, 1167, and was canonized in 1191; his life was written by Walter Daniel, who had been a monk under his rule. *Letter 113.*

Alexander Briant, Blessed, born in Somersetshire in 1553, studied at Oxford where he was reconciled to the Church. He passed over to Douay, was ordained priest in 1578, and in the following year returned to work in England. He was arrested in April 1581, removed from the Counter to the Tower of London, and there subjected to most inhuman tortures. His jailers starved him, thrust needles under his nails, left him on the rack all night and then cast him into a pit for fifteen days. Like another St. Laurence, the martyr—described as a man of angelical beauty of body and soul—mocked his tormentors. He was condemned to be hanged, drawn, and quartered at Tyburn. When proceeding to Westminster Hall to receive sentence of death, he made a cross out of a piece of wood, and bore it like a standard at the head of the band of priests about to be condemned. Being ordered to cast it away, "Never will I do so," he replied, "for I am a soldier of the Cross, nor will I henceforth desert this standard until death." He was martyred on December 1, 1581, aged twenty-eight. *Letter 5.*

Aloysius Gonzaga, St., patron of Catholic youth, was born at Castiglione in Lombardy, 1568, the eldest son of the Marquis of Castiglione, and at an early age showed extraordinary piety, devoting himself to prayer and mortification. After some years at Florence and Mantua, Aloysius and his brother Ridolfo became pages in 1581 to the son of Philip II. His desire to become a Jesuit was strongly opposed by his father; however, upon returning to Italy, Aloysius ceded his rights to his brother and entered the Jesuit novitiate in Rome in November 1585. An ideal novice, he was an example of fervor, love of humiliation, and devotion to our Lady and the angels. He was also a successful peacemaker in various family difficulties. During an epidemic in 1591 he nursed the plague-stricken with assiduous zeal, but though recovering from the plague, he fell into a low fever from whose effects he died on June 21, 1591, the Octave-day of Corpus Christi. *Letters, 45, 108.*

Alphonsus Liguori, St., son of a captain of the royal galleys, was born at Marianella, near Naples, on September 27, 1696. He was a fine horseman, swordsman, an accomplished player of the harpsichord, and a brilliant lawyer. In the teeth of family opposition, he abandoned his legal career in 1724, and two years later was ordained priest. In 1732 he founded the Congregation of the Most Holy Redeemer with the specific aim of evangelizing the peasantry. Appointed Bishop of Sant' Agata de' Goti, he governed this difficult diocese with wisdom and industry from 1762 to 1775, when ill health forced him to resign. From then until his death, he underwent a physical and spiritual martyrdom. A terrible attack of gout forced his chin into his chest, he had to be fed through a tube, he was deaf and almost blind, the Congregation he had founded was rent by schism and dissension, he himself was deprived of all control by the reigning Pope, and his soul was beset by scruples and aridity. Yet he sat quietly revising, expanding, and composing the one hundred and eleven treatises of moral and spiritual theology which remain as his rich bequest to posterity. He died within two months of his ninety-first birthday at Nocera dei Pagani near Naples on August 1, 1787. *Letters 44, 75, 78.*

Ammonas or Ammon, St., was one of the most famous hermit-monks to live in the desert of Nitria. Being forced into matrimony at twenty-two, he and his wife lived as brother and sister for eighteen years; later he retired to Nitria and she established a house of religious women. The mountain of Nitria was the dwelling-place of some 5,000 hermits, some of whom St. Ammonas, on the advice of St. Antony, assembled into a loosely-knit community. The saint may later have become Bishop of Oxyrhynchus, but little certain is known of his life. *Letter 82.*

Anselm, St., was born of noble parents at Aosta about 1033. In 1060 he became a monk at Bec under Abbot Lanfranc, was appointed Prior three years later, and in 1078 was elected abbot. His gentleness and patience won all hearts, and it caused great grief to the community when King William Rufus robbed them of their abbot by appointing him to the arch-bishopric of Canterbury in 1093. The office was no sinecure. Almost immediately Anselm was brought into conflict with the King by reason of his oppression of the Church. He travelled to Rome to lay the case before the Pope, took an active part in the Council of Bari, and returned to England only with the accession of Henry I. The interval of peace and harmony was short-lived. Anselm again contested the royal claim to the right of investiture to bishoprics and abbeys, but after a struggle, the King yielded, and gradually came to revere Anselm as a saint. A man of singular charm, a profound scholar, and the greatest theologian of his age, Anselm died at Canterbury in 1109, where his body is believed to rest to this day. *Letters 84, 90, 100.*

Augustine, St., Bishop and Doctor of the Church, possessed one of the most powerful personalities and brilliant intellects of all time. His writings have deeply influenced the course of Christian thought throughout the ages and are not without relevance to modern needs and problems. He was born in 354 and studied at Carthage and in Rome; the story of his early life, his friendship with St. Ambrose, and his conversion in 387 is well known from his *Confessions.* His battles with the Manichees, Donatists, Pelagians and other sectaries contributed greatly to restore orthodoxy and unity to the Church in Africa, while his sermons and treatises reveal exceptional insight into the truths of God and the workings of the human heart. He died in 430, during the siege of Hippo by the Vandals, leaving an immense corpus of writings and a well-deserved reputation as the most illustrious of the Latin Fathers. *Letters 29, 86.*

Basil the Great, St., Archbishop of Caesarea, Doctor of the Church, Patriarch of Eastern monks, son of St. Basil the Elder and St. Emmelia and grandson of St. Macrina, was born at Caesarea in Cappadocia in 329. Having studied at Constantinople and Athens with his friend St. Gregory Nazianzen, he taught rhetoric for some years in his native city, but renounced a brilliant career to become a monk. In 358 he retired to Pontus where he founded a monastery and laid down the principles by which the monastic life of the Eastern Church has been regulated ever since. The influence of his monastic legislation was clearly marked upon the Rule of St. Benedict. In 365 St. Basil was summoned to defend the orthodox against the Arian heretics, and in 370 he became Archbishop of Caesarea. Here he had to oppose the persecuting Emperor Valens, and later to defend the prerogatives of his see. Meanwhile, by preaching, visitations, and works of charity, he cared for his people's spiritual and temporal needs and made his archdiocese a model of order and discipline. He died on January 1, 379. *Letters 42, 49.*

Bernadette, St., "the weak and foolish" instrument by which God confounded the wise and strong skeptics of the nineteenth century, was born on January 7, 1844, eldest of the six children of François Soubirous, a thriftless and impoverished miller. Delicate and asthmatical, the child grew up illiterate amid circumstances of the direst poverty. On February 11, 1858, while gathering firewood near a cave in the Massabielle cliff at Lourdes, she was granted a vision, the first of many, of the light-encircled, beautiful figure who later revealed her identity in the words: "I am the Immaculate Conception." At the Lady's bidding, Bernadette dug into the ground with her own hands, and there gushed forth the spring that is world-famed today for its miraculous cures. After eight years of incessant interrogation and publicity, Bernadette bade farewell to Lourdes forever when she joined the Sisters of Charity of Nevers. In religion she led a life of complete self-effacement, and underwent the martyrdom of soul and body foretold when our Lady promised that she would make her happy, not in this life but in the next. No amount of suffering, however, could rob her of the merry humor and devastating common sense which have endeared her ever since to millions. She died at the age of thirty-five on April 16, 1879. *Letter 46.*

Bernard, St., the third son of Tescelin Sorrel, a Burgundian noble, was born in 1090 at his father's castle near Dijon. After a deeply religious upbringing, Bernard decided to seek admission to the Cistercian monastery of Citeaux, founded but fifteen years earlier. He induced no fewer than thirty noble companions including four of his five brothers to accompany him, and there, with only one exception, the thirty aspirants made their profession into the hands of the English Abbot, St. Stephen Harding. From the mother-house of Citeaux, Bernard founded and became abbot of Clairvaux, ruling the house for thirty-eight years until his death on August 20, 1153. During those years he made sixty-eight further foundations, assisted at Church Councils, preached a crusade, crushed heresy, reconciled political opponents, defied princes, counseled popes, and became one of the most prolific and sublime spiritual writers of all time. He is known as the *Doctor mellifluus,* the Honey-sweet Doctor, and is reckoned as the last of the Fathers of the Church. *Letters 43, 52, 54, 89, 104.*

Catherine dei Ricci, St., was born in Florence in 1522 and entered the Dominican convent of St. Vincent at Prado at the age of thirteen. While still very young she became novice-mistress, then subprioress, and was elected prioress in 1552. She became famous for her extraordinary mystical experiences, particularly for the series of ecstasies, renewed weekly for twelve years (1542-1554), in which she not only beheld but enacted the scenes of our Lord's Passion. She received the stigmata, and was also given a ring placed upon her left forefinger by Christ in token of her spiritual espousals. In everyday affairs she was a capable administrator, and exercised a wide and beneficent influence all around her. She died on February 2, 1590. *Letters 47, 93.*

Edmund Campion, St., son of a London bookseller, was born about 1540 and educated at Christ's Hospital, popularly known as the Bluecoat School. From there he passed to the newly-founded St. John's College, Oxford, where his brilliance and oratory earned him a great reputation. In 1569, being in doubt as to the validity of the Anglican orders he had recently received, he went to Dublin, and later by way of Douay to Rome where, in 1573, he was admitted to the Society of Jesus. Towards the end of 1579, Fr. Campion and Fr. Robert Persons were chosen to work in England, and on the way there, the high-spirited Campion thoroughly enjoyed himself in Geneva, disguised as an Irish servant named Patrick. However, his whereabouts were soon notified to the English authorities, he was closely watched from the moment he set foot in his native land, and within a short time "Campion, the seditious Jesuit" was hounded to his death, which took place with the usual barbarities at Tyburn on December 1, 1581. *Letter 6.*

Frances Xavier Cabrini, St., Maria Francesca Cabrini, was born on July 15, 1850, at Santangelo in Lombardy. From childhood she felt a strong attraction to the foreign missions but was twice rejected by religious communities on the grounds of insufficient health. In 1880 the Bishop of Lodi, under whom she had conducted an orphanage, gave her this mandate: "You want to be a missionary. I know no Institute of missionary sisters, so found one yourself." She took him at his word, and there sprang into being the Missionary Sisters of the Sacred Heart. At that period Italy, like Ireland, was witnessing mass emigrations of the poor to America, and instead of setting out to evangelize the pagan countries of the East, Pope Leo XIII sent Frances Xavier Cabrini westward with the words: "You will find a vast field for labor in the United States." He spoke truly. In 1889 she set to work among the Italian immigrants in New York City, providing them with schools, orphanages, and hospitals. In 1909 she became an American citizen; she died in Chicago on December 22, 1917. At her death, her Institute numbered sixty-seven houses in Italy, Spain, England, and the Americas. Pope Pius XII declared this "extraordinary woman whose courage and ability," he said, "were like a shining light" to be heavenly patroness of all emigrants. *Letters 7, 12.*

Francis de Sales, St., a Doctor of the Church and one of the most beloved of spiritual writers, was born in 1567, and after studying law at Paris and Padua was ordained priest in 1593 and sent to work among the Calvinists in and around Geneva. Here he encountered many dangers and is said to have converted 72,000 heretics. In 1602 he became Bishop of Geneva with his residence at Anneçy, and in that town he and St. Jane Frances de Chantal founded the Order of the Visitation. A tireless preacher, a fine theologian, and one of the greatest French classical writers, he never refused any demand upon his strength or time. He was a pioneer in devoting his energies specifically to laypeople living a busy life in the world, and as spiritual guide raised many of them to heights of holiness. Perhaps his best known works are the *Introduction to the Devout Life* and the *Treatise on the Love of God.* He also left an immense number of letters replete with excellent advice for his innumerable penitents and admirers. At the early age of fifty-five, he died with the holy name of Jesus on his lips in Lyons on December 27, 1622. *Letters 28, 30, 73, 87, 99.*

Francis-Regis Clet, Blessed, was born at Grenoble in 1748 and joined the Congregation of the Mission at the age of twenty-one. He was appointed novice-master at St. Lazare, Paris, in 1788, and three years later sailed for China, reaching Macao and gradually penetrating to the interior of the empire. Here he worked with heroic fortitude under great difficulties for nearly thirty years, mostly in the province of Hukwang. In 1818, at the Emperor's decree, a period of exceptional persecution was initiated. For a long time Father Clet evaded capture but he was at length betrayed and taken prisoner. After enduring scourgings, cruel confinements, and other torments, he was condemned to death by strangulation. He suffered martyrdom in Wuchangfu, near Hankow, on February 17, 1820, at the age of seventy-two. *Letter 17.*

Francis Xavier, St., Apostle of the Indies and Japan, official patron of all foreign missions, was born in 1506 at the castle of Xavier in Navarre. At eighteen years of age he went to study at Paris where he met St. Ignatius Loyola, and thus became one of that famous band of seven who took the Jesuit vows at Montmartre in 1534. In 1540 he was sent on a missionary expedition to the East Indies, the first of many which included India, Ceylon, Malaya, and Japan. At the end of 1544 he baptized in a single month ten thousand Makuan fishermen in Travancore. The Church regards him as the greatest missionary after St. Paul, and the heroic charity, personal charm, and burning zeal that fill his many letters to friends and brethren in Europe and the mission field have inspired many a young man in succeeding centuries to choose a life of arduous labor, working for the conversion of the heathen. St. Francis died in loneliness and intense suffering at the age of forty-six on the rocky islet of Sancian near Canton, on December 3, 1552. His incorrupt body is venerated to this day at Goa. *Letters 64, 96.*

Gregory the Great, St., Pope and Doctor of the Church, is more especially known and loved as the Apostle of England, for it was he who sent St. Augustine in 596 with his forty monks to convert that nation. He came of a patrician family and was born and brought up in Rome, where he became prefect of the city. In 575 he entered the monastery he had founded in his paternal dwelling, but a few years later he was made deacon of the Roman Church and sent as ambassador to Constantinople. Recalled in 586, he became abbot of his monastery of St. Andrew's, and in 590 was chosen Pope. In this office, not only his great learning and sanctity but also his zeal in putting down heresies and reforming Church discipline was made apparent. His *Cura Pastoralis,* a book on the office of a bishop, became the standard textbook on the subject for centuries afterwards. Other works, well known and justly valued, were his *Dialogues* (in which occurs the *Life of St. Benedict*), the *Homilies,* and the *Morals on Job.* Called upon to face the aggression of the Lombards, St. Gregory in 593 induced King Agilulf to withdraw from Rome, and successfully negotiated a treaty with him. He strengthened the position of the Roman see to such a degree as to be considered the father of the medieval papacy. After crowding a lifetime's work into the thirteen years of his pontificate, St. Gregory died on March 12, 604, having well earned the title of "the Great" by which he is universally known. *Letters 69, 79.*

Gregory VII, Pope St., better known perhaps as Hildebrand, was born in Tuscany of humble parents about the year 1020. He was given a monastic education in Rome, took the habit himself—possibly at Cluny—but like his predecessor, St. Gregory the Great, was soon drawn against his will into the papal service. He acted as counselor and secretary to a succession of popes, until his own election by acclamation in 1073. Well might he feel appalled when the burden of the office was laid on his shoulders. Simony was rife, many of the clergy led dissolute lives, and the Church was under the thumb of the secular powers. The new Pope set his hand to the task of reform with strength and inflexible justice, but in so doing he came into violent conflict with the Emperor Henry IV, who succeeded in driving the Pope from Rome. He died on May 25, 1095. "I have loved justice and hated iniquity," he said "therefore I die in exile." *Letters 70, 80.*

Ignatius Loyola, St., the youngest of eleven children, was born at the castle of Loyola in 1491 of a noble Basque family. The young Spanish hidalgo's thirst for glory sought fulfilment at first in the profession of arms, but a cannon ball brought his military career to a sudden end. While his shattered leg was slowly mending, he was driven in boredom to read some lives of the saints. After fierce self-conflict and temptation, Ignatius resolved to change his life and enroll under the standard of Christ the King. He withdrew into solitude for a time, lived a life of extreme austerity, and at thirty-three years of age sat down with small boys at Barcelona to begin a study of Latin. From Barcelona he passed to Alcala and thence to Paris, where six other students in divinity associated themselves with his spiritual ideals. On the feast of the Assumption 1534 in the chapel on Montmartre, Ignatius and his six companions took the vows of religion which gave to the sorely besieged Church a strong defense in the new and highly-disciplined army of the Society of Jesus. Thus did Ignatius win the glory he had coveted in youth, in a way he never dreamed of. The men he trained—he left behind him one thousand members in twelve provinces—and his little book of *Spiritual Exercises* were, under God, largely responsible for the Pentecostal spirit of revival which swept through the Church of the sixteenth century. No Jesuit province has had a prouder history than the English Province, of which no fewer than twenty-six are beatified martyrs. St. Ignatius died on July 31, 1556. *Letters 53, 67.*

Ignatius of Antioch, St., one of the most famous of the early martyrs, was a disciple of St. John the Evangelist and became the third bishop of Antioch. Having ruled that see for forty years he was condemned to death and sent to Rome during the persecution under Trajan. At Smyrna he met St. Polycarp, to whom he afterwards addressed one of the well-known letters which manifest his ardent desire for martyrdom. He was killed by the lions in the amphitheatre, A.D. 107. In the nineteenth century, St. Théophane Vénard reechoed the cry of this martyr of the second century: "I am Christ's wheat, to be ground by the teeth of beasts that I may be found pure bread." *Letter 20.*

Isaac Jogues, St., was born at Orleans in 1607, entered the Jesuit novitiate at the age of seventeen, and after ordination was appointed to the Canadian mission in 1636. Shortly after landing, he was sent on the Huron mission where he worked with St. John Brébeuf. In 1642 the Hurons were in great distress, and to relieve them Jogues led an expedition to obtain supplies from Quebec. On the return journey he was captured by the Iroquois, the sworn enemies of the Hurons, and there with René Goupil he underwent the terrible torments described in his own letter to his Jesuit brethren in France. After Goupil's martyrdom on September 29, 1642 Jogues remained in slavery until released by Dutch intervention, when he returned to France. Early in 1644 he once more set out for Montreal, and upon arrival was chosen to act as ambassador to negotiate a peace with the Iroquois. With great courtesy they invited him to a meal and treacherously tomahawked him as he entered the cabin on October 18, 1646. *Letter 10.*

Jane Frances de Chantal, St., honored by the Church as wife, mother, widow, and Foundress of the Order of the Visitation of the Virgin Mary, was born at Dijon on January 18, 1562. Her father was President of the Burgundian Parliament, and at twenty Jane Frances married the Baron de Chantal, descended on his mother's side from Blessed Humbeline, St. Bernard's only sister. They had six children of whom a son and three daughters survived, but the ideally happy marriage was broken after only nine years by the accidental death of Christopher de Chantal while hunting. From 1591 to 1604, Jane Frances devoted herself wholly to her children and to works of charity under difficult conditions in the home of her tyrannical old father-in-law. In 1604 she attended the Lenten course of sermons at Dijon preached by St. Francis de Sales, and at once heart spoke to heart. She placed herself under his guidance, and in 1610 inaugurated with his help the new order, founded specifically for women whom health or other reasons would debar from existing religious Institutes. After St. Francis's death in 1622, the government of her eighty-six convents devolved entirely upon St. Jane Frances. She died at Moulins at the age of sixty-nine on December 13, 1641, and her body was buried near that of St. Francis at Annéçy. *Letter 22.*

Jerome, St., Doctor of the Church, a native of Dalmatia, born about 342, studied in Rome and later became a monk in Syria where he practiced great austerities and acquired a knowledge of Hebrew. In 381 he was called to Rome to act as secretary to Pope St. Damasus at whose request he made his first revision of the Bible, and there he became on terms of friendship with a band of noble women living a life of study and asceticism, chief among them being St. Paula and her daughter, Eustochium. He returned to Palestine in 385 and eventually settled in Bethlehem where St. Paula used her immense fortune to build one monastery for monks and three for nuns under Jerome's spiritual direction. Even more important than his controversies with the heretics of his day were his labors in revising, correcting, and translating the text of Holy Scripture, work often undertaken in direct response to appeals from Paula and her companions. The Vulgate, his principal translation, became the standard version of the Bible in use in the Latin Church for many centuries. His Commentaries and his numerous letters show a formidable but endearing personality, capable alike of fierce anger and of deep tenderness. He died at Bethlehem in A.D. 420. *Letters 26, 33, 48.*

John Bosco, St., one of the greatest pioneers in the modern education of boys, was born in 1815 of a poor Piedmontese family, and educated at Chieri and at Turin, where he began his work for neglected and orphaned youths. For them he opened a "festive oratory," then an evening school, a home, and training center. By 1856 there were one hundred and fifty resident boys with four workshops including a printing-press, besides Latin classes, in addition to the oratorios with their five hundred children. His intense sympathy and power of reading hearts gave him an unbounded influence over his boys, whom he ruled with a mildness unusual in his day. His fame as a preacher was enhanced by his reputation for working miracles, mostly of healing, and he also did excellent work in writing popular Catholic books. Deciding to train his own assistants, Don Bosco founded the Salesian Congregation (1859), which was formally approved in 1874 and now numbers thousands of members all over the world. He also founded the Congregation of Daughters of our Lady Help of Christians to do similar work for girls. At length, worn out by illness and incessant work, he died at Turin, January 31, 1888. *Letter 38.*

John Chrysostom, St., Archbishop of Constantinople and Doctor of the Church, surnamed "Chrysostom" or "the Golden-Mouthed" on account of his eloquence, was born about 347 at Antioch in Syria. Having studied law and oratory under the ablest masters, he renounced his career to become a monk and solitary, and was subsequently ordained priest at Antioch in 386. Here he labored assiduously for twelve years, delivering among other sermons the remarkable series "On the Statues," 387. In 398 he was consecrated Archbishop of Constantinople, where he became famous for apostolic zeal, missionary effort, and the brilliance of his preaching. He also founded communities for women, of whom the most illustrious perhaps was the truly noble St. Olympias. Having offended the Empress Eudoxia by his outspokenness, he was irregularly deposed and banished in 403, but soon recalled. As he continued his invectives, he was again banished by the Empress's party in 404 and sent to Caucasus in Armenia. Thence he was transferred to the Eastern end of the Black Sea, but died on the journey at the church of St. Basilicus. Clad in a white garment and having received Holy Viaticum, the Golden-Mouthed Doctor put off his frail body on September 14, 407, with the cry: "Glory be to God for all things. Amen." A large number of his sermons and treatises, still extant, do much to support the view that he was the greatest preacher who has ever lived. *Letters 3, 59, 63, 76.*

John de Brébeuf, St., the Apostle of the Hurons, a Norman by birth, was a man of such superhuman endurance that when they barbarously murdered him, the Indians drank his blood in the hope of infusing his valor into their own veins. Yet when the Provincial of the French Jesuits sent him out to Quebec in 1615, the young Jesuit was in an advanced state of tuberculosis and had never been able to study or keep the observance like his fellow-students. He soon learned the Huron language and set to work to evangelize his strange flock. Amid incredible hardships and dangers he worked often alone and for years at a stretch without making a single convert. Once he had the dreadful experience of having to watch the Hurons torture an Iroquois: "Their mockery of their victim was fiendish," he wrote. "The more they burned his flesh and crushed his bones, the more they flattered and even caressed him." He was witnessing a rehearsal of his own end. After thirty-four years of missionary activity, the Hurons were gradually yielding to grace. The Iroquois, however, remained implacable foes. Within a year after the martyrdom of St. Isaac Jogues, a band of Iroquois attacked the village at which John Brébeuf was stationed. All that Indian cruelty could devise was wreaked on him and St. Gabriel Lalemant, his companion. As if insensible to his necklace of red-hot lance blades and burning belt of bark, St. John calmly preached to his captors until they tore his face to pieces and deluged him in a mock baptism of boiling water. He died on March 16, 1649. *Letter 9.*

John Gabriel Perboyre, Blessed, born in 1802, determined to become a foreign missionary at the age of fifteen. He joined the Congregation of the Mission, founded by St. Vincent de Paul, was ordained in 1826, but because of his brilliant academic qualifications was retained in various employments until 1835, when he at last obtained leave to go to China. He had been there for only four years, devoting himself especially to abandoned children, when fierce persecution broke out. With dreadful fitness, he was betrayed by a neophyte for the sum of thirty silver taels, about fifteen dollars. The torments he underwent cannot be put on paper. On September 11, 1840, almost a year after his capture, his body being a mass of open wounds in which the very bones were all exposed, Blessed John Gabriel was strangled and his body laid beside that of his fellow-Lazarist, Blessed Francis-Regis Clet. *Letters 15, 55.*

John of Avila, Blessed, one of the great religious leaders of sixteenth-century Spain, was the friend of St. Ignatius Loyola and the spiritual adviser of several saints, including St. Teresa. He was born in 1500 at Almodovar-del-Campo in New Castile, studied law at Salamanca, and theology at Alcala under Dominic Soto. As a preacher he possessed extraordinary oratorical powers, and during nine years of indefatigable labor as missioner in Andalusia brought countless souls of all classes to penance and amendment of life, besides directing many in the path of perfection. He later devoted himself to giving missions throughout Spain. His very numerous spiritual letters are among the classics of Spanish literature. He died in 1569 after many years of constant suffering. *Letters 61, 74, 97, 102, 111.*

John of the Cross, St., Carmelite friar and Doctor of the Church, was born of poor parents at Fontiveros near Avila in 1542. After spending some years as an attendant in a local smallpox hospital, he entered the Carmelite Order in 1563. Upon his priestly ordination in 1567, he joined forces with St. Teresa of Avila, and together they achieved the spectacular reform of Spanish monastic life in the face of incredible hardships and opposition. The years following upon St. Teresa's death in 1582 brought a revival of persecution within the Carmelite ranks; the Chapter held in 1591 stripped

John of all dignities and sent him in disgrace to Ubeda, where his fiercest opponent was Prior. There he died after months of terrible suffering, on November 24, 1591. His well-known treatises and poems, *The Ascent of Mount Carmel, The Dark Night of the Soul, The Living Flame of Love,* and *Spiritual Canticle* have established him not only as a sublime mystic, but as a prose-writer of distinction and one of Spain's greatest poets. In its unrest and upheaval, his age closely resembled our own, and through the dark night of bitter experience many today have learned under the guidance of St. John of the Cross the saving wisdom of his stark doctrine of *todo y nada,* and have passed from *nada,* the "nothing" which is man without God, to *todo* the "all," man's high destiny of union in love with Him who is. *Letters 77, 81, 85.*

Leo, Pope St., called the Great, a distinction accorded only to two other popes, St. Gregory I and St. Nicholas I, was probably a Roman, but of his early years there are no records. He was obviously in the papal service, because his election to the papal throne in 440 recalled him from his diplomatic mission in Gaul, where he was endeavoring to make peace between two imperial generals. He immediately set himself to the pastoral work of instruction in Christian doctrine and morals. Ninety-six sermons and one hundred and forty-three of his letters survive, and if no personal anecdotes contribute towards our knowledge of their author, at any rate, their matter and style bespeak the man. In them, sublime, authoritative doctrine is wedded to serene, beautifully resonant language. In 449, he sent to the Council of Chalcedon a pronouncement on the two natures in Christ which called forth from the assembled bishops the cry of admiration and gratitude: "Peter has spoken by Leo!" Perhaps he is most famous for his courageous encounter with Attila in 452, when he persuaded the invader to accept an annual tribute and spare the city. After a pontificate of twenty-one years, one of the longest and most glorious in the history of the Church, St. Leo died on November 10, 461. His body lies in the Vatican basilica. *Letter 27.*

Louise de Marillac, St., born in 1591 of ancient lineage, repressed a youthful desire to become a Capuchin nun, and at the age of twenty-two married Anthony Le Gras, secretary to Marie de Medici. When twelve years of happy married life were brought to an end by her husband's death after a lingering illness, Louise made a vow to devote herself to God's service. It thus came about that when St. Vincent de Paul strove to organize his "Confraternities of Charity," he found upon close acquaintance that in

Mme. Le Gras he had a perfect instrument to hand. In 1633 Louise turned her house into a training center for the first candidates of the Institute known and loved all over the world as the Sisters of Charity of St. Vincent de Paul. Wherever there are sickness, poverty, children to be fed and taught, sinners to be reclaimed, families to be succored, there the grey-blue habit and white cornette of St. Louise's daughters will be found. The only child of her marriage, a son, disappointed his mother's hopes, but under St. Vincent's careful tutelage the boy lived a good life, married, and was with his mother when she died on March 15, 1660, six months before the eighty-year-old St. Vincent de Paul. *Letter 8.*

Peter Canisius, St., Doctor of the Church, has been called the Second Apostle of Germany. He was born in 1521 at Nijmegen in Holland, and after studying at Cologne and Louvain entered the Society of Jesus. He became well-known as a preacher and writer, and attended two sessions of the Council of Trent. Summoned to Rome by St. Ignatius, he was soon afterwards sent to Ingolstadt to counteract the heretical teaching current in the schools. Here he not only reformed the university of which he became vice-chancellor, but also effected a real religious revival among the people. In 1552 he was transferred to Vienna to undertake a like mission, and there won the hearts of all by his ministrations to the plague-stricken. About this time he composed his catechism, or Summary of Christian Doctrine, which speedily won fame and has exercised widespread influence ever since. His life was one long apostolic campaign, during which he founded schools and colleges, preached, wrote works of apologetics, opposed heresy, and restored Catholic faith and life in a spirit of charity and moderation. He died on December 21, 1597. *Letters 2, 91.*

Peter Damian, St., Doctor of the Church, was born at Ravenna in the year 989. He lost his parents in childhood, and suffered much ill-treatment at the hands of an elder brother. Another brother, however, rescued and educated him, and when he came of age, Peter entered the austere eremitical branch of the Benedictine Order initiated by St. Romuald. In 1043 he was elected abbot, but he was forced from his solitude to give his services to a succession of popes, and in 1057 was made cardinal-bishop of Ostia. He did much to remedy the evils of the time, both by word and deed: he fought simony, enforced celibacy on the clergy, upheld monastic discipline with stern rigor, and in his voluminous writings he bitterly castigated all infractions of the law of God or the canons of the Church. Were it not for his beautiful hymns and devotional works, he would remain austere and distinguished, indeed, but a figure to inspire fear rather than love. He died at Faenza at the age of eighty-three on February 22, 1072. *Letter 109.*

Philip Howard, St., son of the fourth Duke of Norfolk, was born in 1557 and married at twelve years of age to Anne Dacre. He grew up careless of his religious duties, went to Court to win Queen Elizabeth I's favor, neglected his wife, and squandered his fortune. In 1581, however, he was so deeply impressed by listening to Edmund Campion's refutation of some Protestant divines, that he returned to his wife and three years later was reconciled to the Church by Fr. William Weston, S.J. He fell under suspicion of recusancy, and in an attempt to flee to Flanders with his family was captured, heavily fined, and imprisoned in the Tower. Although condemned to death, he was left to languish in prison for ten years. His life after his conversion was one of such intense holiness and heroic patience that it would probably have sufficed of itself without the added glory of martyrdom to raise him to the altars of the Church. He died in prison, not without suspicion of poison, at the age of thirty-eight on October 19, 1595. *Letter 105.*

Philip Neri, St., known as the Apostle of Rome, was born in Florence in 1515. At the age of eighteen his thoughts turned wholly to God and he set out for Rome where he lived in seclusion for two years, studied philosophy and theology for three more, then embarked upon an apostolate among the people, with whom his attractive personality and sense of humor made him popular. In 1548 he founded a confraternity of laymen with whose aid he spread the devotion of the Forty Hours and undertook the care of needy pilgrims. He was ordained in 1551, and exercised his apostolate through the confessional with conspicuous success. His power of reading the thoughts of his penitents was notable, and his methods of reawakening a sense of religion included informal conferences, discussions, visits to churches, and spiritual readings. A little later he founded the Congregation of the Oratory with five young disciples, of whom one became the famous Cardinal Baronius. The newly founded community took over the ancient church of Sta. Maria in Vallicella, afterwards rebuilt and renamed the Chiesa Nuova. Here St. Philip took up his abode in 1584 and remained until his death on May 26, 1595. *Letter 4.*

Philippine Duchesne, Blessed, was born at Grenoble in 1769, into a prosperous commercial family. At seventeen, she joined the Visitandine nuns who had educated her but the outbreak of the Revolution prevented her profession, and when the nuns were expelled in 1781, Philippine was forced to return home. When comparative peace was restored with the Concordat of 1801, she acquired her old convent, tried in vain to re-establish a community of Visitandines, and when it proved hopeless, decided to offer the place to Mother Barat who had recently set up her first house at Amiens. It was in this roundabout fashion that Philippine Duchesne became a member of the newly-founded Society of the Sacred Heart, and one of its greatest glories. In March 1818, after much chiseling and polishing at Mother Barat's hands, Mother Duchesne was sent out at the head of a party of five religious to New Orleans. In spite of grim trials and difficulties of every kind, she managed to establish the Society on firm and lasting foundations in the New World. She died at the age of eighty-three on November 18, 1852. *Letter 11.*

Placid Riccardi, St.: Thomas Riccardi, second son and third of the ten children of Francis Riccardi, a businessman of Trevi, was born on June 24, 1844. As a young man he frequented concerts and the theater, was fastidious about food and clothes, fell in love, and showed every sign of settling down to a married life in the legal profession. Having gone to Rome to pursue his studies, he there heard the call to the monastic life; in 1866 he entered the monastery of St. Paul's outside the Walls, receiving the name Placid in religion. His whole life was outwardly as uneventful as that of his contemporary St. Thérèse of Lisieux. He was ordained in 1871; in 1884 he was sent as chaplain to the Benedictine nuns of Amelia where he labored to restore monastic discipline; from Amelia he went to Sanfiano where for seventeen years he lived in solitude, gave spiritual guidance to nuns, attended to the needs of the simple countryfolk both at Sanfiano and at Farfa, and finally returned gravely ill to his own monastery of St. Paul's, where he died on March 15, 1915 in the arms of his devoted fellow-monk and disciple, Dom Ildephonsus Schuster, later Cardinal-Archbishop of Milan. Dom Placid's life, unmarked by ecstasy or miracle, was simply that of a monk who deliberately and unflaggingly conformed himself to his crucified Master. *Letter 32.*

Robert Bellarmine, St., Archbishop and Doctor of the Church, was closely related to Pope Marcellus II. He was born in 1542 at Montepulciano and entered the Society of Jesus in 1560. After studying at Padua and Louvain he returned to Rome where he was appointed to the chair of controversial theology in 1576, a post he held for eleven years during which he prepared his great work, the *Disputations on the Controversies,* in reply to the Protestant *Centuries of Magdeburg.* Later he took the leading part in a revised version of the Vulgate. In Rome he was confessor and friend to the youthful St. Aloysius Gonzaga. In 1597 he was appointed theologian to Pope Clement VIII, at whose desire he wrote his two celebrated catechisms, and who nominated him a cardinal in 1598. His controversies included a famous one with King James I of England on the authority of the Pope. In old age he wrote several more directly spiritual books. He died at Rome on September 17, 1621. *Letters 14, 23, 62, 66, 68.*

Robert Southwell, St., a most attractive figure, writer, poet, and martyr, was born in Norfolk about 1561. He studied at Douay and Paris, entered the Society of Jesus in 1578, was ordained priest in 1584, and two years later sent on the English mission. His active career lasted but six years and was particularly effective on account of his gentle, quiet disposition. In 1587 he became chaplain to Anne, Countess of Arundel, and thus acquainted with her husband, Blessed Philip Howard, then in the Tower. In 1592 St. Robert was betrayed and arrested; he was racked nine times, cruelly tortured by Topcliffe, imprisoned in a dreadful dungeon for three years, and eventually tried and condemned for his priesthood, being executed at Tyburn on February 21, 1595. "The Burning Babe" is probably the best known of Robert Southwell's poems. *Letters 1, 71, 83, 94, 101, 107, 114.*

Sebastian Valfrè, Blessed, was born at Verduno in Piedmont in 1629, of a very poor family. He joined the Congregation of the Oratory at Turin in 1651 and was ordained priest a year later. Successively master of novices and superior of his house, he refused the archbishopric of Turin, and preferred to devote himself entirely to the poor. He possessed a wonderful gift for inspiring enthusiasm in the young, and became famous as a preacher and director of souls. He was indeed the model of a zealous pastor amid surroundings of misery and evil, and many instances are recorded of his supernatural insight and gift of prophecy. He died on January 30, 1710. *Letters 98, 103.*

Simon Hoa, Blessed, a doctor of medicine by profession, was one of thirty-one martyrs of Vietnam. These included fourteen priests, one seminarist, seven catechists, and nine Christian laymen. Before decapitation, Simon was tortured with red-hot and stone-cold pincers. His wife and children were worthy of him. They came to bid him farewell just before his death, his wife bearing in her arms their baby son. "You are very dear to me," he told them. "I have taken care of you to the utmost of my power, but I must not place you before God in my love." He was put to death for having harbored a priest, on December 12, 1840. *Letter 19.*

Stanislaus Kostka, St., born of the Polish high nobility in 1550, was sent at fourteen with his brother Paul to the Jesuit College at Vienna. Stung to rancor by his young brother's purity of life, Paul bullied, ill-treated, and brought him to death's door. Upon his recovery, Stanislaus petitioned to be admitted to the Society in Vienna, but the Provincial dared not receive him for fear of his family. So the boy set out alone on a three hundred and fifty mile walk to find St. Peter Canisius, first at Augsburg, then at Dillingen. St. Peter tested his vocation by setting him to the most menial tasks, and then sent him with letters of warm recommendation to the General in Rome, St. Francis Borgia. Stanislaus' novitiate lasted only nine months. He was taken ill with fever on August 10, and at three o'clock in the morning of the feast of the Assumption, 1568, saw our Lady surrounded by angels, and quietly and with great joy went with her to keep her feast in heaven. *Letter 51.*

Teresa of Avila, St., born at Avila on March 28, 1515 of the noble Castilian family of Cepeda, resolved to become a nun after reading St. Jerome's letters. At twenty years of age, she entered the Carmelite convent of the Incarnation at Avila, which then housed a community of some one hundred and forty nuns. For several years she shared their relaxations, receiving and mixing with many guests, and charming all by her beauty and intelligence. Illness and extraordinary graces recalled her to a life of penance and spiritual striving, and in obedience to God's direction she undertook to reform and renew the ancient spirit of Carmel. At the command of her superiors, she wrote the famous works which have made her a doctor of the spiritual life and one of Spain's classical authors: *Life, The Book of Foundations, The Way of Perfection,* and *The Interior Castle.* St. John of the Cross, St. Peter of Alcantara, and Blessed John of Avila were all associated with her in her work. She founded seventeen monasteries for nuns and fifteen for friars of the Reform, and died at the Convent of Alba de Tormes on October 15, 1582. *Letters 31, 37, 57, 72, 88, 92, 112.*

Thérèse of Lisieux, St., who has evoked a world-wide veneration from every class and type of society in modern times, was the youngest of the five surviving daughters of Louis and Zélie Martin. She was born at Alençon on January 2, 1873, entered the Carmel of Lisieux at the age of fifteen, spent nine uneventful years within its high walls, and there died at the age of twenty-four on September 30, 1897. Humanly speaking there is little more to say. Her life witnesses to the truth of Newman's assertion that if we wish to be perfect, we have nothing more to do than to perform the humdrum daily round flawlessly. *L'histoire d'une âme*, St. Thérèse's auto-biography written under obedience, has made her one of the most powerful spiritual teachers of our time. *Letters 25, 34, 58.*

Théophane Vénard, St., was born at St. Loup in the diocese of Poitiers on November 21, 1829, one of six children of Jean Vénard, the village schoolmaster. In spite of delicate health, Théophane dreamed from child-hood of priesthood and martyrdom, and after receiving the subdiaconate in 1850, he sought admission to the Collège des Missions Étrangères at Paris. Immediately after ordination in 1852, he was sent to Hong Kong and from there to Western Tonkin, where for five years, in spite of violent persecution and unremitting bouts of illness, he labored to serve his flock of ten thousand fervent Christians. He was captured in November 1860 and imprisoned in a cage. His gaiety and sweetness of character attracted even his captors, but did not prevent them from putting him to a horrible death on February 2, 1861. *Letters 16, 18, 21, 35, 50, 110.*

Thomas Aquinas, St., "the Angelic Doctor," and the greatest of the medieval Schoolmen, was born at Aquino about 1226 and educated at Monte Cassino and at Naples. In face of strong family opposition he joined the recently founded Order of Preachers in 1243 and was sent to study under St. Albert the Great. Later he became famous as a teacher of philosophy and theology. He died at Fossa Nova, March 7, 1274. His chief work, the *Summa Theologica*, is a brilliant and methodical synthesis of Christian doctrine which gradually became the standard textbook of its kind and has exercised a determining influence on the thought of the Latin Church ever since. *Letter 40.*

Thomas More, St., born in Milk Street, Cheapside, on February 6, 1478, was educated at Oxford, called to the Bar in 1501, and in 1504 entered Parliament. Having decided that his vocation lay in the world rather than in the Charterhouse to which he was attracted, he married his "uxorcula Mori," Jane Colt, in 1505, and when four years later she died leaving him with a son and three daughters, he took to wife Alice Middleton, a widow seven years his senior. Born and bred in the City, More, who loved London as Samuel Johnson and Charles Lamb loved it, united the common sense of the one with the wit and fantasy of the other; his house, the meeting-place of the intellectual élite of Europe, was also the refuge of the poor and outcast, and quite apart from his death as a martyr, More's character and life have made him for all time the ideal Christian layman, the ideal husband and father, and the ideal Englishman. He rose rapidly in public life, was appointed Lord Chancellor in 1529, resigned office after three years, and finally refused point-blank to take the oath prescribed by the Act of Succession of 1534. He was committed to the Tower and fifteen months later indicted for high treason. The verdict was a foregone conclusion. On July 6, 1535, at the age of fifty-seven, Thomas More was beheaded on Tower Hill. *Letters 36, 39, 41, 95.*

Vincent de Paul, St., the third of the six children of a Gascon peasant, was born April 24, 1581. Since he showed marked ability, he was given opportunity to study and was duly raised to the priesthood at the early age of twenty. In youth he seems to have been somewhat ambitious and while in the service of Queen Margaret of Valois attracted the notice of Pierre de Bérulle. The meeting was to have momentous consequences. Bérulle recognized his potentialities and prevailed upon him to become tutor to the sons of Admiral de Gondi. This led to his hearing the confessions of Court ladies, preaching missions to fashionable audiences, evangelizing the galley-slaves of the Fleet, and eventually to rescuing foundlings and to work in hospitals and prisons. Others joined him in his many labors; in 1633 Vincent was given the old leper-house of St. Lazare in Paris, and there he housed his newly-established priest-helpers, technically styled "Congregation of the Mission," but popularly called Lazarists or Vincentians. By his foundation of seminaries, he gave the Church a holy and educated priesthood, proved himself one of the most powerful opponents of Jansenism, and did more than any man of modern times to bring home to all classes the truth of the brotherhood of men. He died in his eightieth year on September 27, 1660. *Letters 13, 24, 56, 60, 65.*

William Howard, St., one of the victims of the Titus Oates agitation, was grandson of St. Philip Howard and fifth son of Thomas, Earl of Arundel. He was born in 1613, brought up a Catholic, and in 1640 was created Viscount Stafford by Charles I to whom he was a trusted and loyal servant. He was far from being a saint from the cradle, being somewhat crusty and quarrelsome, but he was a good husband and father and is described by his confessor, Dom Maurus Corker, as "ever held to be of a generous disposition, very charitable, devout, addicted to sobriety, inoffensive in his words, and a lover of justice." This tribute may have been true only after imprisonment and suffering had done their educative work, for after being falsely accused by Titus Oates of complicity in an imaginary Popish Plot, he was imprisoned for two years before trial; he was condemned on perjured evidence and beheaded on December 29, 1680. As he stood on the scaffold, he entrusted the letter he had written to his wife that morning to a friend, together with his watch and rosary. *Letter 106.*